DATE DUE

OCT 00			
NO 9 00			

DEMCO 38-296

THE DAY THE
CHINESE
ATTACKED

THE DAY THE CHINESE ATTACKED

KOREA, 1950

The Story of the Failure of America's China Policy

Edwin P. Hoyt

McGraw-Hill Publishing Company

New York   St. Louis   San Francisco
Toronto   Hamburg   Mexico

1 2 3 4 5 6 7 8 9 DOC DOC 9 5 4 3 2 1 0

ISBN 0-07-030632-X

Library of Congress Cataloging-in-Publication Data

Hoyt, Edwin Palmer.
    The day the Chinese attacked : Korea, 1950 : the story of the
failure of America's China policy / by Edwin P. Hoyt.
        p. cm.
    Includes bibliographical references.
    ISBN 0-07-030632-X
    1. Korean War, 1950-1953—China.   2. Korean War, 1950-1953—United
States.   3. United States—Foreign relations—China.   4. China—
Foreign relations—United States.   5. United States—Foreign
relations—1945-1953.   6. China—Foreign relations—1912-1949.
I. Title.
DS919.5.H68   1990
951.904'2—dc20   90-31862
                                                                      CIP

Book design by Eve Kirch

This book is dedicated to Alison Frost in the confidence that by the time she grows up her generation will wonder why in the world the Americans ever got so excited by revolutions in other countries in the twentieth century.

CONTENTS

INTRODUCTION

On the face of it, *The Day the Chinese Attacked* is a book about the war in Korea between the United States and the People's Republic of China, but I have intended it to be much more than that. I dealt with the war as thoroughly as I knew how in my three-volume battle history published by The Military Book Club and Berkley Books: *The Pusan Perimeter, On to the Yalu,* and *The Bloody Road to Panmunjom.* Those books need never have been written, and would not have been had American policy toward China not gone astray in 1945 in the hysteria of anticommunism, and remained that way until rescued by President Richard Nixon in 1972. For more than a quarter of a century America's head-in-the-sand policy toward Communist China precluded any accommodation whatsoever. One did not have to approve of the Communist Chinese, apologize for them, or call them "agrarian reformers," which they were not. They were revolutionaries bent on seizure of power and the transformation of the Kuomintang Party dictatorship into a Communist Party dictatorship. The big difference between the two revolutionary parties was that by 1925 the Kuomintang had abandoned the people's revolutionary policies on which it was founded and Chiang Kaishek had turned the party into a vehicle for personal power, while the Communists gave lip service to the ideals of democracy and many members of the party truly believed that communism would bring freedom to China. By 1947 no one with any knowledge of Chinese affairs could believe that freedom for the people could be achieved under the Nationalist Kuomintang. Until the spring of 1989 people still believed that liberty could be attained under the Communist system as it then existed. The corruption of the Chinese Communist leadership was revealed to the world.

All of this relates to the Chinese-American relationship between 1945 and 1972. I believed in 1945 and I still believe in 1990 that had the United States adopted a different posture toward China in the 1940s, 1950s, and 1960s, the effect would have been to ameliorate the position of the Chinese people. By casting China into the arms of the Soviet Union in the late 1940s, the United States delayed the process of liberalization, so that by 1989 China still had not achieved enough strength to withstand the dying convulsions of the old guard of the Communist Party. The end is yet to come. Ultimately Li Peng will be displaced. It is hard at this juncture to see how Deng Xiaoping will be forgiven for his promises of reforms that were not carried out. But that is another story which I propose to pursue in the next volume of my study of China—*China: The Unfinished Revolution*.

In this volume, *The Day the Chinese Attacked*, I have tried to show American policy as it developed, to explain it in terms of American attitudes and pressures, and to show where it went wrong and what the consequences were. The facts are on the record. The conclusions are my own.

1

The Reach for Victory

Korea. October 1950. It had been a war of lightning thrusts, mostly based on wrong premises. The North Koreans, eager to see the unification of their homeland, had ignored the American tradition in that winter of 1949–1950. Instead they believed a speech by the U.S. Secretary of State in which he foolishly opened the door for aggression by telling the world that Korea was outside the American sphere of influence. That statement had turned on a green light for the North Koreans, and they acted within a matter of months. They had crossed the border into South Korea in June and driven south with all their strength, knowing that it was essential to win a quick victory and present the world with a fait accomplis.

Once this invasion occurred, the American military had second thoughts, and President Harry Truman decided that Korea was, after all, within the American sphere. General Douglas MacArthur, the commander of American occupation forces in Japan, was ordered to resist the North Korean thrust and fight back. This move was approved by the United Nations, and the war became a UN "police action" against "North Korean aggression." MacArthur summoned his slender resources—occupation troops, not combat-ready troops—and in a series of desperate stands managed to prevent the smothering of South Korea. Then, in September, he made a lightning stroke and invaded far behind the North Korean lines at Inchon and began to cut off the North Korean armies from their supply sources. The North Koreans rolled back, back, back, above Seoul, above the 38th parallel, the old demarcation line. And the United Nations forces kept pushing.

1

All this had been regarded with growing dismay in Beijing. Mao Zedong's Communist government had a healthy fear of the Americans, engendered by an American policy that was seen as dedicated to the return of Chiang Kaishek and the destruction of the Communist Chinese government. As the tide in Korea turned, the meetings in Beijing proliferated, but of course the Americans who had no relationship at all with Beijing, and did not seem to read the neutral press, ignored or were oblivious to the signs. By September the Chinese had decided that they must intervene if the Americans were bent on the destruction of the North Korean government, and from Tokyo General MacArthur trumpeted that message. Coming from MacArthur the message was unmistakable; he was on record as advocating the destruction not only of the North Korean People's Republic, but of Communist China's government as well.

Message after message was sent to the West by Premier Zhou Enlai, as is noted elsewhere in these pages. All were ignored. And, not understanding Chinese concerns, the Americans forged on to what seemed to be an inevitable victory, blind to all in their scent of quick victory and the revamping of East Asia in the mold they wished to create.

On October 25, 1950, the Republic of Korea First Division was moving along the road from the Chongchon River to Unsan. General Douglas MacArthur had ordered a general advance to the Yalu River to mop up the fleeing remnants of the North Korean People's Army, which was now in shambles, following MacArthur's brilliant landing behind the North Korean lines at Inchon in September. It seemed the ROK First Division—comprising the best of South Korea's troops—might be the first unit to reach the Yalu and there to stop, on the borderline between Korea and China.

The 15th Regiment of the First Division passed through Unsan, and the Sixth Tank Battalion led the way forward. Once the United Nations forces reached the Yalu and consolidated their positions along that river, it seemed certain that the Korean war would end, just four months after the North Koreans had shocked the world by invading South Korea.

A mile and a half northeast of Unsan the ROK troops came to a bridge, and as the first tank rolled onto the bridge, it was suddenly hit with heavy mortar fire. The ROK infantry that were traveling with the tanks jumped into the ditches on the sides of the road and began firing. Half an hour later they reported that they faced about three hundred enemy troops. And there was something else. These troops they faced were Chinese.

Chinese?

When that word was passed back to General Walton Walker's Eighth Army headquarters at Pyongyang, no one believed it. The Chinese were not involved in the Korean war. General MacArthur had said that all the recent talk about their becoming involved was so much propaganda.

The troops were Chinese, said General Paik Sunyup, commander of the ROK First Division. He should have known. He had fought Chinese Communists in the 1940s when he was a soldier of Japan.

Then, said the high officers of the Eighth Army, these soldiers must be individual Chinese volunteers. The Chinese were definitely not in the war.

General Paik and his men did not know anything about that. All they knew was that they were fighting troops that fought with a will and that they were Chinese. True, they were wearing North Korean uniforms, but they were definitely Chinese.

There must be something wrong, insisted General Walker. They could not be Chinese.

And for the moment, that was that.

If those were Chinese troops fighting the United Nations forces in Korea, and they most definitely were, then how and why did they come to fight in this war? After all, they had not been attacked or even threatened by the United Nations, which was in charge of this "police action" designed to restore peace to the Korean Peninsula.

The answer lies in the course of American policy and actions toward China from 1945 to 1950 and in the statements and attitudes shown towards China by a number of American leaders in that period. Of such stuff is foreign relations made, even though by and large when Americans speak out in their freedom, they are unconscious that the rest of the world is listening very closely.

This book tells how and why the Chinese happened to appear as fighters in Korea on October 25, 1950, and how and why the people of the United States and China were cast into a war as antagonists, a position that very few people in either country wanted.

The story begins in 1945, as the war against Japan is just ending. . . .

2

Days of Hope in China

America's close involvement in modern Chinese affairs really began in 1940. We had missed the opportunity to halt Japanese aggression in 1931 when the Kwantung Army seized Mukden and then all of Manchuria and turned it into the puppet state of Manchukuo. At that time, the Japanese record shows, if the United States had acted, Japan would have backed away. And if that had happened, civil control of the Japanese government might have been retained. Another missed chance: 1932, when the Japanese attacked Shanghai. Again, strong western action would have caused the Japanese to stop their aggression against China. The failure of the Americans and British to act was a signal to the Japanese army to go ahead with the conquest of China.

When what the Chinese call the War of Japanese Aggression began in 1937, the Americans were still not ready to act, although growing public sympathy for China filled to overflowing the China Relief boxes in every Chinese restaurant in the land. After the occupation of Canton (Guang-zhou), American supplies began moving to China over the last remaining route of supply, the Burma Road, which runs between Lashio in North Burma and Kunming in Yunnan Province of China. Yet so slight was American concern then that when the British, then overlords of Burma, closed the road as a gesture of appeasement to Japan, America did not protest. We had our own appeasement. After the Japanese attacked and sank the American gunboat Panay *in the Yangtze River, President Roosevelt ordered the gunboats off the western sector of the river, where the*

5

Japanese were driving Chiang Kaishek back to Chongqing, because he did not want a confrontation with Japan.

The first strong action the United States took in relationship to China was to cut Japan's lifeline of oil in 1940 after the Japanese occupation of French Indochina, which came on the heels of the fall of France into the hands of Japan's partner Germany. This American action set the wheels of war going in Japan and made inevitable the Japanese drive south into the Dutch East Indies to secure the Sumatra and Borneo oil fields.

After that, in 1941, Americans resumed deliveries of supplies to China on a cash basis, and the American aviator Claire Chennault organized the American Volunteer Group of mercenary pilots to fight the Japanese in the air. American backing of this move was shown in the permission given U.S. Marine, Army, and Navy pilots to fight for China and then later to resume their commissions in the U.S. services without penalty.

And what were the basic motivations behind this slowly emerging American policy? One was the preservation of American financial interests in China, which included newspapers, tobacco companies, petroleum companies, shipping, banking, and insurance. Another was fear of Japanese expansionism, which had already declared for "Asia for the Asiatics" and against the Western presence. And finally there was the emotion encouraged by missionaries and the sons of missionaries. The most voluble of the latter was Henry R. Luce, the magazine publisher, who had grown up in China as the son of missionaries, and who had a highly romanticized view of the Chinese Republic. His influence as a major figure in "the China lobby" would be pervasive in the decision of the United States government to back the Nationalists long after they had shown themselves as venal and incapable of reform.

Americans tend to hold an oversimplified and romantic assessment of their country's relationship with the Chinese. Secretary of State Dean Acheson enunciated this clearly enough in 1949 in his prefatory letter to the compilation of papers about China that has come to be known as the China White Paper.

Despite the distance and broad differences in background which separate China and the United States, our friendship for that country has always been intensified by the religious, philanthropic, and cultural ties which have united the two peoples, and has been attested by many acts of good will over a period of many years, including the use of the Boxer indemnity for the education of Chinese students, the abolition of extraterritoriality during the Second World War, and our extensive aid to China during and since the close of that war.

All that Secretary Acheson said was true; it did not, however, represent the whole truth.

To be sure, many American missionaries went to China, and while distributing the Gospel, they also brought medical supplies, foodstuffs, and social welfare. The Rockefeller Foundation established the Peking Union Medical College, which in its time was a wonder of China and a major contribution of the West to Chinese welfare. And, yes, the Boxer indemnity was used to educate Chinese students. But just as large an impact in China was made by American businessmen, who sold oil and groceries, ran newspapers and insurance agencies, shipping lines and cable companies, and who were perceived by the Chinese to be a part of the colonial establishment of Europeans who dominated the treaty ports in the nineteenth and early twentieth centuries.

It was true that the Americans abandoned extraterritoriality in China during World War II, but they had enjoyed the privilege until that time, and a nationalistic China, smarting under the yoke of colonialism, found little to differentiate the American attitude toward colonialism from that of the British, French, and Germans. This has been true from the days of the Chinese empire until the present.

Much of the American attitude toward China is founded on fantasy stemming from the ardent and effective publicity campaign of Madame Chiang Kaishek during World War II, the journalism of Henry R. Luce, and the writings of the American novelist Pearl Buck. Except during World War II, when American assistance kept the Republic of China going in the war against Japan, United States policy toward China has been largely irrelevant to that country's development, and in that period, the United States ended up backing the wrong side—not just the losing side, but the dead-wrong side. The Kuomintang, by that time, represented a failed revolution that had become corrupt and venal, and had lost the support of the Chinese people.

The foreigners, and this included the Americans by and large, were interested in preserving the status quo in China. They sided with the Qing Dynasty to put down the Taiping Rebellion. When Dr. Sun Yatsen went to America to seek assistance for his rebellion against the Qings, he was not very successful. When Dr. Sun's revolution did get underway in the 1920s, it received more help by far from the Soviet Russians than from the Americans.

The Chinese revolution was a real revolution, and neither Dr. Sun nor his military advisor Chiang Kaishek were afraid of being called "red" in those days. The Communists were very much a part of the Kuomintang Party and were welcomed in the early 1920s. It was only in 1927, when Communist-led troops captured the Wuhan area and Chiang took Shanghai, that the rift occurred. Chiang saw that he had to "eat or be eaten," and he allied himself with the notorious Green gang of Shanghai and the foreign business community, which wanted stability and was willing to pay for it. The Communists accused Chiang of selling out to the enemy and betraying the revolution; many of the left wing of the Kuomintang, including Soong Chingling, the widow of Dr. Sun Yatsen, agreed. These feelings contributed to Chiang's own uneasiness, which caused him to begin a campaign to exterminate the Communists in China and seize control of the country for the Kuomintang.

But in dedicating his efforts to eliminating the Communists (which he very nearly succeeded in doing), Chiang Kaishek sacrificed his revolution, the basic ideas of land reform, and the other revolutionary principles of San Min Jui, which was to the Chinese revolution what the American Declaration of Independence was to the United States.

The Communists had settled into communes in central China, but then for survival they undertook the "Long March" that took them first south, then west, then north along the Tibetan frontier, and finally back northeast to the barren lands of Shaanxi Province.

They settled in Yanan, so remote and so unfriendly an environment that even in the 1980s it remained a backwater and was not connected to any other part of China by rail.

In the middle of the 1930s American policy in a China beset by Japan was geared very closely to American business interests. For example, it is now known that the United States or Britain could have stopped the Manchurian takeover by Japan, by a dispatch of warships to the Far East. The Japanese government was prepared to back down. But no strong action was taken. Yet, when the Japanese proposed in 1934 to establish an official petroleum monopoly to distribute petroleum products in Manchukuo, on behalf of Standard Oil Company and other firms that had enormous interests in China and Manchuria, the U.S. government sent a strong protest.

By 1937 the Japanese penetration of China covered the eastern seaboard, and the American government was taking issue with much Japanese activity. The Chinese were fighting the Japanese, but in their own ways. Chiang Kaishek's Nationalists fought here and there, retreated steadily, but maintained their government's integrity. Chiang did not put his full force against the Japanese, because much of it was lined up against the Chinese Communists, and the extermination campaign continued, in principle if not very effectively in fact.

As for the Chinese Communists, Mao Zedong and his comrades shrewdly assessed the future, and found that by enlisting the help of the peasantry in Japanese-occupied lands they could achieve two objectives: first, to secure the assistance and adherence of the people; and second, to fight the enemy and establish bases for future control of large areas of China.

This considered policy of "United Front" was begun in January 1936, before the Marco Polo bridge incident of 1937 that began the long anti-Japanese open war. Chiang paid no attention to the "hand of friendship" extended by the Japanese. He recognized that it would be the handshake of convenience only, but he erred in underrating the Japanese threat and overrating his own ability to fight two wars at once.

In December 1937, on a visit to Xian, Chiang was kidnapped by Generals Zhang Xueliang of the Manchurian Army and Yang

Hucheng of the Northwestern Army. Holding Chiang, they forced agreement to make a common front against the Japanese.

This alliance was never very real, and was never made formal. The Communists in theory accepted Chiang's authority as supreme military commander, but in fact maintained their own strength and cohesion; and when Chiang tried to move their troops around to his own advantage, they balked. Chiang, for his part, did pay the Chinese Communist armies some money, and gave them some ammunition, but it was not enough to make a vast difference in the balance.

The basis of the agreement, such as it was, went back to the 1920s program and mutual adherence to the principles of Dr. Sun Yatsen. But by 1941, when the war was extended by Japan to include the whole Pacific Basin, the idealism of the Kuomintang was in shards, and the government was controlled by a handful of families who milked it for their own purposes, and generals who used their armies to unify the country and put down all the war-lords who had been frustrated by the Japanese war. Chiang did not prosecute the war except sporadically, and then only for limited objectives, usually having to do with the future control of postwar China. By 1942, with the United States in the war, Nationalists and Communists were both certain that the Allies would triumph against Japan, and both wanted to be in position to take advantage of all opportunities to emerge from the anti-Japanese war with strength for what they knew would be the coming struggle for control of China.

To propitiate the Kuomintang in the war against Japan, and also to make their own administration of "liberated areas" easier, the Communists had temporarily halted their oppression of land-lords and forcible redistribution of lands. They contented them-selves with controlling rents and working with the peasants, some of whom approached the landlord class in the size of their holdings.

After Pearl Harbor, the United States began supplying the Chinese government in Chongqing with money and military goods. General Joseph W. Stilwell was given military control of the Chinese armies, at least in theory.

In fact, Stilwell found it very difficult to move the Chinese, and with the exception of a campaign in Burma in the spring of 1945, the Americans never did move them much. Stilwell developed a personal animosity toward Chiang Kaishek, which was returned by the Generalissimo.

In the fall of 1944, President Franklin D. Roosevelt sent General Patrick J. Hurley to China to encourage a real coalition between Nationalists and Communists. Hurley's other task, equally important, was to ease the differences between Chiang Kaishek and General Stilwell.

Hurley stepped into a tenuous and most delicate situation. At about the time he was going, Congressman Mansfield of Montana returned from a trip to China with an apt assessment of the situation: "It appears to me that both the Communists and Kuomintang are more interested in preserving their respective parties at this time and have been for the past two years than they are in carrying on the war against Japan."

Nationalists and Communists did face a real dilemma. Each party had as its long-range goal the absolute control of China. The American position of 1944 and early 1945 was that the more important matter was the war against the Japanese. President Roosevelt and all his advisors pressed Chiang and Mao to come to some accommodation to that end. The Nationalists relented to the point of opening talks, to which the Communists assented. Zhou Enlai maintained a mission in Chongqing for the purpose of negotiation.

Meanwhile the American observers on the China scene, from Ambassador Clarence Gauss on down, indicated that the Nationalist government was deteriorating every day in its ability to control and enlist the support of the people.

One of Chiang's potent arguments against linking with the Communists was their allegiance to Moscow and international revolution. This was a very telling argument. But in 1944, American observers detected a new note in the Chinese Communist line. It was a note of nationalism which ultimately would rise to the point of a direct challenge from Beijing to Moscow for leadership of the "Marxists" in the world. The basic difference was in the form of revolution: The Russian revolution had been one of urban workers; the Chinese revolution was a peasants' revolt taken over by the Communists. The Chinese brand of communism was bound to develop on different lines.

However, this truth was not readily apparent in 1945 and was given small credence by American political leaders. They felt that the American China experts were too close to the forest, too much opposed to the Kuomintang to have level heads. So, although the China experts made a set of recommendations, the political and military leaders generally ignored them.

On April 17, 1944, the Japanese began a campaign to open the Beijing-Hankow railway. They fought across the Yellow River. On May 18, they captured Loyang, and with the capture of Kaifeng a few days later the Chinese Honan Province front collapsed completely. Before the end of the month, the Japanese were moving in the Yangtze region again, and soon captured Changsha and then Henyang. They then started an offensive against the Allied air base at Guilin.

By November, when Guilin fell, the Japanese were swarming through Hunan and the Nationalist war effort was about to collapse. Only in Burma, where General Stilwell had direct command of the Chinese army, did the Nationalists make an effort to fight the Japanese. Out of this problem had come the Hurley mission. Patrick Hurley, a general officer in World War I, was a Republican politician from Oklahoma who served President Franklin Roosevelt in several capacities during the U.S. coalition government of the World War II years. In addition, General Stilwell was promoted to command all the Chinese armies, but this strategy did not work. By autumn Stilwell and Chiang were at swords' points. Said General Stilwell:

> Chiang Kaishek has no intention of making further efforts to prosecute the war. Anyone who crowds him toward such action will be blocked or eliminated. . . . Chiang believes he can go on milking the United States for money and munitions by using the old gag about quitting if he is not supported. He believes that the war in the Pacific is nearly over, and that by delaying tactics he can throw the whole burden on us. He has no intention of instituting any real democratic regime or of forming a united front with the Communists. He himself is the main

obstacle to unification of China and her cooperation in a real effort against Japan. . . .

Stilwell, now an obstacle, was removed, and General Albert C. Wedemeyer was brought in. Wedemeyer was naive and sufficiently anticommunist for anybody. Besides this, Wedemeyer was never placed in command of the Chinese forces. Thus, Chiang Kaishek had once more gotten his way with the Americans, but the American government was now aware of the problem of getting China to fight and also to reach some accommodation with the Communists that would prevent the immediate outbreak of civil war in China upon defeat of the Japanese. This really was a positive development, and it was marked by the travel of Americans to Yanan and some minor cooperation between Americans and the Red Chinese over weather reporting for the American submarines scouring the China seas.

General Hurley also had the right idea. He saw as his mission in September 1944 the unification of the Chinese Nationalist and Communist forces to fight the Japanese.

In November 1944, General Hurley did manage to secure from the Communists at Yanan a draft agreement of five points between Nationalists and Communists:

1. Unification of military forces.
2. Coalition government.
3. Return to the Sun Yatsen Three Principles of the People.
4. Obedience of military forces to the coalition management.
5. Recognition of the legality of the Communist Party.

In the fall of 1944 this agreement seemed to point the way to a real solution to China's future. Hurley believed this was a good plan, and one that could bring about the unification of China. But the Nationalists rejected it and instead offered a three-point plan that first of all called for the Communists to turn over their armies to the Nationalists for reorganization—which had to mean control by the Nationalists. Second, the Communists would have membership on the national military council, which would control the armies, but the plan did not say how much membership. And third, the government did agree to return to the Three Principles of the People enunciated by Dr. Sun Yatsen.

The Communists rejected the three-point plan as one which in no way called for a coalition government, but only for Communist subordination to the Nationalists.

Zhou Enlai also wrote to General Hurley, pledging Communist cooperation with the American war effort, and thanking him for his concern over China. This was, in a way, a high point in American relations with the Chinese Communists.

The exchanges continued, with Hurley trying to expand the narrow Nationalist offer, and Zhou Enlai maintaining his five-point plan as a basis for discussion. Hurley said then that the sticking point was Chiang's insistence on one-party control of the government.

The discussions limped along, but in January 1945, Zhou Enlai did return to Chongqing, after several refusals to do so, to reopen talks. The problem, always, was Chiang's demand for control of all the troops, and the Communist refusal to give it over until abolition of one-party rule and establishment of a real coalition government.

Still, nothing happened of any real significance for the future. General Hurley, newly created ambassador to China, then recommended against shipment of arms to the Communists, which still further decreased their faith in the United States.

Early in 1945, Hurley went back to Washington for consultations. While he was there, Chargé d'Affaires George Atcheson sent a long message to the State Department summing up the observations made by the professional staff of China watchers over a long period of time.

They observed that the Communists were aware of the attitude of Chiang Kaishek, which had grown tougher since he now once again felt that he had the United States in his pocket. They recommended some tough talk and action by the U.S. government, because Chiang had just recently been appointing many strong anticommunists to high places.

And here is a key:

On their part the Communists have arrived at the conclusion that we are definitely committed to the support of Chiang

Kaishek alone and that Chiang's hand will not be forced by us so that we are unable to assist or cooperate with the Communists.

Because of this, the Communists were taking an action they forecast the year before: Linking America with their enemy, they were moving ahead to strengthen their position in south China and elsewhere, so that when the war ended they could protect their holdings and increase them.

And, said Atcheson:

Despite the fact that our actions in our refusal to aid or deal with any group other than the Central Government have been diplomatically correct, and our intentions have been good, the conclusion appears clear that if this situation continues, and if our analysis of it is correct, the probable outbreak of disastrous civil conflict will be accelerated and chaos in China will be inevitable.

The recommendation of the professionals was that Chiang be told that the Americans would help the Communists because they were fighting the Japanese. Aid to Chiang would not be cut. It should also be pointed out to Chiang that it would be better to have the Communists helped by the United States than by the USSR.

A tremendous internal pressure for unity exists in China, based upon compromise with the Communists and an opportunity for self-expression on the part of the now repressed liberal groups. Even inside the Kuomintang, these liberal groups such as the Sun Fo group and the minor parties were ignored in the recent negotiations by the Kuomintang, although not by the Communists, with whom they present what amounts to a united front, and they are discouraged and disillusioned by what they regard as an American commitment to the Kuomintang's existing reactionary leadership.

But here, at this juncture, General Hurley went wrong. He opposed any aid to the Communists. He told Roosevelt that the

United States should stick with its commitment to the Chiang Kaishek regime. Along that road lay disaster, but Hurley could not see so far.

Hurley was not in fact a fool. He was duped by Stalin, with whom he had a long conversation before he returned to China. Stalin and Molotov both told him that they did not regard the Chinese Communists as true Communists, but as "agrarian reformers." Thus the term, introduced by Josef Stalin and which he knew was a lie, was used in the discussions in America.

Stalin suggested to Hurley that he would support the Chinese Nationalists. Hurley returned to China with that idea, and feeling that backing the Nationalists was the easiest way for the United States.

Hurley went back to Chongqing and began talking tough to the Communists. They were not surprised. They had long since developed a strong disbelief in the logic of foreigners and in their reliability to live up to their apparent commitments and promises. Hurley believed that the Soviets would support Chiang Kaishek because he had been told, or thought he had been told, just that by Stalin. George Kennan, a professional diplomat and expert on the USSR, had warned the State Department after the Hurley-Stalin meeting that Hurley's impressions were not reliable, given Stalin's thinking and use of words.

What happened to General Hurley during his stay in China could have happened to any political—as opposed to professional—diplomat. He had gone to Yanan and there had been convinced by the Communists that there must be a coalition government before there could be a laying down of Communist arms. He went back to Chongqing, where T. V. Soong convinced him that only the Chiang Kaishek faction had the interests of China at heart.

General Hurley went to Yanan, but he did not go to the new territories, where it was possible to see what Chinese Communist policy had done, and what attitude the people had towards the Chinese Communists as opposed to the Nationalists and the warlords and landlords who had controlled their destinies in the past. When he returned to the Nationalist territory, seeds of suspicion were sown with him against the foreign service personnel in

China who disagreed with his views. That winter he got John Davies transferred out, and John Stewart Service of the State Department, who had been reporting from Yanan, was warned. Service and others had traveled around inside Communist-held territory and noticed the difference between the adherence of the peasants to the Communist cause and the apathy in the Kuomintang areas.

Several observers, such as Raymond Ludden, had traveled extensively through Communist territory. Ludden spent four months moving 1200 miles in Red territory.

In the spring of 1945 Ludden and Service were both attached to the military headquarters of General Albert Wedemeyer, who had succeeded General Stilwell in China.

Ludden reported on his trip to Wedemeyer, who asked for a written report. So Ludden and Service collaborated on a joint report, dealing with military policy and the problems posed by Chiang Kaishek's priorities: He was more interested in keeping up troop strengths in the Communist areas than in fighting the Japanese.

General Hurley and General Wedemeyer left China in February 1945 to go to Washington; the implication was that serious policy matters would be decided in the next few weeks.

While Hurley and Wedemeyer were away, the Chinese Communist Party convened its 11th National Congress, and political advisor Service attended. He reported that the Communists had been hearing Chiang Kaishek's anticommunist speeches and that they were unfavorably impressed.

Also while Hurley was away, Chargé d'Affaires George Atcheson drafted a message that told what was going on in China from the point of view of professional observers.

In Washington Special Ambassador Hurley met with the new president, Harry S. Truman, who succeeded in the spring when President Roosevelt died. Ambassador Hurley had undergone a major change of heart regarding the Chinese situation. Perhaps it was engendered by his belief that what Stalin had said was true, and that the Russian Communists did not regard the Chinese as coming from the same mold. Also, the ambassador was subjected to the same pressures from the China lobby that were used to persuade all political figures toward the Nationalist position.

On November 26, 1945, General Hurley, who was a Republican politician, resigned as Special Ambassador to China. Since 1942 Hurley had served the Democratic administration in what was, in fact, an American coalition government formed for the prosecution of the war. Republican leaders had agreed to forego differences in matters of foreign policy in the interest of maintaining a single national posture. But as in Britain when the European war ended, the government of national unity ended in America shortly after the surrender of Japan.

Thus Ambassador Hurley's letter of resignation is an extremely important document showing the change of American foreign policy. The Republicans were now going back into opposition, and developing the policies that would win the victory in the American Congressional elections to the 80th Congress in the autumn of 1946. One of their key campaign issues would be American policy in China, and the Hurley resignation was one of the opening guns in the battle.

"The astonishing feature of our foreign policy," wrote Ambassador Hurley,

is the wide discrepancy between our announced policies and our conduct of international relations. For instance, we began the war with the principles of the Atlantic Charter and democracy as our goal. Our associates in the war [Hurley meant Soviet Russia, but the same was true of Chiang's China] at that time gave lip service to principles of democracy. We finished the war in the Far East furnishing lend-lease supplies and using all our reputation to undermine democracy and bolster imperialism and Communism.

The most important of Hurley's charges, and the most damaging to the Democratic Administration, was the ambassador's claim that American foreign policy was undermined by the professional diplomats in the State Department. This startling charge was made in all seriousness in relation to the aims of the Administration: trying to keep China in the war in 1944 and 1945 and to soothe troubled relations between Chiang Kaishek and the American military.

> While these objectives had the support of the President and the Secretary of State, it is no secret that the American policy in China did not have the support of all the career men in the State Department. The professional foreign service men sided with the Chinese Communist-armed party and the imperialist bloc of nations whose policy it was to keep China divided against herself. Our professional diplomats continually advised the Communists that my efforts in preventing the collapse of the national government did not represent the policy of the United States. These same professionals also advised the Communist-armed party to decline unification of the Chinese Communist army with the National army unless the Chinese Communists were given control.

The men of whom Ambassador Hurley spoke, John P. Davies, John Service, Richard Service, and others, knew China very well. Some of them, such as the Service brothers, had been born there and spoke at least one of the languages.

But one aspect of their attitude that put Hurley off was their nearly uniform view that the Kuomintang was falling apart and the Communists were offering the only viable alternative to chaos in China. The fact that they were dead right was no excuse; it only helped inflame Ambassador Hurley and the China lobby.

The most destructive aspect of General Hurley's letter of resignation was his blanket charge that the American foreign service was weak and riddled with Communist sympathizers. Certainly there had been Communist sympathizers and even agents in the State Department in the past. But by 1945 this problem really did not exist, although for the next four years America would devote an enormous amount of collective energy to an anticommunist witchhunt in government. The real internal threat from the Soviets in the 1940s was their effort to secure the atomic bomb.

General Hurley saw a strange dichotomy of American policy: supporting the Communist world on the one hand and the imperialist nations of Europe on the other. It is the word "support" that makes this position difficult to understand.

> Instead of putting our weight behind the charter of the United Nations we have been definitely supporting the Imperialist Bloc. At the same time a considerable section of our State Department is endeavoring to support communism generally as well as specifically in China.

Perhaps a better word than "support" would have been "accept." The Americans were *accepting* the return of their Western Allies to their wicked colonial ways, and not only accepting but defending and then picking up their burden, as America did in Indochina with the French, in effect becoming the colonial power that carried the war against the Vietnamese Revolution.

But in Eastern Europe the United States "accepted" the Soviet fait accompli of takeover. Some would argue that the United States did not have to accept it; that was true only if America did not mind risking war and extending its self-appointed role as policeman of the world.

In China the professionals of the State Department saw something (also seen by the majority of journalists) that the makers of American foreign policy did not see: the coming collapse of a Kuomintang government that had wasted the good will of the Chinese people to the point of exhaustion, that had wasted its resources, and whose leaders had all too often stolen those resources. The fact was that by 1945 the Chinese people had very little confidence in their government, and the high taxation and corruption of the next two years raised the stink of death to hang over the Kuomintang.

This was the time at which the reporting of the China experts of the State Department would have been invaluable. But already in 1945, the Hurley mission had disrupted the State Department Far Eastern Section, and those people who were not being harried were running scared and protecting themselves as best they could. In 1946 this tendency became more noticeable; thus American policy was made largely in a void, and too often dictated by short-range military considerations rather than long-range diplomatic thinking.

Despite the intransigence of the Kuomintang on the major issue of coalition government, the Americans continued to hope that some solution could be worked out.

As the State Department White Paper on China put it:

After the successful termination of the war against Japan and at the time that General Hurley left Chongqing, there were several elements of the situation which plausibly argued that the prospects for peaceful reconstruction in China were reasonably good. The Nationalists and the Communists were still talking, and they both seemed to be talking the same language. Both participants in the negotiations still professed their desire and intention to seek a political settlement and there could be little doubt that the overwhelming popular demand was for peace.

Economically there seemed to be real hope. The inheritance from the Japanese in Manchuria and north China and the Shanghai area was promising for the future. No one then could dream of the venality of Chiang's wife, relatives, and friends that would cause them to personally take over whole industries to add to their personal fortunes.

In the military sphere both Nationalists and Communists were accepting Japanese surrenders and taking over the territory and arms. Theoretically all these belonged to the Nationalist government, but the country was really in a state of suspended civil war, with frequent military clashes. American policy held that the Nationalist regime was the only legitimate government, which was a good legal view but a very bad political one. It created an "Alice in Wonderland" world for American policy in China, high on moral intent, and very low on potential performance.

For example, the Chinese central government was legally entitled to occupy Manchuria as the Japanese surrendered. But Chiang Kaishek was totally unprepared for such an occupation. General Wedemeyer suggested to Chiang that he content himself with trying to consolidate north China and central and south China, and wait on Manchuria. This was a sensible solution to an otherwise insoluble problem. It should also have been recognized that the Communists had already moved into Manchuria with major army strength from north China. The Communists, then, by strength and the default of the Nationalists, now had this important area of China to add to their holdings and negotiating power. It was of little use to argue the fine legal points. Possession was nine points of the law.

Instead of treating the China situation as one where existed a legitimate government and a pretender, America would have been much wiser to accept the facts. There were, as of 1945, two Chinas: one strong, but riddled with corruption, and one weak, but strengthened by unity of purpose.

3

The Marshall Mission

By the time the Pacific War ended, Americans, generally speaking, had divided into two factions regarding China, personified by two American generals. One, General Claire Chennault, commander of the 14th U.S. Army Air Force, was fiercely loyal to Chiang Kaishek and applauded Chiang's wartime policy of keeping his best troops on the borders of Communist-held territory. The other general, Joseph Stilwell, regarded Chiang Kaishek as a failure and a liability. Ultimately both generals fell afoul of higher American authority because of their views. Stilwell was the first to go. Before the war ended, he was withdrawn because of his views that the Nationalists were on the verge of collapse. Major General Albert C. Wedemeyer was brought in to replace him. But just before the end of the war, Chennault was also ordered out through the influence of General George C. Marshall, who was angered by Chennault's politicking in favor of the Nationalist cause.

The division within the American community deepened. It affected every level, including the political reporting that went on inside the State Department establishment. It was not that the American diplomats were not doing their jobs. But at the upper levels the officials of the State Department had begun to distrust their representatives in China, and they were pressed by the China lobby to get rid of the representatives who warned that the Nationalist government was growing more venal all the time. General Patrick J. Hurley, the special ambassador representing President Truman, adopted this view and cut the ground from beneath his principal advisors,

old China hands who saw clearly the coming collapse of the Nationalist
government from its own corruption. . . .

———

After the surrender of the Japanese, the Chinese once more took
control of their own country. But the control was anything but
unified. China was divided into two major political elements, both
armed, with a few warlords still to be dealt with. For example,
Yunnan Province was the center of American military activity during the war; here were the headquarters of the 14th Air Force
and the Services of Supply for all China. Yet Yunnan's links with
the Kuomintang government were very slender. They always had
been since the heyday of the warlords. Yunnan paid lip service to
the Nationalist cause, but not much else. Indeed, while the rest of
China went on daylight saving time to conform to the American
system, Yunnan Province remained on standard time as a gesture
of defiance.

When the war ended, Chiang Kaishek decided it was time to
take control of Yunnan. He arranged to have the Yunnan army,
under the command of the half-brother of the governor, General
Lu Han, sent to occupy northern Indochina. It was an enormously
attractive opportunity, a chance to loot, so Lu Han's army went to
Hanoi. As soon as the soldiers were out of Yunnan, Chiang Kaishek
sent in troops loyal to himself, and took control of the province
for the first time. This little tale is indicative of the major problem
China had faced since the 1920s. Chiang never was able to unify
China, although he did come close before the Japanese interrupted
his plans.

After the war ended in 1945, the Nationalists controlled the
south, with the exception of Canton, which was a Communist
stronghold, and Hainan Island, which was disputed territory.
Chiang also was able to replace the Japanese in Anhui, Hube, and
Hunan, except for the triangle around Hankow, which had always
been Communist country. The Communists held most of east
China north of Chekiang Province, and almost as far east as Ning-
hsia and then north to the Soviet border. When the Russians entered the Pacific War, they undertook the occupation of
Manchuria's six provinces, and the Communists were active in most

of them, particularly in Heilongjiang and its capital, Harbin. Indeed, within a few months Zhu De, the commander of the Red Army, established a strong force in and around Harbin, with Japanese weapons turned over by the Russians.

General Wedemeyer saw Chiang's problem very clearly. Chiang could stabilize his situation in the south and part of central China if he would reform his government and employ foreign technicians to put industry and finance to rights. But Chiang would have to deal with the Communists on a political level, and that meant negotiation and reform. These old adversaries, Chiang and Mao Zedong, knew one another very well. They had both come up the revolutionary ladder before their paths parted and crossed again with weaponry. As Wedemeyer saw it, there was no substitute for the political solution if Chiang was to succeed. Otherwise, said General Wedemeyer, Chiang would not get control of Manchuria.

Wedemeyer was practical and not very hopeful. On the basis of the record, it seemed most unlikely that Chiang would reach an accommodation with the Communists. And as the weeks after the Japanese surrender wore on, the problem grew worse, because the Communists gained strength. This strength was not just in the territories where the Communists accepted Japanese surrender, but also in the south, where Chiang Kaishek failed completely to bring about the reforms needed. The Nationalists marched in, took over from the Japanese or the troops of Wang Chingwei's puppet government at Nanking, and immediately dissipated the enormous good will that was waiting for them through looting and mistreatment of the Chinese people, who had lived so long under Japanese occupation, as though they were an occupying power. The Kuomintang seized factories and gave them to Kuomintang officials. They grabbed the money from the banks. Within weeks the KMT had established a reputation for venality that turned the people of east China against them and towards the Communists.

Recognizing all this, General Wedemeyer suggested that the United States, Britain, and the USSR establish a trusteeship over Manchuria. Then, if the Nationalist government reformed, and could achieve a political settlement with the Communists, Manchuria could be returned to Chinese control. Otherwise, Wedemeyer predicted, the Chinese Communists would take control.

The Nationalists' behavior in Manchuria was in sharp contrast to that of the Communists, who were punctilious, carrying out some land reforms, but gently. They not only promised, but delivered, help to the farmers who had been oppressed for so long under the Japanese.

This was the problem that Chiang Kaishek posed for his American ally in the fall of 1945.

Hurley's resignation had been submitted on November 26, 1945, and was immediately accepted by an angry President Truman, who understood the Republican declaration of political warfare it implied. The President's answer was the appointment of General George C. Marshall, probably one of America's most respected men, to go to China and use America's influence to bring about a peaceful settlement of the political problems.

At the time such a settlement was a perfectly legitimate aspiration. The United States had supported the Nationalist government of China throughout the latter stages of the war against Japan, beginning well before the Pearl Harbor attack. In Yanan such representatives as John Stewart Service, who was General Wedemeyer's advisor, had also created genial relations with the Communists (for which Service was charged by Hurley and others with trying to promote communism).

The America of 1945 had a very close relationship with China; the United States was, in fact, responsible for making China, quite illogically, a member of the Security Council with veto power over UN affairs when, in fact, China had much less claim on membership in the Security Council permanent group than did France or Canada. What Americans and others did not realize then was that China was not a unified country, its government did not have control of its territory, and its fiscal condition was disastrous to the point that it could only be propped up by enormous grants in aid.

All this justified and made important the attempt of the United States government to interfere in Chinese affairs as a friend to both sides, and thus to try to bring about peace and unity. No one could gainsay this attempt, and the Chinese Communists welcomed the effort, while the Chinese Nationalists pretended to do so.

On December 15, General Marshall was instructed publicly to go to China, with the understanding that the United States would not intervene in military affairs. The only reason for American troops to continue in China, said President Truman, was to disarm and evacuate surrendered Japanese forces there.

Truman advised the Chinese to call a national meeting of all the political elements in the society, to bring unification and political representation to all views. He promised that as China moved toward peace and unity, the United States would give assistance to the economy and to the unified military organization that would be established. With these instructions and views in mind, General Marshall set out for Chongqing.

The groundwork for representative government in China had already been laid. President Chiang Kaishek had indicated that a year after the war ended, a national meeting was to be held, and that the Kuomintang, which had been carrying on a one-party dictatorship, would then lose all its special privileges. A constitution would be promulgated. A committee of 53, including two members of the Communist Party, had been appointed to prepare for constitutional government. Any questions that the meeting could not resolve were to be referred to a Political Consultative Conference. This key group would convene at Chongqing on January 10, 1946.

That autumn another consulting group was established. From the Nationalist side came General Chang Chun. From the Communist side came General Zhou Enlai. General Marshall was chairman. The task of this small committee was to discuss matters relating to the cease-fire of Communist and Nationalist troops.

The first matter to come before that committee was the movement of Nationalist troops into Manchuria, which was then held by the Soviets, since they had marched in during the final days of the Pacific War. General Marshall announced that the United States would transport the Kuomintang troops to Manchuria, and General Zhou offered no objection. This move conformed to the announced American policy and to the Sino-Soviet treaty signed in August 1945, in which the Soviets had agreed to support the Nationalist government.

On January 10, 1946, the committee of three also agreed on a cease-fire between Communist and Nationalist troops. It was to take place in three days. That same agreement also provided for the establishment of an Executive Headquarters at Beijing. Three commissioners would serve there: one American, one Nationalist, and one Communist.

The month of January thus opened with bright prospects. The Political Consultative Conference opened in Chongqing on January 10 and lasted three weeks. Chiang Kaishek announced the immediate grant of amnesty for political prisoners, and freedom of speech, association, and assembly.

Indeed, all looked promising—except that the announcement of these grants started a rumble of discontent within the right wing of the Kuomintang Party. Still, the Generalissimo had ordered the drafting of a constitution and a bill of rights. As far as the Americans were concerned, everything was on the right track. A constitution was being prepared, a national assembly was to be called, and it appeared that democracy and unity were coming to China.

But then specifics caused difficulties. The Communists said they should have at least fourteen of the forty assembly members for themselves and their friendly parties. Since certain functions could be carried out by only a three-fifths majority, this would give the Communists a sort of veto power. Again, the right wing of the Kuomintang objected violently.

The question of the army was to be decided by General Marshall and a Communist and a Nationalist general. Within eighteen months, the idea was, the Nationalist army would drop to sixty divisions, fifty of the Kuomintang and ten Communist. These would be integrated. General Marshall spoke strongly for a nonpolitical military force, a democratic army that would represent the nation and no particular group.

All this was done, and the Chinese public was very pleased.

In the winter and spring of 1946, Chiang faced an incipient rebellion within his own party. The Kuomintang had maintained a dictatorship since 1927, and the diehards saw no reason for it to end. Then, too, there was the problem of the generals, some of them not long out of the warlord stage, who saw no reason to give any ground to the Communists they had been told for years were an enemy to be wiped out. So the Nationalists stalled on bringing the changes into law, and the Communists stalled on approving the changes before the Nationalists had shown their approval. All matters were put off until November 1946.

In early March of that year, feeling that it was time to consult personally with President Truman, General Marshall returned to Washington. It seemed that the major differences between Communists and Nationalists could be resolved, and Marshall saw the need for a large amount of economic assistance to put a new China onto its feet.

That spring of 1946 the focus of events narrowed on Manchuria. There the Russians were busy looting whole factories that had belonged to the Japanese. They were supposed to move their troops out, but they did not seem to be in any hurry to go.

There had been reports of Nationalist-Communist clashes at the port of Hingkow, but Chiang wanted to preserve his freedom of action in Manchuria, so it was not until the day that Marshall left for Washington that a team was sent up there from Executive Headquarters. There were other troubles, with the Communists complaining about the Nationalists and vice versa. The Communists claimed that the Nationalists had encircled 60,000 Communist troops in the Guangzhou region and were trying to starve them out. The Nationalists claimed that the Communists were constantly enlarging their area of control in Manchuria with Russian help. That also was true. But the Nationalists were entrapped by their own eagerness. The Soviets were asked to speed up their withdrawal, and they did, leaving vast areas without troops. The Nationalists did not have the troops and could not move fast enough, and so in many areas of Manchuria, the Communists slipped in to fill a vacuum, with relatively small numbers of troops, augmented by militia they picked up and trained on the spot.

By April 1946, the Manchurian problem dominated the political discussions of the Nationalists and the Communists. Until it could be solved, nothing could be done to create a unified government.

The Communists protested the transport of Nationalist troops to Manchuria by American naval convoys. But the Americans were also transporting Communist troops out of the Guangzhou encirclement and up to Communist areas of north central China.

By the spring of 1946 it was apparent that the Communists

were gaining ground to the point that they now felt competent to contest almost every change that tended to bring territory under Nationalist control. On April 15, 1946, the Russians evacuated Changchun, the old capital of Manchukuo, and the Chinese Communists immediately attacked the city and occupied it, in pure violation of the agreement to cease hostilities.

As the American White Paper reported, this action had two serious results. First, it made the Chinese military men both overconfident and more reluctant to agree to a sharp reduction of their forces. Second, it angered the Kuomintang, and increased the influence of the diehards who still thought the only good Communist was a dead one.

General Marshall returned to China on April 18, after an absence of less than six weeks, but by that time the political situation had deteriorated enormously. Nationalist generals and politicians were clamoring for civil war. Communist generals were willing.

Only the top Nationalist leadership and the top Communist leadership prevented the outbreak. Mao Zedong agreed to submit to further military dispositions by agreement, but only if the fighting was terminated. The Nationalists, believing time was on their side, refused to stop the fighting in Shantung and other areas. As General Wedemeyer had pointed out, Chiang Kaishek did not have the military power to take over Manchuria, although he had legal authority. There was no compromise in the air.

At this point the Chinese Communists urged the Americans to move out, because American naval and military presence in north China inadvertently gave support to the Nationalist strength throughout the Beijing-Tianjin areas. It was good advice, and had the Americans followed it, the situation in China might have been clarified very quickly. In those six weeks of Marshall's absence, the Communists sensed the political failure of the Nationalists, and their loss of support in centers such as Shanghai and Beijing. Everywhere, Nationalist leadership was driving the Chinese people into the arms of the Communists.

General Marshall was completely cognizant of the growing crisis. He began by pointing out to Chiang and his associates that all this could have been avoided had they taken his advice in the beginning to work out a political settlement. By this time, the spring of 1946, the political atmosphere was deadly; neither side believed the other. Now it was no longer a case of negotiating for agreement, but of marking time, gaining strength, and preparing for war.

Marshall pointed out, to each side, its own violations of the cease-fire agreements and political agreements. Then he announced that since both were quarreling over Manchuria, and the future of that area would determine the future of China, he was withdrawing from mediation attempts.

That spring of 1946 the world of China changed, when so suddenly the situation altered so drastically in Manchuria. There, except in the Liaoning Peninsula and the Changchun corridor, the Communists had control of all the area that had been so important to the Japanese for fifteen years. In other words, circumstances delivered into the Communist hands what was the equivalent of a whole country, and gave them an enormous new power—a fact even they, much less the Nationalists, did not realize fully.

Now both sides saw how they might use the Americans to their own advantage. The outside parties, the Democratic League and others, were also eager for the Americans to remain as a means for achieving a real peace.

But Manchuria proved to be the furnace in which the fires of freedom were smothered.

The atmosphere of weakness and mutual dependence, which had been forced to a degree on the Chinese Nationalists and the Communists during the years of the Japanese occupation, had now completely disappeared.

The Chinese Communists, seeing that they had gained an enormous advantage in Manchuria, were reluctant to relinquish it. They asked for a drastic realignment of Nationalist and Communist troops under the proposed government of unity. The Nationalists were even more cocky.

Although General Marshall had temporarily withdrawn from his attempts at mediation, he did continue to give advice to both sides. He advised the Communists to give up Changchun, which properly belonged to the Nationalists. He advised Chiang Kaishek to move slowly.

The Communists agreed to let the Nationalists occupy Changchun. General Marshall was gulled by Chiang Kaishek. Marshall allowed himself to urge Chiang Kaishek to act, and when Chiang did act, stating he was going to look at the Changchun situation, Marshall lent him his own aircraft, thus making it appear that he was supporting the Generalissimo.

Chiang Kaishek flew to Manchuria. He went to Mukden (Shenyang). At that same time his armies up north, freed from Communist threat, marched into Changchun. The appearance was that of a great Nationalist victory. No one mentioned the Communist agreement to withdraw. The Communists looked foolish. They had by this time acquired much sensitivity to outside opinion. So they were confused and angry and resentful.

By pretending that Changchun was a great military victory, Chiang strengthened the right wing of the Kuomintang, and perhaps let his own ego run away with him. He had not won a victory. He had been granted one. His arrogance, which from this point seemed to increase even as he lost power, was such as to annoy the Communists, who now were stronger, and to decrease the chances for peace. Following the easy capture of Changchun, the Nationalist troops began marching east toward Harbin. The Communists immediately reacted, and they began to wonder if General Marshall was not leading them down a path to destruction.

The fact was that General Marshall's effectiveness as a mediator had ended. In spite of this, General Marshall allowed himself to be persuaded that there was still hope, when actually there was none. Chiang Kaishek had deluded himself into believing he had the strength to conquer China and eliminate the Communists by force of arms. The Communists meanwhile were subject to their own cockiness. They began to believe they could hold against a major Nationalist assault on the territory and that they could then win the civil war.

On June 6, 1946, Chiang Kaishek returned to Marshall. He admitted that he had made a very serious error, and he now seemed willing to accept advice. He ordered the end of Nationalist troop advances. The Communists were to have a period of about two weeks to prove their sincerity in the plan to reorganize the army, a plan which had been pending for months.

The hope for peace during this period grew dim. All sides had lost faith in one another. In some areas of China Chiang was capable of moving, and he did not try very hard to restrain his generals, yet Marshall continued to believe in the possibility of the success of his mission.

After the capture of Changchun, the Communists were standing still, but the Nationalists were growing more aggressive. At this time, the Communists finally lost faith in the United States.*

American intent and American performance were suddenly brought into question in that summer of 1946.

---

*I know this from my own experience. I happened to be in the Kalgan area at the time, visiting the "new liberated territories." At a school one day children staged a parade, but not for me; the blackboards were filled with crude drawings of Uncle Sam clutching atomic bombs and threatening the world. This was the first time I had seen anti-American propaganda.

4

Unyielding Truce

When the Pacific War ended, the United States enjoyed a brief period of international popularity unmatched by any nation in history. An American could go anywhere with impunity. I recall that in late August of 1945, I was sent to Hanoi by United Press Associations to cover the insurgence of Ho Chi Minh against the French and the activities of the Chinese army of occupation. I found Hanoi to be an armed camp, with French Foreign Legionnaires skulking in their barracks. The white faces and the khaki uniforms worn by legionnaires (and Americans) were not popular. One night I was riding in a ricksha on the Boulevard Gambetta, a shady tree-lined thoroughfare in residential Hanoi, but also a very dark street at night. I heard slipper-clad feet running up behind the ricksha, and a voice demanded of my ricksha-man whom he was carrying.

"American," he said, and the footsteps died away.

Later I asked a French settler what would have happened if the ricksha-man had said "French."

"You probably would have had your throat cut," he said cheerfully. "You Americans have charmed lives."

But the charm ran out in China in the summer of 1946, when, as noted in these pages, the Chinese Communists perceived correctly that the U.S. government was talking out of both sides of its mouth, supporting the Nationalists with money and with guns. . . .

The American failure to recognize what had happened in Manchuria in 1946 would certainly have been understandable, even had the Americans been more familiar with Chinese history and the special importance of the northeastern provinces. The possession of most of Manchuria gave the Communists a new sense of importance and changed their approach to the question of unification. They continued to negotiate with the Nationalists, but now the negotiations went very slowly because neither side would yield on the matter of troop redistribution.

That spring fighting also broke out in Shantung Province, where the Communists were strong, but where the Nationalists had again moved in many thousands of troops. This further delayed negotiations. Then Chiang Kaishek, now in control of Changchun, said he would negotiate on political matters. But the Communists resisted regional political settlements, saying they first wanted an overall settlement.

By this time the Communist strength was such that their desire for a political settlement was far less than it had been a year earlier. Had Chiang really wanted a political settlement in 1945, he could have had it; by the spring of 1946, settlement seemed doubtful.

By mid-June Chiang Kaishek had prepared a list of demands for withdrawal of Communist forces from areas taken over since the end of the war. They included Jehol and Chahar provinces, Chefoo and Weihaiwei in Shantung, and a number of cities in Manchuria. The demands were presented to the Communists, and Zhou Enlai informed General Marshall that they were rejected.

Thus the negotiations reached an impasse, just a few days before the truce would expire.

Chiang Kaishek then agreed to extend the truce. By the end of June, there did seem to be some progress. Hostilities ended in Manchuria and the machinery was established for settlement of local issues: A team of three—a Communist, a Nationalist and an American—would interpose, and the American would have the deciding vote on all issues.

Chiang Kaishek wanted first of all to resolve the military problem, which would bring an end to the separate Communist army. But the Communists again insisted that the political problems be solved first. Who was going to run the government? And how?

They flatly refused to participate in the organization of a single army until these questions were answered. The impasse continued.

General Marshall tried valiantly to mediate. He drafted a complex army reorganization plan, but it failed because the Nationalist generals insisted on having military control of the areas that would be evacuated by the Communists, while the Communists insisted that these areas be demilitarized and governed by civil government. Nationalist supporters rallied and paraded, advocating the use of force for settlement of the dispute with the Communists.

Meanwhile the Communists complained that the United States was committed to support of the Nationalist government no matter what happened. Just then the American Congress was considering a China aid bill. The Communists said the bill persuaded the Nationalists that the Americans would back them, thus making the Nationalists less eager for serious peace negotiations. There certainly was food for thought in this complaint; the right wing of the Kuomintang party agreed with the Communist interpretation.

A delegation of citizens set out from Shanghai for Nanking, to petition Chiang Kaishek to end the threat of civil war by peaceful means. They were set upon at the Nanking railroad station by Kuomintang secret police, who arrested them, held them in rooms in the station for several hours, and beat most of them severely.

By July the military incidents were increasing. On July 7 the Communists issued their first "official" denunciation of American policy, complaining that the Americans were committed not to peace but to the Nationalists. At about the same time two members of the Democratic League, a serious "third force" in Chinese politics but one that did not have an army, were assassinated by Chiang Kaishek's secret police.

The break point came on July 29.

Since war's end the United States Marines had returned to China, where they had been seated for many years prior to the Japanese occupation. (After the Boxer Rebellion of 1900 the Marines had considered North China to be almost a home post, as the United States participated in extraterritoriality and a colonial attitude toward China.) Since the end of the war, the Marines had run regular convoys up and down the Beijing-Tianjin Road without incident. Everyone knew their comings and goings; they traveled through territory occupied by the Nationalists and territory occupied by the Communists without concern.

Then, on July 29, the Marine convoy was ambushed by Communist troops at Anping. Three Marines were killed and twelve wounded. The ambushing party then withdrew.

The Marine Corps conducted an investigation to find out what had really happened. The Communists conducted their own investigation.

Executive Headquarters launched a third investigation. When the investigations were complete, the Communists' set of facts was at variance with those of the Americans. The Communists claimed the Americans had fired on them. The Marines found no evidence indicating provocation. There had been none. The Marines were traveling close together, in good order and under discipline. They had done nothing to provoke the attacks. The Marines proved to their own satisfaction that they had not fired at all until the ambush was under way and the Communist firing was half over. They also proved that there were no Nationalist soldiers who could have taken part in this incident anywhere in the area.

The Anping Incident marked the absolute end of America's effectiveness as a mediator of the Chinese civil dispute.

General Marshall thought of returning to the United States—and he should have. If, in the summer of 1946, the Americans had said that as their assistance was no longer welcome, they were leaving the Chinese to resolve their own problems, the outcome would have been almost precisely the same—except that the Americans would have had no responsibility, the Communists would have borne them no further animosity, and the Korean war probably never would have occurred at all.

But instead of extricating themselves from an impossible situation, the Americans dug in deeper. Perhaps General Marshall could not bear to lose. Certainly the American preoccupation with the perceived dangers of communism and its threatening spread around the world had much to do with what happened next.

General Marshall recommended the continuation of American efforts to bring peace to China. On his recommendation, President Truman appointed J. Leighton Stuart as U.S. ambassador to China. Stuart was the president of Yenching University, a famous school located in Beijing before the war, but which traveled west with Chiang Kaishek as he fled the Japanese. Many Yenching graduates had joined the Communists. Thus the University's reputation with the Communists and with the Nationalists was unexceptionable.

Almost immediately after the appointment, Zhou Enlai suggested that an unconditional order for cessation of hostilities be issued by both sides and that Ambassador Stuart then meet with Communist and Nationalist representatives. The results of this meeting to reorganize the government would be handed over to the People's Consultative Committee to get on with the job of democratizing the government, after which the military problems could be solved.

At this point the situation was already grim. For a while, in 1945, Chiang Kaishek had seemed to hold himself aloof from the more venal elements of his party, and offered himself as a leader beyond party. But with the military activity in the spring of 1946, he stepped down from his pedestal. Chiang still wore the mantle of the Kuomintang bequeathed to him by Dr. Sun Yatsen, but by this time it had become very bedraggled.

General Marshall again warned of the deteriorating situation in China. The defalcations of the Soongs and Kungs had left China bankrupt and the Nationalist government in no condition to prosecute a civil war. Marshall warned the Nationalists that their military commanders were leading them to war, and he stated bluntly (though wrongly, as it turned out) that the United States would not underwrite the Nationalists in a civil war.

Marshall also counseled that the policies being followed by Chiang Kaishek were very likely to lead to a Communist government of China.

Ambassador Leighton Stuart became embroiled in the details of Chinese politics with a proposal for a State Council, another organization in which the Nationalists and Communists were to work together. It was now August 1946, and still the fighting was spreading. General Marshall and Ambassador Stuart issued a statement of warning, but instead of heeding it, Chiang Kaishek issued his own statement throwing all the blame for trouble on the Communists. The Nationalists' talk now was not for the purpose of reaching agreement, but to justify their stiffening position.

During the summer Chiang Kaishek made several demands on the Communists:

1. Evacuation of Jehol and Chahar provinces.
2. Occupation of Chefoo and Weihaiwei by Nationalists.
3. Reinforcement of Qingdao by one Nationalist army.
4. Nationalist occupation of all areas of Shantung taken by the Communists since the war's end.
5. Reinforcement of Tianjin by one Nationalist army.

Later Chiang added another demand: withdrawal of the Communists from the Jinan-Qingdao railroad.

In August Chiang Kaishek defied the right wing of his party enough to sanction formation of a five-member committee to pave the way for formation of the State Council, which would represent both Communists and Nationalists in the new government. The conclusions of this group were to be presented to the Political Consultative Council, and that Council's decisions would be binding. But the Generalissimo had put up so many roadblocks in the form of conditions that Zhou Enlai told General Marshall that, as far as he could see, the Generalissimo's approval was simply a smokescreen and nothing would come of it all. General Marshall had to agree, in view of the fact that Chiang Kaishek insisted that the Communists first stop fighting.

The fighting did not stop. Chiang Kaishek had demanded that the Communists, who held most of Shantung Province, leave the rail line from Tsinan to Qingdao. The Communists did not. The Nationalists drove them off.

The Nationalists also captured Chengte, the capitol of Jehol Province.

The Communists attacked along the Lunghai railroad and launched an attack against Tatung. Inside the Communist camp existed the same sort of stubbornness shown by the Nationalist right wing. In brief, the attitude was, as Mae Zedong put it: "Stop the talking and get to fighting. We will overcome the rotting Kuomintang."

In August President Truman became so concerned about the lack of progress in the peace talks that he told Chiang Kaishek that the United States would have to redefine its position on China unless matters improved. On August 31 Truman told Chiang that a prompt end to the quarreling would make it possible for the United States to start the major economic aid program. The implication was very clear: that aid would not start until the quarreling ended. It was a very strong American position which, unfortunately, the Administration did not maintain. Indeed the wheels were already moving to destroy the American position.

The first U.S. act of open support of the Nationalists against the Communists was the signing of an agreement on August 30, 1946, giving the Nationalist government, for virtually nothing, all the surplus equipment abandoned by advancing military forces in the American drive across the Pacific during World War II. The Communists objected strongly. General Marshall put the best face on the deal that he could, telling Zhou Enlai that the equipment was only machinery, motor vehicles, communications equipment, rations, and medical supplies. The alternative, said Marshall, was to deprive the Chinese people of these materials. But that was not the only alternative open to the Americans. If they were going to supply one side, then they could have supplied the other as well. If they were seriously interested in achieving peaceful settlement, the matter of balance was extremely important.

In the Pentagon were people not at all interested in balance but in promoting the cause of the Nationalists over the Communists. Marshall was put in an untenable position, trying to mediate between two adversaries while his government was helping one against the other. He should have resigned, but again he temporized.

Thus, by the end of August 1946, the mediation attempts of America had failed. The superactivists among the Communists had already shown their enmity toward America in the Anping Incident, and now this was amplified by Chairman Mao Zedong's acceptance of a national anti-American propaganda campaign in reaction to American aid to the Nationalists. The time for American withdrawal had definitely arrived, and yet the Americans did not withdraw.

The Administration could not bring itself to quit. To better the situation, the government refused licenses for export of military combat weapons to the Nationalists. But a few weeks later this stricture was lifted; the Pentagon sent C-47 and other cargo aircraft to the Nationalists. One could argue that the C-47 aircraft was nothing but a Douglas DC-3 passenger cargo plane with a coat of olive drab paint, but everyone in China knew that the C-47 had been the workhorse of the American Air Force, used for everything from dropping supplies to dropping bombs. The Communists were not fooled.

By November 1946, the Nationalists had achieved all the aims set forth in their "five demands" on the Communists—but by force of arms. With American assistance the Nationalist army had achieved the highest point of military strength it was to hit. Only then did Chiang Kaishek issue an order for cessation of hostilities against the Communists.

That autumn of 1946 the political discussions between Chinese Nationalists and Communists continued, but it was apparent that the positions of the two parties were irreconcilable. The State Department White Paper recapitulated the policy events of the period:

> General Marshall and Dr. Stuart had endeavored to break the deadlock through the proposal for the five-man committee as a step leading to the cessation of hostilities. They had exerted strong pressure on the Generalissimo in an effort to obtain his concurrence to this proposal only to meet with Communist refusal to participate in the meetings of the committee. Propaganda campaigns, as usual, played a part in the wrecking of their efforts, as they led to confusion and misunderstandings; the most bitter of these campaigns was that directed by the Communist Party against the American government and the surplus property transaction. Communist distrust and Communist practices of distortion and disregard of the truth imputed to the transaction an evil purpose intended to further the civil war in China, which was utterly contrary to the facts.

This last statement is probably true, although it is difficult to believe that anyone could have been so naive as to expect the

Chinese Nationalists to do anything but what they did do with the surplus equipment and supplies. Items that the Nationalist military could use were taken over by the military. Those that the military could not use were sold on the black market, either to enrich the sellers or to gain cash to buy supplies to carry on the war against the Communists. To have expected the Communists not to react badly to such a proposition would have been even more naive. But that, unfortunately, is the position in which the American government found itself. Certainly the Communists were guilty of excesses, questioning the integrity and honesty of General Marshall while privately asking him to continue to mediate the dispute.

The fighting grew more serious again. The Nationalists launched a campaign against Kalgan, that Communist show city not far from Beijing. The Communists refused to attend any more meetings until the attack was stopped.

By October 1, General Marshall, who had exhibited almost saintly patience, told both sides that he had nearly reached the point beyond which he could not continue to mediate. He was particularly annoyed by the Kuomintang government's campaign against Kalgan, which "could be justified only on the basis of a policy of force." And he told both sides that unless a basis for agreement was found without further delay, he would recommend to President Truman that he be recalled and that the United States terminate its efforts to mediate the dispute.

This was followed by much verbiage from Chiang Kaishek, but no termination of the attack on Kalgan. So General Marshall did recommend to the President that he be withdrawn—or, rather, he started to. He prepared the message, but Chiang Kaishek said he would hold up military advances against Kalgan for five days, and once again General Marshall allowed himself to be gulled.

Then came more talk.

Chiang extended the truce on Kalgan to ten days.

By this time the cause of peace was really lost. The Communists demanded the withdrawal of the Nationalists to the positions they held before the Kalgan campaign began. Everyone knew the Nationalists would not comply.

General Marshall made one last effort: He went to Shanghai, where Zhou Enlai was staying, and tried once more to reason.

Memoranda flew back and forth like pigeons. The Generalissimo used the Double Ten Holiday (October 10) to make a propaganda statement calling on the Communists to abandon their "plot" and join the government—on Nationalist terms, of course. The Generalissimo kept making proposals that virtually no one could understand and that the Communists would never accept. The fighting continued in north China, but the ominous sign for the future was the withdrawal by the Communists of their offices in Nanking, Shanghai, and Chongqing. There was no secret about the withdrawal. They went to Yanan in American planes supplied by Executive Headquarters.

On October 24, Zhou Enlai told Ambassador Stuart that the Communists would not accept the new proposals made by Chiang Kaishek.

The Communists now asked the Americans to withdraw from China. Even at this late date, withdrawal would have demonstrated American good faith and would have ended the growing American military involvement with the Nationalists. But it was not done.

By the autumn of 1946 the prospects for peace were gone. The Democratic League and the other "third force" elements were trying to mediate. The Americans had stepped into the background, but not out of the China picture. Kuomintang troops were moving north along the Beijing-Hankow railroad, and they had begun a drive to capture Antung in Manchuria.

The Communists virtually deserted the Executive Headquarters, making the truce teams inoperative. They continued to demand that the United States withdraw its troops from China.

The State Department White Paper describes the situation succinctly:

> On October 28 in a discussion of the situation with the Generalissimo, General Marshall described the deep-seated distrust the Communist Party had of the motives of the Generalissimo and the Kuomintang leaders, to which had been added the distrust of the American mediators. He pointed out that the Communists had no intention of surrendering, and that while they had lost cities, they had not lost armies, nor was it likely that they would lose armies since they had no

intention of making a stand or fighting to the finish at any place.

And so the American efforts to mediate the civil war were a complete failure, but General Marshall continued to hope, and thus to drag the Americans even further into the mire of China. Again, this is understandable, because every time Marshall announced total failure, the Generalissimo would seem to make some concession and the Communists would respond, so that the Americans continued, like toys on a string, to jerk back and forth.

The concession of November was to call a meeting of the National Assembly, a body which had representatives from all elements of Chinese society. The meeting produced nothing of note.

Still, even now, as the darkness of civil war loomed over China, Zhou Enlai offered a glimmer of hope: He asked Marshall not to disband the Executive Headquarters just then, just in case. . . .

General Marshall asked Zhou to get an answer from the Communist leadership: Did they or did they not want Marshall to continue to try to mediate? On the basis of the propaganda campaign, which accused Marshall of favoring the Nationalists, he would leave. But privately Zhou Enlai had always assured Marshall that he should stay. General Marshall, the optimist, continued to hope.

On November 19, Zhou Enlai went back to Yanan, and that was the end of the mediation.

To Marshall's mind the failure lay largely with the Nationalists. Why, then, did the Americans continue to support the Nationalists, particularly when they could see the growing corruption all around them, and the evidence of the coming collapse of that government? Since summer the Kuomintang had increased its military expenditures and its level of attack on the Communists. Military expense was taking 70 percent of the government funds. Just now Washington was considering the Kuomintang's request for more help, thus proving correct the Communist accusation.

But General Marshall did not lay the entire blame on the Nationalists.

On the other side, the Communist Party had defeated itself through its own suspicions, refusing to agree to possible procedures which might well have resulted in a settlement of the issues. This had been particularly true of the rejection of the five-man committee under Ambassador Stuart which might have led to the organization of the State Council and the carrying out of the other PCC agreements.

Kuomintang officials were approaching General Marshall to secure his support for more aid. Marshall turned a cold shoulder to them, saying that the corruption, the waste, and the determination of the reactionary clique that ran the Kuomintang to use force made it useless for the Americans to pour money into China.

And so the Marshall mission came to an end, with a final meeting between the General and Chiang Kaishek, in which General Marshall warned of the impending financial collapse of the Nationalist government. The large Communist element in China could not be ignored, said Marshall. For over a quarter of a century Chiang had shown that he could not "exterminate" them, much as he had tried.

General Marshall left China in January 1947, and he did not return.

5

The Prophet

When General George C. Marshall gave up and left China in January 1947, announcing the failure of his mission to bring a unified government to China, that should have been the end of the problem for the United States. But the China lobby was persistent, and the Republicans made much of Marshall's failure. Reluctantly, and largely for political expediency at home, the U.S. government continued to support the Nationalists, thus driving the wedge deeper between America and the Communist Chinese.

The Nationalists were able to ride a growing tide of anticommunism in America. The American media were full of spy stories. Americans were being told that their State Department was alive with Russian agents. The Russians were caught stealing secrets concerning the atomic bomb. The cases of the Rosenbergs, accused as Communist spies, and Alger Hiss, a highly placed State Department official accused of lying, were brewing. These were the days when it was becoming apparent in Germany, in Austria, the Balkans, Poland, and Korea that the United States and the Soviet Union were traveling collision courses. One of the most popular radio programs was "I Was a Communist for the FBI." The Communists were strong in Italy and France, and for a time it appeared that they might gain the strength to take over these governments. This was the year that Winston Churchill characterized Soviet policies in Eastern Europe as an "iron curtain." It was also the year in which America, fearing a Communist victory in China, scrapped its Japanese policy of tearing down the power of the Zaibatsu, or industrial cartels, and began to think about

46

rebuilding Japan to become an American bastion in Asia. So when General Marshall spoke of the need for reform in China, Chiang Kaishek listened politely but consulted the newspapers to see what was going on in America. . . .

———

The departure of General George C. Marshall from China might have signaled the end of American involvement in the Chinese Revolution—for, of course, in hindsight it became apparent to many, as at the time it was apparent to a few, that the deadlock between Communists and Nationalists in China was a part of the continuing Chinese Revolution that had begun in 1911. A survey of university students taken in Beijing at about this time showed that the vast majority of them opposed both Nationalist and Communist policies, and wanted a truly democratic, free, and united China. But the students did not have armies, and the Communists and Nationalists did. The fate of China would be determined by military strength; it was apparent to General Marshall and other China watchers that the attempts to bring a peaceful end to the conflict had failed.

Before General Marshall left China in January he had one last word for Chiang Kaishek. If the Generalissimo really wanted to stop the Communists, the best policy would be to carry out reforms and gain the support of the people of China; nothing less would do. Even as Marshall said these words he was sure they would not be heeded, for to his eye, Chiang Kaishek was now irretrievably associated with the right wing of the Kuomintang, and this wing was in control of the government.

On January 7, President Truman appointed General Marshall to be U.S. Secretary of State. At that time the Executive Headquarters closed, and the American marines moved out of the Beijing-Tianjin corridor, leaving only a guard at Qingdao, where Americans continued to train the Chinese navy. Certain U.S. projects to aid the Chinese government also continued, which meant that the United States failed to disengage from the Chinese civil strife. There were no aid projects for the Communists. The U.S. government still paid lip service to a very sensible policy, as stated in the White Paper:

The termination of the American mediation effort did not change the traditional attitude of the United States toward China. The effort had failed to bring peace and unity to China. There was a point beyond which American mediation could not go. Peace and stability in China must, in the final analysis, be achieved by the efforts of the Chinese themselves. . . . It was General Marshall's belief that the United States should continue to view sympathetically the problem facing the Chinese and should take any action, without intervening in China's internal affairs, that would assist China in realizing those aims which represented the hopes and aspirations of the Chinese people as well as those of the United States.

Noninterference in Chinese affairs was the key to that policy statement. How, then, would the Americans achieve the distancing of the United States from the unfinished Chinese Revolution, when the United States never stopped interfering in Chinese internal affairs?

The continued existence of the Chinese naval program at Qingdao was interference, helping the Chinese Nationalists build up a segment of their armed forces in time of looming civil war, and not helping the other side. Other American programs for China, in the agricultural and economic fields, did not stop. The Communists could and did argue that every bit of help the Americans proffered to the Nationalists government in some way aided their military effort against the Communists. The charge was fair; much of the economic aid simply disappeared into the Nationalist war machine.

In January 1947, Chiang Kaishek continued to pay lip service to peace. He enlisted the aid of Ambassador Stuart to keep in touch with the Communists.

The Communists, on their side, announced a major change in policy, aligning themselves with the Soviet Union in matters of foreign policy. This was a major defeat for American foreign policy; had the U.S. mediation not failed, the Chinese Communists would not have decided that the United States was their enemy.

Ambassador Stuart summed up the position now taken by Chiang Kaishek: The Generalissimo, Stuart said, now expected the

United States, because of the powerful anticommunist feeling in America and the new alignment between the Chinese Communists and the USSR, to continue to furnish assistance to the Nationalists.

Of course, as it turned out, Chiang Kaishek was an accurate prophet.

——— 6 ———

China and American Anticommunism

For a time it looked as though the Americans would be able to resist the China lobby's importunations, but . . .

———

In March 1947, American political and military involvement in China reached a low ebb. Generalissimo Chiang Kaishek was doing everything that General Marshall had advised him not to do. The Nationalists captured Yanan, but the Communists had already moved out of their old capital, so the capture was symbolic only. The Nationalists began a drive in Shantung and suffered a major defeat with the loss of 40,000 men to the Communists' loss of 20,000. The Communists began a drive in Manchuria and reached the gates of Changchun, but were stopped there with a loss of 20,000 men to the Nationalists' 10,000. The Nationalist economy was in shambles, and students were calling for a national general strike to show their lack of confidence in the government. Repression was growing everywhere in Nationalist China, and the Kuomintang was once more talking about "annihilating" the Communists.

From every part of China came evidence of growing deterioration of the Nationalist government, corruption, and incompetence. The American consul in Mukden reported "a picture of government corruption, inefficiency and aimlessness in the face of a major disaster." Rivalry between General Xiang Shihui, the Generalissimo's representative, and General Tu Liming, head of the Northeast Combat Command, reached the stage of open enmity. Nationalist military forces and civil administrators conducted themselves as conquerors, not as fellow countrymen, with the Manchurians. The consul reported that they had brought in a carpetbag government, and that the local people had begun to hate the Nationalists. The civil administrators were requisitioning grain from the people and paying official controlled prices, then selling the grain on the black market for personal profit.

Not just in Manchuria, but throughout China, the corruption grew worse each day.

The government talked incessantly about "reform," but there really was no reform. "We must exert all our efforts in effecting national reforms and improvements," said the Generalissimo; "while we are suppressing the Communist brigands with military means, the nation must also at the same time effect internal reforms." But the venal right wing and the Soongs and Kungs were still running the Chinese economy for personal gain, and the Generalissimo was unable to control the Kuomintang. Therefore such statements were absolutely meaningless.

What was meaningful was a resolution on general national mobilization adopted on July 4, proclaiming the Communists to be in open rebellion against the government and demanding that the resources of all the country be devoted to their suppression. Thus came to an official end the period of uneasy but not quite inimical relations between the Nationalists and the Communists that began with the kidnapping of Chiang Kaishek by Zhang Xueliang at Xian in 1937. Chiang had once more declared outright war on the Communists and vowed to exterminate them.

Two days later, General Marshall made a statement as Secretary of State:

> In the final analysis, the fundamental and lasting solution to China's problems must come from the Chinese themselves. The United States cannot initiate and carry out the solution of these problems and can only assist as conditions develop which may give some beneficial results.

On August 11, Ambassador Stuart repeated the plea for radical reforms. He contrasted the misery and confusion of Nationalist China with the conditions in Communist China, which had no outside assistance at all:

> The more intelligent country people live not so much in actual discontent or hardship as in fear of what might happen at any time. The others accept relative economic insecurity and the regulations imposed upon them rather passively. The children are growing up with more or less enthusiasm for the existing regime, and are taught to believe all that is evil of the National government and America. The situation is still somewhat plastic but will become fixed with time. Economic distress is widely prevalent but there is food for everyone.

So the Communists, without resources, were proving to be the better masters of their environment, and the Nationalists were losing supporters every day.

In the summer of 1947 American foreign policy was definitely on the defensive. The Soviet Union had made satellites of Poland, Bulgaria, and Rumania, and were working on Hungary and Czechoslovakia. Greece was in an uproar, with a Communist revolution threatening to dislodge the government. Yugoslavia had become Communist under Marshal Tito. The fire of communism seemed to be rising everywhere, and the Americans had vowed to extinguish it, singlehandedly if necessary. But vowing and succeeding were two different matters.

In the Far East, a Communist rebellion flourished in the Philippines. The British were fighting in Malaya to put down Communists; in Indochina the Vietminh revolution was led by Ho Chi Minh, an avowed Communist. Japan, the defeated enemy, was under American military occupation. Korea, which by this time should have been a united country after free elections, was split in two at the 38th parallel, and the Russians were creating a North Korean People's Republic, which was another satellite.

A look at the map showed China, huge land mass that it was, joined with the USSR and the satellites on east and west. If you painted it all red, the red shadow would dominate the planet.

In this atmosphere, deathly afraid of Soviet imperialist expansion, which seemed to be succeeding everywhere, the men who governed America began to panic and reconsider all their past reliance on such concepts as freedom, truth, and human rights. America was desperately seeking allies in the lineup of East and West.

Into this atmosphere the China question was injected anew. By this time the Nationalists' China had become an oligarchic dictatorship, not at all unlike Soviet Russia, with a new campaign of oppression of the people illustrated by the dissolution of the Chinese Democratic League, one of the third parties on which such men as Ambassador Stuart had placed much hope. It was the same as in South Korea, where the United States ignored the center parties and built up the right wing of Dr. Syngman Rhee to take over the government of the half-country.

A debate began in Washington about the Chinese question. The Republicans, in particular, saw in China an issue that might bring them control of the White House in the 1948 elections. Charges began flying that the Truman Administration was "soft on communism," and that the Department of State was "riddled with Communists and Communist sympathizers" who were bent on turning the world over to the Reds.

President Truman then consulted with Secretary of State Marshall, who repeated all his arguments that the Chinese really had to solve their own problems. But, said the President, the Chinese were not solving their problems; unless something were done, it seemed sure that the Nationalist government would collapse, and then the China lobby and the right wing of the Republican Party would have a field day against the Democrats. Since the Republicans controlled the 80th Congress, the issue was already making life most difficult for President Truman, a man of good will and good intention, who was like a tightrope walker.

Out of these concerns and discussions came Truman's appointment of Lieutenant General Albert C. Wedemeyer to return to China and make a survey of conditions.

> You will proceed to China without delay for the purpose
> of making an appraisal of the political, economic, psycholog-
> ical, and military situations—current and projected. In the

course of your survey you will maintain liaison with American diplomatic and military officials in the area. In your discussions with Chinese officials and leaders in positions of responsibility you will make it clear that you are on a fact-finding mission and that the United States government can consider assistance in a program of rehabilitation only if the Chinese government presents satisfactory evidence of effective measures looking towards Chinese recovery and provided further that any aid which may be made available shall be subject to the supervision of representatives to the United States government.

In making your appraisal it is desired that you proceed with detachment from any feeling of prior obligation to support or to further official Chinese programs which do not conform to sound American policy with regard to China. In presenting the findings of your mission you should endeavor to state as concisely as possible your estimate of the character, extent and probable consequences of assistance which you may recommend, and the probable consequences in the event that assistance is not given.

In China the reaction to the announcement was mixed. The Nationalists were delighted. This appointment meant a major change in American policy toward China. American involvement had ended with Marshall's previous observation that the Chinese had to help themselves and that unless major reforms were made, the Nationalist cause would be lost. China was not helping itself, and there were no major changes. And yet, as the last paragraph of the appointment letter made clear, America was coming back. As everyone involved with China recognized, without enormous infusions of American aid, the Nationalist government would certainly collapse within six months. The Nationalists knew this. So did the people of the center, who saw in the American action only a prolonging of the civil war, before the Nationalists finally collapsed. And so did the Communists, who saw very clearly that this new policy letter of the President's said absolutely nothing about the Nationalist need to come to grips with the political problem of relations with the Communists. Anticommunism was now the basis of American foreign policy, and Truman was just hitching up to the Nationalists once more. Indeed it was of enormous significance that the Nationalist-Communist split was not even mentioned in the letter, nor was there a single mention of the Communist Party with which General Marshall had dealt for nearly a year, and which now controlled a large part of China.

7

America Leaps into the Morass

The Wedemeyer mission to China was billed as a fact-finding mission. In fact it was a sales job to secure American public support for a new China policy: Bolster Chiang Kaishek at any price. The justification for this was that the Chinese Communists were, as Communists, in league with the Russians in an effort to create revolution and take over the world. The Chinese Communists were well aware of what was happening, and the shift in U.S. policy renewed and strengthened all their suspicions of the Americans. It was hard to believe that only two years earlier the Chinese were helping the Americans fight the Japanese and hoping for American support, or at least for noninterference, in China. It was hard to believe that in World War II the United States had stood for the right of self-determination for all peoples. Now America stood for the right of self-determination for all peoples—except those that wanted to create a Marxist society. They were aligning themselves with Chiang Kaishek, Syngman Rhee, and the French in Indochina. Only one issue was important in American assessment of any nation's policies: Was the government actively anticommunist?

At the end of July 1947 General Wedemeyer's party left for a month-long tour of China. The Communists predicted, quite rightly, that this was the beginning of a campaign to prop up the collapsing Nationalist government in the interest of American foreign policy, that policy now having shifted to the Cold War stance.

56

From the American point of view the justification was that the Chinese Communists had cast their lot with the Soviet Union. It would not be for another two or three years that the Americans would learn, through the breach of Yugoslavia with Moscow, that the Comintern had failed and that the international nature of communism was a Russian dream never to come true.

General Wedemeyer did not march blindly through China. On the eve of his August 22 departure, he gave a major address to a large number of Chinese organizations and leaders, in which he was strongly critical of the Nationalist failure to carry out reforms. The government would never defeat the Communists by force of arms, Wedemeyer said, but could only stop the civil war by improving the political and economic situations.

As Wedemeyer left China he made a final statement, noting the apathy, lethargy, and defeatism, and the need for inspirational leadership.

The Nationalists could still succeed, said the general, by removing incompetent and corrupt officials.

> To regain and maintain the confidence of the people, the Central Government will have to effect immediately drastic, far-reaching political and economic reforms. Promises will no longer suffice. Performance is absolutely necessary. It should be accepted that military force in itself will not eliminate communism.

Repetitious as its theme had become in the preceding two years, it was an excellent speech. But, of course, the reaction of the Nationalists was annoyance. They had no intention of following the advice, no intention of stopping the fighting. They still believed they could win the civil war.

General Wedemeyer went back to Washington to recommend that the Americans give aid to the rotting Chinese government—particularly, as the Communists noted, military aid. The weak excuse that the military aid would be provided outside tactical areas did not impress anyone. The United States was being asked to leap into the middle of the Chinese civil war.

The venality and the corruption and the incompetence and the military foolishness continued. On September 27, the American Consulate in Shanghai reported that the right wing of the Kuomintang had taken over the economic milking of China.

On October 11, a group of American congressmen from the House of Representatives Military Affairs Committee toured China. Chiang gave them his "grade A" treatment, telling them what they wanted to hear: The Chinese Communists were real Communists; just like Russians, they took their orders from Moscow. Chiang put on his longest face and repeated his plea for American aid. If the Nationalist government was defeated, said Chiang, it would not be because of Russia or the Chinese Communists, but because of the failure of America.

The remark reached the ears of Ambassador Stuart. He listened, and then said he had no reason to change his opinion, laying the responsibility for what had happened and was happening in China squarely at the door of the Kuomintang.

The situation in Manchuria, for which Chiang Kaishek blamed the United States and about which generals Marshall and Wedemeyer had previously warned Chiang, continued to grow worse for the Nationalists. The Central government controlled only one percent of Manchuria and only ten percent of north China, north of the Yellow River. The Communists were growing stronger, too, in central and south China. Chiang was about to reap what he had sowed. And yet, such was the climate in America in the fall of 1947 that the Congress and State Department were preparing to shovel more money into China to support a lost cause. In February 1948, Congress received the State Department's draft of the China Aid Bill, calling for more than a half billion dollars over a fifteen-month period.

The United States had leaped back into the Chinese morass.

In March 1948, an event occurred that showed how drastically American political thinking had altered in the two years since the Truman Administration tried through mediation to bring about a coalition government in China and thus prevent the civil war.

In Nanking, a newspaper correspondent interviewed Ambassador Stuart, whose remarks created a sensation when he indicated that "the best thing that could happen to China would be a coalition government."

Coalition? With the Communists? The sensational story was splattered over front pages all across America, and aroused protest. So short were American memories that it seemed somehow disloyal for Ambassador Stuart to admit doing in 1947 what everyone tried to do in 1945 and 1946.

One of the members of the House of Representatives Foreign Affairs Committee raised the question: Was it still America's foreign policy to seek an accommodation in China? At Secretary of State Marshall's press conference on March 10 a reporter asked that question again.

Marshall went into the background, relating how he had spent nearly two years trying to seek just such an accommodation. Yes, he said, that was certainly still American policy.

Reporters rushed away from Marshall's press conference, and a few hours later the front pages again erupted with headlines indicating that Secretary of State Marshall advocated the accommodation with *Communists*! Again the implication was clear: The Administration was selling out to the Reds.

It was an election year. In another seven months Americans would go to the polls to choose a President and a new Congress. The American atmosphere was deadly with fear of "international communism," and this fear was reflected and magnified in much of the American press.

Within twenty-four hours, the Department of State issued a "clarifying" statement which begged off the issue.

In view of misunderstandings that have arisen concerning the Secretary's statements about China at this March 10 press conference, it is pointed out that the Secretary referred to President Truman's statement of December 15, 1945. That statement expressed the belief of the United States that "peace, unity, and democratic reform in China will be furthered if the basis of this government is broadened to include other political elements in the country." The Secretary says that the statement still stands. When asked specifically whether broadening the base of the Chinese government meant we favored the inclusion of the Chinese Communist Party he replied that the Communists were now in open rebellion against the government and that this matter [the determination of whether the Communists would be included in the Chinese government] was for the Chinese government to decide, not for the United States government to dictate. . . .

Brave-sounding words, these last, but hardly truth. Long before, General Marshall had warned Chiang Kaishek that his government would rise or fall on its ability to resolve the political problem of Chinese communism. America, he advised, could not pour money into China unless the problems could be resolved.

And now, in the spring of 1948, internal political exigencies had changed the whole picture, and the United States was embarking on a program of aiding the Nationalist government in its civil war against the Communists. This was the point at which American policy went seriously wrong, doing what Truman and Marshall had said they would never do: becoming embroiled in the internal affairs of China.

Now came the window dressing: The Nationalist government held presidential elections, and Chiang Kaishek said he would not stand for President. So, of course, he was "drafted."

As for change, there was no real change.

During the summer of 1948, as the Nationalist government continued to waste its resources, American policy, once designed to encourage Nationalist-Communist cooperation, now had turned in exactly the opposite direction. On August 12, 1948, Secretary Marshall made two points:

1. The U.S. government would not encourage or accept a coalition government between Nationalist and Communist elements in China.
2. The U.S. government would not offer its services again as mediator in China.

There was a reason for the American volte-face in China. It had nothing to do with the particular situation in China, but everything to do with international communism.

In 1947 Hungary and Czechoslovakia had coalition governments with the participation of Communists, Socialists, and others.

Both countries fell swiftly in Communist takeovers that were assisted by the Soviet Union. To the Americans this provided a pattern on which they could now project the Chinese situation.

What we did before, said the Americans, was wrong, and now we shall put it to rights. But by the fall of 1948 the Nationalist government was slipping fast, the economy was in shards, and the Communists had begun winning more military victories.

What all this proved was that the Americans had been right in 1945 to encourage the Nationalists to compromise, and right in 1946 to warn that without major political and economic reforms there was no hope for the Nationalist government. Now, although the Nationalists remained unchanged, the Americans poured money into the country to achieve the impossible, and by interfering in China, lost the friendship of the Chinese people.

8

The Wrong Compounded

Perhaps no one ever stated the American dilemma in China more clearly than Ambassador John Leighton Stuart was to state in his remarks about the China problem in the fall of 1948. The real difficulty was that the American policy was all based on a premise that had already been proved to be erroneous: that all Communists were made in the same mold and that they all owed blind obedience to Moscow. Just that summer of 1948 Marshal Josip Broz Tito had taken Yugoslavia out of the Moscow bloc. Americans did not have enough understanding of the desires of the Chinese people to see that they would never give loyalty again to the morally bankrupt Nationalist government that was so mercilessly exploiting them. . . .

On October 28, 1948, Ambassador John Leighton Stuart summed up the most enlightened official attitude towards China and the Communists.

> What we really object to in communism is not its admittedly socialized reforms, but its intolerance, its insidious reliance on fifth column and similar secretive methods, its ruthless suppression of all thought or action that does not conform, its denial of individual human rights, its unscrupulous reliance on lying propaganda and any other immoral means to attain its ends, its fanatical dogmatism, including its belief in the

necessity of violent revolution. All these evils plus the fact that policy is directed from Moscow, apply to Chinese Communism as truly as elsewhere. Our problem is how to retard or expose their influence in China.

Evil in communism is moral or political rather than military. Predominence of the latter aspect in China is largely a historical accident. Even if we had been able to assist the Chiang government by military means to clear an area of militant communism—which is all we could have hoped to do at best —we would still have been obliged to assist in educational and other processes by which the non-Communist section would be able to demonstrate superiority of genuine democracy. Otherwise military gains would have proved self-defeating.

Most of what Ambassador Stuart had to say was certainly true. The Chinese Communists did resort to lies in their propaganda against the United States. They had begun an enormous campaign of terror, which they would carry out in the 1950s, killing perhaps fifty million people and depriving virtually every landowner of most of his land. The charges of intolerance, denial of human rights, suppression of thought, and the belief in the need for revolution were all justified charges. But what really upset the Americans about communism in the world was the belief that it was all directed from Moscow—and this proved not to be true. As for the other charges, they could almost word for word be levied against the Nationalist government. The secret police, under General Li Dai, were notorious for their ruthless suppression of ideas and for their brutality. The government recruited soldiers by kidnapping. It denied human rights, and continued to deny them after it went to Taiwan; many who questioned the Kuomintang's activities were murdered out of hand. Chiang promised everything in the way of reform and delivered nothing.

The real question America faced was: Is it necessary, in a revolutionary situation, for the United States to choose sides at all?

Yes, decided the Congress and the Truman Administration. It was necessary to choose sides. Why? To fight communism. For America had taken upon itself the task of protecting the status quo. At the end of World War II, when the colonial powers were divesting themselves or being divested of empire, the United States alone undertook to protect empire. The reason was neither clear nor cogent. It welled up from within the American system: a great revulsion against communism that for nearly thirty years would dominate American policy and keep the nation politically and morally stagnant. It is ironic that this policy was begun in a liberal Democratic administration, and ended in a conservative Republican one.

As 1948 drew to a close, the Communists began to gain ground in the civil war. Earlier that year Chiang Kaishek had been very confident, because his armies outnumbered the Communists' by about two to one. But he was finding that numbers did not matter when the people opposed him. Riots and demonstrations in Shanghai and other cities sucked the spirit out of the Nationalists, who put down the demonstrations with increasing violence, which only made things worse for Chiang.

The Communists continued to be elusive. In the areas where Chiang massed strength, the Red armies disappeared. The Communist First Field Army, threatened in the Huanglong mountain area, dispersed to do "field work." That meant mingling with the people and setting up the conditions for future resistance. But by the end of 1948 the Communists were also planning a major attack on Taiyuan, the industrial capital of the north, in Shaanxi Province.

Chiang asked for more American military assistance, even the appointment of American officers to lead the fight. But the Americans wisely refused to become militarily involved in the civil war. There could be no real increase in American assistance, because Chiang's government was too ineffective to absorb it.

As 1949 began, the Communists were growing ever stronger. In the Pengpu area, north of the capital at Nanking, the Nationalists had now withdrawn to the south bank of the Yangtze River. Soon they withdrew all along the front. Major General Barr, director of the U.S. military advisory group in China, recommended against more waste in the form of U.S. aid.

Chiang's next step was to seek American mediation again. But President Truman had been that route once and he knew it would not help. The request was refused.

On January 21, 1949, the Generalissimo did what he had done

many times before: With a flourish he announced that he was quitting public life and retiring to his birthplace at Fenghua. He turned over all authority to Vice President Li Tsung Jen. His action was greeted with enormous relief by the people of China, who wanted nothing but peace.

The depth to which the Nationalists had sunk was indicated by the next development. Finding themselves unable to secure any more help from America, the Kuomintang turned to Russia. The Russians were willing to give the Nationalists help (so much for the idea that the Chinese Communist policy was directed in Moscow) but only under certain conditions: The Chinese must promise neutrality in any future international conflict, they must eliminate American influence in China, and they must establish a real basis of cooperation with Russia, economically and otherwise.

Li Tsung Jen agreed to these Russian demands, disregarding the "eternal friendship" of the Nationalists and the Americans. Then Li had the brass come to Ambassador Stuart and ask for a public statement of support of this plan by the United States. America was to be deprived of all influence of any sort in China. And the Americans were to endorse the plan.

Actually it might have been a good idea if the United States had used this excuse to wash its hands of China. Another chance was missed.

At the same time, Acting President Li took a delegation to Beijing, now captured by the Communists, and tried to discuss peace terms. But with victory behind them and more victory before them, the Communists were unyielding. They had offered peace before, at a price:

1. Strict punishment of war criminals (Chiang Kaishek was Number One).
2. Abolition of the Kuomintang constitution and of the Kuomintang legal system.
3. Reorganization of Nationalist troops along democratic lines.
4. Confiscation of bureaucratic capital.
5. Land reform.
6. Abolition of "treasonous treaties" (U.S.-China treaties).
7. Convocation of a political consultative conference with no

participation by reactionary elements; establishment of a democratic coalition government.

All this was anathema to the Chiang Kaishek wing of the Kuomintang. The Kuomintang would be made just another party. The old leaders, Kungs, Soongs, and the CC clique would be stripped of their stolen wealth. The government that came out of this probably would have been Communist, but it might have been a limited communism of the sort that began to appear forty years later.

In any event, the talks came to nothing. And behind the scenes, Chiang Kaishek continued to pull the strings with America, even though he had no more credit left with the Chinese people.

The American capacity for self-deception when the Red flag was waved continued to be phenomenal.

The Chinese asked for more aid. The American business community in Tientsin asked the embassy not to give any more. Once again the people on the scene sent home valuable advice:

Americans in Tientsin who had the unhappy experience two months ago of witnessing the capture of Tientsin by Communist armies equipped almost entirely with American weapons and other military equipment, handed over practically without fighting by the Nationalist armies in Manchuria, have expressed astonishment at radio reports from the U.S. during the last two days to the effect that a bill may be presented to the Congress to extend further military and economic aid to the Nationalist government in the sum of a billion and a half dollars.

Americans in Tientsin feel the only result of further U.S. aid to a government which has proved so ineffective that most of our previous aid has passed to the Communists will be to further strengthen the Communists. They feel that the apparent retirement of the Generalissimo has had little effect on the character of the Nationalist government, particularly in view of the reported selection as new Premier of Ho Ying-chin, considered the archetype of the Chinese who have brought the National Government to its present sorry state. They feel that our global policy of opposition to communism should not oblige us to support a hopelessly inefficient and corrupt government which has lost the support of its people. They believe that at this juncture it would be useless to extend further aid to a government which is so far gone. They feel that the present situation must be solved by the Chinese and that for the time being we should adopt a hands-off policy. . . .

And on March 22, the U.S. Embassy officer in Guangzhou (Canton) said much the same:

I have been given the impression of the utter inability of China to cope unaided with the situation. In other words, the sole means of turning the tide in China, would, as the Department suggests, require the use of large U.S. forces in actual combat, contrary to our traditional policy and our national interest.*

In April the Nationalist government fled from Nanking, and the Communists advanced across the Yangtze River on April 20. It was very easy: Nationalist troops laid down their arms, and the Nationalist government moved to Canton.

The Communists moved swiftly south. Why not? Over the past three years they had been given or captured 80 percent of the war materials the Americans brought in for the Nationalists. The speed with which they moved was only controlled by their own ability to move and to take control. In the confusion many innocent and many not-so-innocent Chinese were slaughtered, but the big fish got away. Chiang Kaishek emerged from the woodwork of "retirement" as everyone knew he would, and having arranged for the looting of the museums and treasury, he flew to Taiwan to set up a government in exile where the Communists would not get at him. Immediately he demanded, and received, American naval protection. The Americans, it seemed, would never learn.

At the end of the Mainland life of the Kuomintang government, when the Chinese Communists crossed the Yangtze, Ambassador

---

*Here is the beginning of the change in that traditional policy, a change that was to lead the United States to the unfortunate and avoidable war in Korea and the morass of Vietnam.

Stuart made a halfhearted attempt to establish some sort of normal relations with the Communists, but it was unsuccessful. The Communists had their own excesses which led them into emotional traps, one of which was the virulence with which they had been portraying the United States for the past two years. There was nothing to be done but for the American Embassy to take down its flag and the diplomats to wend their way home. The American presence in China, which had been continuous since July 3, 1844, when Americans and Chinese signed the Treaty of Wangxia, came to an abrupt, inglorious end. On October 1, 1949, Mao Zedong proclaimed the People's Republic of China, and the "eternal friendship" between the Americans and Chinese also came to an abrupt end.

In that year, 1949, the U.S. Department of State made its appraisal of the American China policy of the past four years. The facts were all there for anyone to see. In his letter of transmittal, Secretary of State Dean Acheson noted that it was not so much that the Communists won the civil war; it was that the Nationalists, no longer having any faith in their central government, lost the war.

"The Nationalist armies did not have to be defeated, they disintegrated," said Secretary of State Dulles later. "History has proved again and again that a regime without faith in itself, and an army without morale, cannot survive the test of battle."

And, he added: "The unfortunate but inescapable fact is that the ominous result of the civil war in China was beyond the control of the government of the United States." Said Dean Acheson: "Nothing that this country did or could have done within the reasonable limits of its capabilities could have changed the result; nothing that was left undone by this country has contributed to it. It was the product of internal Chinese forces, forces which this country tried to influence but could not."

Secretary Acheson had more words of wisdom:

And now it is abundantly clear that we must face the situation as it exists in fact. We will not help the Chinese or ourselves by basing our policy on wishful thinking. We continue to believe that, however tragic may be the immediate future of

China, and however ruthless a major portion of this great people may be exploited by a party in the interest of foreign imperialism, ultimately the profound civilization and the democratic individualism of China will reassert themselves and she will throw off the foreign yoke. I consider that we should encourage all developments in China which now and in the future work toward this end.

By 1949 the estrangement was complete. Since V-J Day the Americans had spent two billion dollars on China, almost all to shore up the Nationalist government. Worse than that, American policy had thrown the Chinese Communists into the hands of the Soviets, although in 1945 Mao had said that what the Communists wanted was not a close relationship with Russia but one with the United States.

The State Department's White Paper told the story, but the leaders of Congress ignored the facts in that White Paper, and particularly ignored, because it was impossible for them to believe, the idea that American policy and American involvement anywhere could be pointless. And so for the rest of 1949 and the early months of 1950, American policy toward China consisted of shoring up the Nationalists on Taiwan, and particularly in sword brandishing by the U.S. Sixth Fleet while safely ashore in Taiwan. Chiang spoke of the day that he would gather his forces and invade the Mainland. There was only one way that could ever be done— with massive support from the Americans; the China lobby in Washington kept that concept alive.

What American policy had been it might become again, the Communists believed. They knew General Douglas MacArthur, commander of the American forces in the Pacific, as well as chief of the occupation of Japan, and they knew his belief in wiping out Communist governments in Asia. By 1950 the Chinese Communists regarded the United States as their major enemy in the world; they did not fear Chiang Kaishek in his island stronghold of Taiwan, except as an agent of American policy.

——— 9 ———

Trouble in Korea

One of the problems of the Republic of the United States of America is that its leaders talk too much and not always with one voice. In 1950, as the Korean war began, the stridency of such talk was apparent almost from the first. And notable among the people who talked too much was General Douglas MacArthur, whose world was made up of good guys and bad guys. The good guys were America and its friends, including Chiang Kaishek and Syngman Rhee, and the bad guys were the Communists of the world. In his heart MacArthur would have welcomed a battle à l'outrance with the Communists, to end up at the gates of Moscow. In the summer of 1950, even as the UN troops struggled to stay alive on the Pusan perimeter, MacArthur telegraphed his coming campaign and its aims to Beijing, apparently with no thought at all about what the Chinese reaction would be. . . .

———

The North Korean invasion was the result of a convolution in American foreign policy. After the establishment of the two Koreas by the Yalta Agreement of 1945, the Americans had found President Syngman Rhee of the Republic of South Korea a difficult ally; and in an impatient moment early in 1950, Secretary of State Dean Acheson indicated that the Americans did not regard Korea as within their sphere of influence. This was an invitation to the North Koreans to solve the "two Koreas" problem by military

70

means, and on June 25, 1950, they marched across the 38th parallel
that divided North from South Korea.

At first the North Korean forces moved at will, slicing south,
led by fast, well-trained armored divisions that were equipped with
a very new weapon, the Soviet T-31 tank. The training of the men,
as well as their equipment, was superior to that of the South Koreans and their American allies, who came belatedly to the South
Korean rescue in what, by a fluke, became a United Nations police
action to halt aggression.

The condemnation of the action was widespread outside the
Soviet bloc. Most countries of the world reacted negatively to the
North Korean use of force. The United Nations was able to express
this general feeling because the Soviet Union, one of the four
powers holding a UN Security Council veto, happened to be in a
sulk and was boycotting Council meetings when the Korea issue
suddenly arose.

The North Koreans drove the forces of the Republic of South
Korea and the United States nearly to Pusan, the southernmost
port of the Korean peninsula and the last bastion of defense. Here,
along a perimeter about fifty miles from the end of the peninsula,
the Allies finally pulled themselves together and held.

But General MacArthur, commander of the U.S. and UN
forces, did not plan simply to hold a line. He drew up an audacious
plan for invasion of the South Korean territory now held by the
North Koreans. On September 15, 1950, United Nations forces
landed at Inchon, the port of Seoul, completely surprising the
North Koreans and threatening to cut them off from their supply
bases and isolate them for capture or destruction. A massive North
Korean retreat began.

By this time many members of the United Nations had sent
military forces to fight in Korea against the Communist invasion.
Principal supporters were the nations of the British Commonwealth; even pacifist-inclined India sent a medical team. The
Turks sent a force of fierce fighting men. The French sent a
battalion. To the discomfiture of the Communist powers, the UN
action truly represented United Nations feelings, at least in the
beginning.

Ten days after the Inchon landings, the UN forces captured

much of Seoul, and to all intents and purposes restored the status of Korea that had existed before June 25, 1950, just three months earlier.

What now? The North Korean invasion had been stopped. The problem of the two Koreas remained, however. How would it be approached?

The Americans and the world already knew General Mac-Arthur's opinion on the subject. When the American forces were just barely holding on to the Pusan perimeter, in August, Mac-Arthur had stated his views at a press conference at his head-quarters in Tokyo's Dai Ichi Building:

> If we lose this war to communism in Asia the fate of Europe will be greatly jeopardized. Win it and Europe will probably be saved from war and stay free. Make the wrong decision here, the fatal decision of inertia, and we will be done. I can almost hear the ticking of the second hand of destiny. We must act now or we will die.

Oddly, in Beijing the leaders of China had a similar view, but their announced enemy was the United States. For two months the men in Beijing had watched the Korean conflict carefully. In August, when North Korea's drive bogged down at the Pusan perimeter, Zhu De, the leader of the Chinese Communist armies, called a strategy meeting in Beijing. At that meeting he told his generals to make contingency plans to enter the war if the situation changed. There was nothing peculiar or sinister about that. The People's Republic of North Korea was their ally—or at least, they recognized it officially. The fact that the recognition had come just eleven days before the war began was an indication of how little North Korea really meant to China. Had the American relations with China been different, the Chinese attack might never have occurred.

Out of that Zhu De meeting came a reevaluation of the strengths and weaknesses of the People's Liberation Army, and the beginning of preparations to invade North Korea on behalf of the North Koreans, if China was itself threatened.

From mid-August, the Chinese began moving troops up along

the Manchurian border into General Lin Biao's Fourth Army bailiwick.

On September 29 General MacArthur symbolically shepherded President Syngman Rhee of the Republic of South Korea back to Seoul and, in a dramatic speech, turned the capital of his republic back to him.

But what MacArthur wanted was much more than the restoration of the situation that existed before the North Korean attack. The general wanted to unify Korea under Dr. Rhee's government by destroying the North Korean People's Republic. To do so the UN forces had to occupy Pyongyang, the North Korean capital. They accomplished this, but then decided to go even farther, to the borders of North Korea and Manchuria, thus driving the North Koreans completely out of their own country.

MacArthur's desires were completely in line with the attitude of South Korean President Rhee. In summer, even as he retreated steadily toward the end of the peninsula, Rhee blustered that he would not be bound by any settlement of the Korean issue that left Korea divided.

Two principal Far Eastern advisors to Secretary of State Acheson, John Foster Dulles and John M. Allison, both advocated the use of military force to settle the Korean question because diplomacy had failed since 1945. Allison, in particular, made one point that appealed to President Harry Truman's midwestern Calvinist conscience: The North Koreans had committed an act of naked aggression in invading South Korea and trumpeting their plan to convert the south by force of arms. Allison said they deserved punishment. Harry Truman agreed.

The U.S. State Department's professional diplomatic planning staff suggested that for the American forces to go above the 38th parallel was potentially disastrous. Such an action might bring the Chinese Communists and even the Soviet Union into the war, they said, and thus create World War III.

The leaders of the Republican Party, which controlled Congress then, said this attitude represented "appeasement" of the Communists. They were supported by powerful elements in the Democratic-controlled Department of Defense, who also advocated unification of Korea by military means and the sanctification of the conquest by the United Nations Organization. Thus, these hawks argued, the Communist teeth would be drawn. The Communists would hardly dare risk the wrath of the united forces of the rest of the world.

In the autumn of 1950 this reading of the situation had no discernable basis in fact. The Communist world had no reason to trust the Western powers or their mercy. American action since 1945 had been consistently powered by anticommunism. If some action would injure or embarrass the Communists, it was acceptable to the American hawks for that reason alone. The Chinese Communists had come to believe in 1946 that America was their enemy, and thereafter America so behaved.

In the eyes of Beijing, there was nothing to be gained by appealing to American good will—and perhaps there was much to be gained in Moscow by defying it.

Further, the men in Beijing understood one fact: General Douglas MacArthur was their implacable enemy, and General MacArthur was running the Korean war. MacArthur had advocated preventive strikes against the Communists and the restoration of Chiang Kaishek, by American force, to the Chinese Mainland. He had visited Chiang early in the Korean war in what was, and was regarded in Beijing as, an effort to bring Chiang into that war—an effort fortunately resisted by President Truman.

What Beijing observed in Washington in the fall of 1950 was the ascendance of the MacArthur view of the world. This view held that communism was the same everywhere, that the Communists of China and of Korea were subservient to Moscow, and that these governments should be destroyed by the West at almost any cost. This message was clear throughout Asia. Nor was MacArthur alone in his beliefs. There was a strong element in America that viewed the Soviet Union as the ultimate enemy; and the head of the American Legion, a veterans' political organization, had advocated a preventive war against the USSR.

By September 1950, views of this nature were very popular in Washington. The idea of extending the Korean war at least to the boundaries of Manchuria was American policy. As always with the United States, the debate raged in full public view, and thus was well known to the Chinese.

Until mid-September President Truman had held out against this opinion wave. He went so far as to discharge his Secretary of Defense, a notable hawk, and install General George C. Marshall in that post. Marshall was known in America as a man of moderation. But in China, where he had attempted mediation between the Communists and Nationalists for more than a year at the end of World War II, Marshall had been caught in the middle of an American foreign policy dispute and had been tarred by the Communists as a backer of Chiang Kaishek. So to the Chinese of Beijing, the appointment of Marshall to the defense post only confirmed their worst fears. And in the Korean war General Marshall proved to be more a general than the statesman he had apparently become in 1947 with his enunciation of the Marshall Plan for the reinvigoration of war-torn Europe. Marshall joined the cabal that favored letting MacArthur march north and destroy the North Korean government. This debatable attitude was accepted by the President largely because of his respect for General Marshall. It became American policy on September 27, the day that Truman approved the U.S. Joint Chiefs of Staff decision to authorize MacArthur to carry the war above the 38th parallel. But even at this point Washington reiterated several important warnings to MacArthur:

1. No forces would cross the Manchurian or the USSR border.
2. Only South Korean ground forces would approach the Manchurian and Soviet borders.
3. There must be no violation of Soviet or Chinese air space.

General MacArthur appeared to agree to these conditions. He replied to the Joint Chiefs of Staff that the Eighth Army under General Walton Walker would attack up the west side of the Korean peninsula while the X Corps would attack up the east side. Both spearheads would consist of South Korean troops only.

The plans were secret, but they were leaked to the press. The *New York Times* editorially backed the move north. And in Pusan, President Syngman Rhee called for an advance north to the Manchurian border.

As of late September, then, the Communist world knew that

the UN forces were committed to the destruction of the North Korean government. This course was completely unacceptable to the Chinese Communist government at Beijing, a fact which would have been apparent to the Americans if they had been paying attention to Red China over the previous two years. But unfortunately, by 1949 the adversary relationship that had developed between the United States and China both precluded normal relationships and blinded the American government to the realities of Asia. Thus, in blindness the Americans forged ahead along a path to disaster, dragging along with them allies who were growing increasingly leery of the policy set by Americans.

From the beginning of the Korean war the CIA and other intelligence-gathering organizations had made assessments of the world military and political situations as they might affect the war. The verdict in the summer when the North Koreans were winning was that the USSR would support the North Koreans logistically as they had been doing, but that they would not actually join the war effort.

In regard to China, the CIA was off base. One of the earliest of CIA estimates (July 8) pondered a question: Would the USSR employ Chinese troops in Korea?

The question was ridiculous and showed how little the Americans knew about relations between the Chinese Communists and the Russians. The Chinese Communist relationship to Russia was nowhere nearly as close as the American relationship to the Nationalists.

There was no way the Russians could control the China of Mao Zedong. To suggest otherwise, as the Americans did, was to misunderstand the fundamental independence of the Chinese Communists and the difference between their agrarian revolution and the shopworn proletarian revolution of the Russians. Other reports indicated a close military relationship between the Russians and the North Koreans. But the relationship between the North Koreans and the Chinese Communists was much more complicated. Many North Koreans had fought in the ranks of the Chinese Communist armies against their common enemy, the Japanese. Thus most of the leaders of the North Korean army had learned their trade with the Chinese. But the two governments had just recently established government-to-government relations.

At the end of September 1950, Prime Minister Zhou Enlai of China warned publicly that China would not sit by and see the North Korean government destroyed.

On October 1, General MacArthur called on the North Koreans to surrender everywhere.

The Americans should have known that the Chinese would not sit back and watch the destruction of the North Korean government and the passage of total power in Korea to what they considered to be an American vassal state. Some Americans advocated a reasonable relationship with the de facto government of Mainland China, but by 1950 most of these people had been shouted down by the "anticommunist" elements. There was virtually no voice of dissent left in the demoralized State Department.

If it was true, as some moderates said, that the United States was committed only to Chiang Kaishek's defense, that point was lost on the Chinese Communists, who argued that what happened in China was China's business and not America's.

From the point of view of American global strategy, the situation of Red China represented an enormous blind spot on the globe. Deprived of normal diplomatic relations after the Communist military victory of 1949, the Americans simply did not know what was happening inside Mainland China, nor did they know the views of the Communist leadership on changing affairs.

The fact was that the Chinese army was too big and was suffering from unemployment, now that the Nationalists had been defeated. In that summer of 1950 the Communists had five million men under arms. They were very short of the sinews of modern warfare—tanks, trucks, artillery—and what materiel they had came largely from the Americans, by capture or surrender from the Nationalist armies. As early as August, when the Americans were holding their tenuous line along the Pusan perimeter, the Chinese leadership was concerned about the war, and about the North Korean miscalculation. America was not supposed to fight for Korea; earlier, Secretary of State Acheson had said America would not fight, and now the United States was fighting that Pusan line.

The successful American landings at Inchon, the speedy capture of Seoul, and the movement of the UN forces north brought even greater concern to Beijing. Premier Zhou Enlai went to the

USSR to consult with Stalin about the problem. Out of that meeting came the Chinese decision to intervene in the war if necessary, and the Soviet indication of support for such intervention.

The Chinese were under no illusions about the enemy. They knew that as the United States was the world's most powerful nation, China might lose the war, in which case the Communist movement would be back to its condition of the 1920s, just before the "Long March." But so strong was the feeling that the "imperialists" must not be allowed to take over North Korea that the Chinese were willing to take the risk.

First, however, Mao and the rest of the leadership agreed that every effort would be made to persuade the Americans not to threaten the existence of North Korea.

On October 3 Zhou Enlai warned the Indian ambassador to Beijing that if the UN forces crossed the 38th parallel, China would enter the war. That warning was transmitted to Delhi and thence via London to Washington, where it arrived at 5:30 on the morning of October 3.

On October 4, as General MacArthur was using all pretexts to extend or circumvent the orders that limited his operations, the Chinese were becoming alarmed by the MacArthur insistence on a rush to the Yalu River. The Yalu was of enormous economic importance to the Chinese, because of the system of dams and reservoirs concentrated there that were built by the Japanese in the years of the Manchukuo adventure.

At a meeting of the Party Central Committee, Mao Zedong began to discuss the dangers and problems of Korea.

10

China Prepares for War

The following Chinese account of the discussions and decisions that brought China into the war is, or should be, an object lesson to the American military to keep its collective mouth shut about military plans. It is also indicative of the failure of the American intelligence organizations between 1947 and 1950 to keep track of Chinese official thinking and of an American arrogance of the period that assumed that the Chinese were incapable of action. One of the most interesting facts about this period when the Chinese were gearing up to attack was that their principal source of information about MacArthur's forces and movements was the intercepted dispatches of the war correspondents, which speaks highly of the accuracy of the reporting but does not say much for the security of the military. And of course the biggest security risk of all was General MacArthur. . . .

In 1950, the soldiers of the Chinese Red Army, unlike their American counterparts, had been fighting for the past two years. The civil war against the Kuomintang had ended in the fall of 1949, but after the surrender the Red Army still had to defend against some four hundred thousand Kuomintang guerillas who remained on Chinese Mainland territory. Furthermore, that fall Mao Zedong had just ordered the investment of Tibet, which China claimed to be a basic part of Chinese territory, and the movement was under way to carry out his wishes.

Peng Dehuai, the field commander in the far west, was the man who was supposed to carry out Mao's Tibetan campaign, but he was diverted to the more important matter of the Korean war. At the end of September 1950, Chairman Mao's concentration on the Tibetan problem was disturbed by the turn of affairs in Korea. As noted, the UN forces had captured Seoul, returning the South Korean capital to the South Korean government, and General MacArthur was determined to wipe out the Communists of North Korea. On October 4, as the Americans were preparing to drive on to the Yalu, the Chinese Communist Party Central Committee was meeting in the Zhongmanhai, a part of the old Imperial Palace of the Qing dynasty.

Marshal Peng Dehuai was summoned from his army headquarters in Xian to Beijing. The summons was urgent. A plane from Beijing was waiting for him at the Xian airport, he was told.

Late that afternoon, Peng Dehuai arrived. He went to the meeting but he did not speak. Peng, who had made the investigation of the army's readiness, listened to discussions by various leaders of their objections to commitment in Korea. That evening he went to the Beijing Hotel and spent most of the night worrying over the problem.

Marshal Peng wrote later in his memoirs,

I could not fall asleep that night. I thought it might be because I could not enjoy the soft, cozy, spring bed, so I lay down on the carpeted floor. But sleep still did not come, and a train of thoughts flashed across my mind. The U.S. occupation of Korea, separated from China only by a river, would threaten northeast China. Its control of Taiwan posed a threat to Shanghai and east China. The United States could find a pretext at any time to launch a war of aggression against China. The tiger wanted to eat human beings; when it would do so would depend on its appetite. No concession could stop it. If the United States wanted to invade China, we had to resist its aggressions. Without going into a test with U.S. imperialism to see who was stronger, it would be difficult for us to build socialism. If the United States was bent on warring against China, it would want a war of quick decision. While we would wage a protracted war, it would fight regular warfare and we would employ the kind of warfare we had used against the Japanese invaders. As we had a national government and Soviet assistance, our situation was much better than it had been during the War of Resistance to Japanese Aggression. We should dispatch troops to Korea to safeguard our national construction.

Next day, Peng went to the Yiniantang Hall in the Zhongman-hai for the next session of the Central Committee.

This time Peng spoke, and although he had earlier said that China's army was not prepared to fight the Americans, now he said they must do so for the national interest. Peng was chosen to lead the forces in Korea, and it was decided that they would be called volunteers to lessen the international significance of the act of sending them in.

As the Chinese leaders were deciding, the American-led forces were driving on above the 38th parallel. Their objective was the Yalu River, and the right-wing press and hawks of America were crying for the UN forces to "go all the way."

What would have happened had the Chinese not opted to send their troops into Korea and the Americans persisted in driving to the Chinese border? No one knows, but it can be assumed that the presence of United Nations forces along the long border between Korea and China would have been a constant irritant.

The sad fact was that virtually no responsible persons in America saw the Chinese objections, or made any attempt to see them. While Marshal Peng Dehuai left his western army and moved into Manchuria with leading units of the Chinese People's Volunteers, the responsible elements of the American government were claiming that the Chinese statements that they would enter the war if the Americans moved north were so much propagandistic bluster.

On the very day that Marshal Peng had been summoned to Beijing, U.S. Secretary of State Dean Acheson was trying to stiffen British morale. The British believed what the Chinese were saying. Not so, said Acheson. A great risk would be to show any timidity. As noted, Acheson then knew that Premier Zhou Enlai had been telling the Indian ambassador to Beijing, K. M. Pannikar, what would happen and how, and Pannikar had faithfully reported.

The reports got to the Americans, but the American high command would not believe them.

That next week, the American Central Intelligence Agency reviewed the situation in Asia and came up with some surprisingly accurate estimates. By going to war with America, China would endanger the whole Chinese domestic program, which was just beginning. To the CIA it seemed unlikely that the Chinese would do so.

But there again, the CIA suffered from the recent lack of communication with China. It was not aware of the very real fears of the Chinese that the Americans were just looking for an excuse to attack them, so that Chiang Kaishek could be brought back into control of the Chinese Mainland.

Those October days were odd days in the American camp. What you believed could depend more on what you wanted to believe than on the facts. In Tokyo, Rear Admiral Arleigh Burke, deputy chief of staff of the Far East naval command, looked over the intelligence reports and said the Chinese were already in Korea. Indeed they were, for by the end of the first week of October, some troops were filtering in through Lin Biao's Manchurian command to various points along the border.

But General MacArthur's intelligence officer, Major General Charles Willoughby, saw it all quite differently. Although the daily intelligence summary, prepared by officers of the lower ranks, indicated that the Chinese were in Manchuria in force and that they could move in at any time almost anywhere along the border, the high command stuck with its stubborn view that the Chinese would not come in, based on the belief that the Russians pulled all the strings, and that the Russians did not wish to risk a general war.

What General Willoughby and his associates did not understand was the degree of concern in Beijing, the degree of fear that the United States' designs were far-reaching and evil and would result in the return of Chiang Kaishek. At about this point Mao remarked that although a Chinese Communist intervention in Korea could put the Communists back fifty years, still it had to be done. From the Chinese point of view, the presence of America on their border was intolerable.

And so, because of basic failures in understanding, and because of General MacArthur's powerful personality and his belief that communism must be wiped out, America and China marched toward war.

In the third week of October, Field Marshal Peng Dehuai moved into an old wooden building on a mountainside, the office of the mine in a gully northwest of the town of Bukjin, which was now abandoned, the whole village of workers down below having fled the war zone. From the top of the mountain the elevated cableway hung down, the buckets rusted and disused. Marshal Peng was getting ready for action.

So far the Chinese had behaved with enormous skill. Peng, Lin Biao, and all the other generals knew that they faced the most modern army in the world in that of the Americans, equipped not only with the atomic bomb, but with powerful field artillery, the most important aspect of their fighting power to the Chinese. American artillery (coupled with the American mastery of it) was indeed a formidable weapon.

Field Marshal Peng was considering his problems and his options. He had been thinking about them steadily since he flew into Shenyang (the old Mukden of Japanese days), where on October 8 he had met with Lin Biao and other high-ranking officers of the Chinese Communist forces to consider strategy.

He had selected the divisions to go in first, and those to come later. Then he had flown back to Beijing on the night of October 11, to report personally to Chairman Mao on his preparations for the fighting. On the next day he had flown back to Shenyang.

Next had come brief meetings with the North Koreans, who had been almost pleading in their request that the Chinese get into action before it was too late. Their concern was real, because the Allied forces of the United Nations were moving very rapidly toward the borders of North Korea, forcing the North Koreans into Manchuria.

Peng and his staff had moved into Korea on October 18th, going by motorcade with the North Korean foreign minister. The minister rode in a car, and Marshal Peng and his bodyguards and a secretary rode in a jeep. Behind the jeep came a truck, carrying the communications radios that were essential to Peng's operations, and behind them came trucks carrying the chief of staff, the staff, and the officers and men of the support units. They drove for two days to Kim Il Sung's headquarters, a farmhouse right on the side of a road. What a comedown for the chief of state of the North Korean People's Republic! Pyongyang, the battered capital, seemed far away, and the future grim.

Marshal Peng and Kim Il Sung were old comrades in arms, for Kim had fought shoulder to shoulder with the Communists in the Red Army during the days of the war against Japan. They talked for a while and agreed to establish a joint headquarters—more for show than anything else, as a matter of socialist solidarity; as all knew, the North Koreans were near the end of their rope, and the war, if it was to be continued, would have to be the responsibility of Field Marshal Peng and his support forces in Manchuria.

To fight the Americans, with their highly mechanized army, their air umbrella, and above all, that fearsome artillery, was a very stiff proposition, and the consideration of it had already created the lines of tension in the field marshal's face, although the battle had not yet begun. At the Central Committee meeting they had discussed the prospects if they lost this war: The Americans would restore Chiang Kaishek, and the revolution would have to be won all over again.

This grim, deep-seated fear was not even suspected by the Americans, who liked to consider themselves as republican in origin, democratic in nature, and never colonial. The Americans still did not see that they were, in their new postwar alliances, setting themselves up as the guardians of the status quo against the colonial peoples who were demanding freedom on their own terms. In this the Korean war had become a complicated anomaly, begun to preserve the freedom of the South Koreans, and now prosecuted to destroy the freedom of the North Koreans.

From the Chinese point of view, the prospects of the moment were depressing. There was no hope of saving Pyongyang. It had already fallen to the Americans and the South Koreans. The Republic of Korea Army had garrisoned the North Korean capital.

To Peng, the movement of his troops into position in North

Korea was agonizingly slow. They traveled by foot, with virtually no mechanized equipment, moving at night and holing up in the forests in the daytime to avoid the prying eyes of UN aircraft. That they did this skillfully was to be expected. It was the same tactic they had used against the Japanese for ten years.

In the meeting with Kim Il Sung, Peng had tentatively offered the Mao plan—a defense line that would run from Kusong, to Taechon, to Kujang-dong, Tokchon, Yongwon, and Oro-ri. But the advance units of the UN forces were now only 80 miles from the China border, and it did not seem that this line could be established. Most of Peng's headquarters troops were still on the road, along with the communications equipment.

Peng Dehuai had established a command post at Shenyang. He now moved to Manchuria and assembled his armies. On October 18, as night was falling, the armies crossed the Yalu River and silently disappeared into the forest. They marched to the Ragocho power station, arriving on the morning of October 19. Peng had set up his headquarters in the mine northwest of Bukjin.

Peng may not have realized that he had one great advantage: the American overconfidence and lack of understanding of what was just now happening in Korea. Everyone was talking about getting the European and American troops home for Thanksgiving. On the morning of October 20, General Willoughby was in Tokyo, writing an intelligence summary for General MacArthur. "Organized resistance on any large scale has ceased to be an enemy capability," said the general. The Chinese Communists, said Willoughby, would not enter the war. They were far too much concerned with the enormous domestic problems their government faced in the rebuilding of a shattered Chinese economy.

General Willoughby's estimate was thoughtful and restrained, and by all the laws of military warfare it should have been accurate. But the Chinese were not following the logic of sensible military stance. Mao had said that perhaps China would lose the coming struggle. But if that were to happen, he also said, then the Communists would once again retreat at they had before the Japanese and the Kuomintang, and rebuild for the future generations.

Had the Americans understood the depth of the Chinese feeling, certainly they would have restrained General MacArthur. But the Americans did not understand at all.

As the various units arrived on October 21 and afterwards, Marshal Peng greeted their officers. He was watching and waiting.

In a meeting with Marshal Peng before he set out for Korea, Mao had made some suggestions. Most important was that Peng establish a defense perimeter along the Kuson, Taechon, Yongwon, Oro-ri line. But, as the unit commanders reported, the troops instead wended their way carefully between enemy units so as not to be detected. Thus Peng still had the surprise factor working for him, although the clean defense line envisaged by Chairman Mao was an impossibility.

On October 23, the situation report from Kim Il Sung's headquarters brought a new assessment of the UN dispositions. It was hard to maintain accurate assessments Peng's staff officers could see, because the UN troops were moving very fast. They were, in fact, all mixed in with the Chinese in the west, although the Chinese were still being extremely careful to maintain the secrecy of their movements, and so far had been completely successful.

Marshal Peng spent much of his time these days wandering up the mountain and looking down into the valleys, lost in thought. The mountain path along which he traveled from the mining camp was covered with red and yellow leaves. Fall was ending, and soon the blasts of winter would rip along this trail.

From the top of the mountain Marshal Peng looked to the south, where the UN forces lay, and watched hundreds of refugees streaming along that road from Pyongyang and other cities. Here they were coming very nearly to the end of the path, and their only further refuge could be to cross over the river into China. As Peng watched on October 23, American planes came down to strafe the road, killing what Peng believed to be some civilians. Marshal Peng watched as the American P-51 Mustangs strafed the road and killed, and he cursed.

Peng waited. Then at dusk, the vanguard troops arrived.

Here is a conversation reported long after the war in a magazine article. All the names of people and units except Marshal Peng's are false, an indication of the strong Chinese sense of security even now.

Peng's chief of staff, Lin Qing, took the commander of the army, Deng Jun, to see the marshal. Deng Jun was an old soldier from the "Long March" days. He had lost an arm.

Lin Qing made the introductions.

"This is Commander Deng Jun of the vanguard regiment of the Fifth Army."

The marshal beamed. He rose and was going to shake hands until he saw the empty sleeve. He came around and shook Deng Jun's left hand.

"What, a one-armed general!"

Deng smiled.

"Is this the first time we've met?"

"No. I saw you during the 'Long March.' I heard your mobilization report before we attacked Lanzhou."

[Lanzhou was one of the decisive battles of the Chinese civil war, won by the Communists.]

"You fought at Lanzhou?"

"I lost an arm there."

"Oh. I heard it said that there was a regimental commander who was very good at fighting and who loved to run ahead fighting with a machine gun and that he was later seriously wounded. Was that you?"

Deng Jun blushed and laughed.

"You've come at the right time," said Marshal Peng.

"Weren't you allocated scores of vehicles?"

"Almost all of them were destroyed by bombing by enemy aircraft," said the commander. "We marched on foot afterwards. The soldiers carried too much. Added to the grain and field rations it came to fifty to sixty catties [sixty or more pounds] altogether."

[This whole section is incomprehensible, unless one presumes that the UN aircraft thought they were attacking North Korean troops, for there was absolutely no UN report of air action involving UN planes and Chinese troops.]

Peng had another question.

"How is morale?"

"Pretty good. However their understanding is not that good. Some people think nothing of the American army, some people don't know what to expect because they are fighting the Americans for the first time. A small number are nervous about going into battle."

"You must especially strengthen political work and bring our superiorities into full play," said Peng. "The present situation is critical. The enemy is already in our rear on one route. Your task has not changed. You are to go to Kusang as soon as possible. If Kusang has been taken by the enemy you are to set up positions north of Kusang and screen the deployment of troops in the rear."

"All right," said General Deng.

Peng shook his hand.

"I want you to tell the comrades the life or death of a nation friendly to us, the safety of our motherland, and also the honor or disgrace of our armed forces are all at stake in this war."

So the Chinese Communists were in no doubt at all about what they were fighting for—which gave them a big advantage over the UN troops, many of whom were now thoroughly confused by the changed American war aims.

For Marshal Peng, up on his mountaintop, the "First Campaign" of the new Korean war began on October 21, when a division of Chinese of the 40th Army, passing through Bukjin, encountered ROK troops. But since the Chinese dressed in North Korean uniforms and since they were careful to retrieve all their dead and wounded, and there were no prisoners, the South Koreans did not know who had hit them.

It was very vexing those days after October 21 when Marshal Peng had reached his command post but the radio, carried on a truck, had not arrived. Finally the radio came, with Chief of Staff Xie Fang. It was a great relief, for without the radio, Peng felt quite lost. For an American commander, of course, lack of modern communications was virtually unthinkable. But to the Chinese, accustomed to every possible hardship of war in the 1940s, it was merely an enormous inconvenience. Peng needed his radio to make his final plans for assault on the UN forces.

"Did the enemy discover our movements?" the field marshal asked Chief of Staff Xie.

"No," said Xie.

"Did you read the news from the foreign wire services?"

"I read them all. The Americans not only didn't see the troops, but said several times we couldn't send troops."

The field marshal was amused.

"There was one Associated Press wire which said there was a conjecture over whether or not we would send troops before Seoul was occupied. . . . However it was now believed that we could not. . . ."

"Why?"

"They said if the Chinese Communists planned to intervene in the Korean war, they would have done so when Seoul was in Communist hands or at least when Pyongyang was in their hands. Everyone concluded that after the two capitals were taken, China had no intention of intervening. . . ."

"Fools, didn't we publicly tell them we could not ignore it?"

"Right," said the chief of staff. "However, they have their logic. The wire also said that Chinese officials, including Mao Zedong and Zhou Enlai, had made sharp ringing statements that are unquestionably significant in meaning, and even though they cannot allow Communist Korea to disappear from the map, many experienced observers believe there are two reasons they cannot accept these statements literally. First, because if they officially send troops, it will kill the Communists' hopes of getting a United Nations seat; second, because they believe Mao Zedong to be very cunning and will never pull the Russians' chestnuts out of the Korean fire. . . ."

Marshal Peng grunted. "These bourgeoisie, even their body cells are egotistical. . . ."

"The Americans didn't believe we sent troops. A spokesman for the UN X Corps said: 'China cannot send large scale ground forces because they would be interdicted by our air force first.'

"Our army crossed the river without anyone knowing it. And up to now the enemy hasn't discovered them at all. In military history, this deserves to be called a miracle."

But Marshal Peng was too old a hand at war to be proud. "We can't be careless about this," Peng said. And then he paced back and forth, lost in thought.

Mao had asked him to hold the Kusang line until spring. But already there was no Kusang line; the enemy had penetrated at half a dozen points. So an entirely new plan had to be worked out, and it was Peng's responsibility to work it out right there in the field.

"The situation has changed. The enemy is presently underes-timating us and is making a rash advance with forces divided. This is really a favorable opportunity for us to destroy him. We can use tricks we are good at, fighting mobile warfare and fighting a battle of annihilation, selecting weak routes of the enemy and destroying him."

The chief of staff wanted to draft a plan, but Peng said to wait until the commanders had reported in. Then Peng would draw the plan and report to the chairman of the military commission of the Communist Party, and if it was approved, they would move.

The following day the generals arrived, and Peng held a series of meetings. At the end of the day, a plan had been approved.

Peng personally framed the telegram to Beijing, and the chief of staff supervised the sending. It was October 24. Next day the Chinese moved, and at last the UN forces discovered they were in Korea.

11

The Red Army Moves

How in the world did the Chinese put more than 350,000 men into North Korea in the eleven days between October 14 and October 25, 1950, without giving a clue to the American military command?

One answer, as indicated in the following account, is that the Americans in Tokyo were so occupied with their vision of total victory that they still were not listening to the warnings emanating from Beijing. But that is not the entire reason—far from it. The MacArthur command had never bothered to study the Chinese Communist methods of making war. It was inconceivable to them that a nineteenth-century peasant army—for that is really how one had to characterize the Chinese Red Army of 1950—without air power, without significant artillery, without tanks and armored vehicles, without motorized transport, without even enough rifles for the infantry, could even attempt to challenge the strongest country in the world. This reality was not even considered, although the Communists had without many arms succeeded more or less in the war against Japan. But in the war with the Japanese the Red Army was much weaker and fought a guerilla campaign. In the Korean war Mao Zedong chose to put force against force; his force of human hordes against the American force of modern weapons and technology. Against the technology Marshal Peng used cunning. His men marched into Korea on their own feet for the most part, at night. Behind them the rear guard carefully brushed the tracks out of the snow. They concealed themselves in the deep forest, kept quiet, and did not even show a fire. There was another factor too, which should have remained a

permanent lesson to the Americans but which they ignored again in Viet-
nam: It is no good going to war against an indigenous population fighting
for its life, because the intelligence factor is all on the side of the native
army. And make no mistake, the Chinese and their North Korean allies
knew that if they lost this war they would lose their independence. Mao
Zedong and the rest of the Chinese Communist Party Central Committee,
believing this absolutely, were willing to sacrifice millions of men, and see
their dream of modernizing their country set back for 50 years, to maintain
their independence. The American people, who did not realize that
MacArthur was a threat to China, were blissfully unaware of the Chinese
attitude, and the leaders in Washington really knew no more. . . .

As the days marched on, so did the Chinese armies, heading for
Manchuria. During the third week of October some three-quarters
of a million Chinese troops were massed on both sides of the North
Korean border, and many of them were inside that border. An
American logistics officer could laugh at the Chinese: They were
woefully short of artillery, signal equipment, and supply vehicles.
Earlier in the year Peng Dehuai himself had made a long report
on the need for modernization, cuts in manpower, and enormous
expenditures of cash to build up the armed forces (the report was
made in connection with the Chinese desire to resolve the Tibet
and Taiwan problems expeditiously). So Peng knew exactly where
he stood in terms of supplies and manpower.

But Peng also knew the determination of Chairman Mao and
his fellow leaders of the Communist Party not to be put down by
the Americans. The Chinese leaders were willing to sacrifice huge
numbers of soldiers on the battlefield, to stop the enemy by the
age-old method of putting so many men in his way that he could
not proceed.

Manpower was the Chinese key, and manpower almost alone.
In many regiments only one man in five had a weapon. The others
were told to use grenades until they managed to capture a rifle—
there were plenty of grenades and plenty of mortar tubes and
mortar shells, all cheap to manufacture.

Marshal Peng had a plan, responsive to the demands being
made by Zhou Enlai, to counter the United Nations forces. He did
not want to launch a major assault immediately. The purpose of

China's action was to stop the Americans, not to fight them any harder or any longer than was necessary.

"Our first response to the American invasion of North Korea should be limited," he said. "The PLA has not the equipment, the supplies, or the time to launch large-scale operations deep into Korea."

The plan was to lure the foreigners north, if that is where they wanted to go, with the Chinese remaining concealed until the last. Peng Dehuai debated whether or not the Americans would be so foolish as to overreach themselves. He did not think they would. His staff officers disagreed. His staff, this time, was right. The Americans, flushed with success, would allow themselves to be lured deep into the mountains, extending their line of supply, falsely secure in the belief that the Chinese would not enter the war.

But on October 14, the Chinese had begun crossing the Yalu River, over the twin bridges at Dandong. First went the men of the 38th Field Army, just as the UN forces were crossing the 38th parallel. Next moved the 42nd Field Army, at Manpojin, 100 miles to the east. And soon at Dandong would come the 39th and 40th field armies, with their divisions reinforced by one division each from the 41st Field Army. This would be the 13th Army Group, under General Li Tianyu, and its area of operations would be the west coast on the Chungchon River front, 700 miles below the Yalu. The enemy here would be General Walker's Eighth Army.

The 42nd Field Army would move along the east coast of Korea to stop the UN troops from taking that region.

Behind the advance units came the 50th and 66th field armies, which would cross later in the month at Sakchu, near the Suiho Dam. The 20th, 26th, and 27th field armies were coming up to enter Korea at Manpojin and Singalpojin during the first week of November. Each of these was reinforced by a division from the dismembered 30th Field Army. This new group, to be employed only if the Americans did not listen to Zhou Enlai even after the preliminary attack, would comprise the Ninth Army Group.

Thus, as Field Marshal Peng contemplated his command and his procedures, he had 380,000 men on their way into North Korea to launch a major attack if need be.

His most effective weapon had to be surprise. To achieve surprise, the Chinese would have to move like the wind, with the silence of the night, and leave no more tracks than a vanishing wave on a rocky shore. Ironically, this was possible because the Chinese had virtually no mechanized equipment; only three regiments of artillery from Russia, a few truck-mounted rocket launchers, and a few trucks. The vast majority of the supplies were hand-carried.

As the soldiers moved into Korea, the messages came to Field Marshal Peng: The surprise element was on their side; the Americans were unaware of their coming. Monitoring of the American radio indicated no awareness of any change in the military situation.

Unit after unit crossed the steel bridges, watching for American aircraft and freezing into silence when they came. Silence was the theme of the march, silence and darkness. At night they gathered in the forests and ate and slept, waiting for the march to begin once again.

Up in the old mining camp, Marshal Peng waited. From the radio which connected him with his forces he learned that the UN forces had moved up north to pass, at places, the line Marshal Peng had selected for defense; they would not be able to use that line.

The best news was that the enemy had not learned of their existence as yet, and the element of surprise was still with them. The Americans did not know that they were infiltrated, and in some areas surrounded, by Chinese troops, not by intent, but by the accident of armies moving in different directions simultaneously. Now this factor could be a big element in achieving surprise.

On October 25, 1950, from the vantage point of General Douglas MacArthur in Tokyo, the Korean war was really over, it seemed. It was just four months after the North Korean People's Army had crossed the 38th parallel to try to do by force what neither of the two Koreas had been able to do otherwise, and the powers entrusted with the job at Yalta had also failed to do: to reunite Korea as one nation under one government.

The North Koreans had had their innings. They had counted on a lightning victory against an inferior Republic of Korea military machine, and "promised" noninterference by the United States.

They had gambled, and they had lost. It was now the time of the South Koreans, buttressed by the military force of the United States and UN allies.

On October 25, 1950, at last Marshal Peng had his wish: On orders from General Douglas MacArthur, the UN forces were driving toward the Yalu River, to destroy the North Korean military machine and, it was easy for anyone to infer, to destroy the North Korean government.

General MacArthur had removed all restrictions on the use of UN forces to press forward. In obedience the ROK Sixth Division was racing along the valley of the Chongchon River, and its forward element passed through Onjong. The Yalu River was just fifty miles farther. Late on the afternoon of October 24 they reached Kojang, just 18 air miles south of Chosan, and stopped to bivouac before driving on to the river the next day.

On October 25 the ROK First Division tanks and infantry began fighting troops they said were Chinese. By nightfall the first Chinese prisoner was brought down to General Walker's headquarters in Pyongyang by the South Koreans, as proof of their claim that the Chinese had entered the war.

At first the Americans would not believe that the Chinese were Chinese, since that first contingent of Chinese, infiltrating into Korea, had all adopted the North Korean uniform. Even Marshal Peng Dehuai was in North Korean combat clothes. This first prisoner had no marks to distinguish him from the troops the UN forces had been fighting all summer; he was small, slender, wearing cotton clothing and tennis shoes. But he could not speak a word of Korean, a fact the ROK troops who had captured him had ascertained hours earlier.

He could be a fake, said General Walker's intelligence officers. Yes, of course, said the South Korean intelligence officers. But . . . this man spoke fluent Mandarin Chinese, and virtually none of the North Korean troops spoke any Chinese.

That night the word was sent to Tokyo that Chinese soldiers in significant numbers had been found inside Korea.

At first the officers of General MacArthur's staff scoffed. But the confirming factors kept arriving: prisoners from the eastern side of Korea.

At Peng Dehuai's headquarters there was another sort of confirmation that night. The men from the eastern front reported on the capture of an American army lieutenant, Lieutenant Glen C. Jones, undeniably American, undeniably serving the Korean forces, and undeniably far above the 38th parallel.

As Marshal Peng now knew very well, the UN forces had come north of the 38th parallel in spite of the warnings.

Now what was going to happen?

The nature of the Chinese Red Army, with its paucity of modern military equipment, placed a great deal of responsibility on unit commanders, they were to follow the general plan if they could, but not be afraid to deviate if it seemed appropriate. Thus, although Marshal Peng said that the First Chinese Communist Campaign ended on about October 25, it really lasted several days longer, because local units were engaged and could not easily be withdrawn.

On the night of October 26 the Chinese attacked Onjong and routed the South Koreans. At the end of the fight not a single unit of the ROK Second Regiment remained intact. Still, on that morning of October 26 the ROK Seventh Regiment did reach the Yalu River, as ordered to by General MacArthur—the only element of the UN force ever to get so far. It reached Chosan that day, fighting only against fleeing North Koreans.

Everywhere on the Eighth Army front the Chinese were now on the attack. Hundreds of thousands of Marshal Peng Dehuai's men had filtered into North Korea under the noses of the UN forces. The movement had been very skillful. So unknown were these movements that the Eighth Army intelligence officers still believed that these Chinese soldiers were individual volunteers, enlisted by the North Koreans.

"There are no indications of open intervention on the part of Chinese Communist forces," said the Eighth Army intelligence estimate that day. General Paik Sunyup, the commander of the ROK First Division, told Eighth Army intelligence that his men faced at least 10,000 Chinese, but General Walker's staff still did not believe.

Two days later the Eighth Army was stopped and made no further progress anywhere.

General Walker ordered the First Cavalry to attack and reach the Yalu River. They pushed northward.

The collapse of the ROK Second Corps left a hole in the UN line. The U.S. Eighth Cavalry came up to support the line, but made no progress, and the 12th ROK Regiment fell back through that cavalry unit. That afternoon the troops of the Eighth Cavalry discovered that the troops they were fighting were Chinese.

The 24th Division, mindful of General MacArthur's command to drive to the Yalu, had reached a point 18 miles from that river, still fighting North Koreans, or so they believed. Then, the number of prisoners confirmed as Chinese, the defeats in the south, and the reports of more Chinese moving towards Korea changed the weight of the evidence. General Walker was finally convinced that he faced a new and powerful enemy. He ordered the troops to retreat back to the Chongchon line and there consolidate the line and await orders.

Marshal Peng claimed victory. The limited ambitions of this "First Campaign" had been achieved in a few days. The United Nations was now warned. As the Chinese units across the broad front could be reached they were told to break off action. Marshal Peng settled down at the old mine to await developments.

The results of Marshal Peng's First Campaign were strangely mixed, and thus very hard for the UN field commanders to evaluate. Unfortunately, as noted, such men as John Service of the Department of State and Lieutenant Colonel Evans Carlson of the U.S. Marine Corps had been forced out of public service. These were men who had lived with the Chinese Communist armies during the war against Japan, and knew their tactics. There remained no one in authority or even close to it in the American military hierarchy who really knew much about the Chinese.

The result was an odd mixture of optimism and caution. General Walker had now become cautious, but some of his division commanders were still talking about "having the boys back in Tokyo to do their Christmas shopping." The Far East Air Force bomber command complained that it had run out of targets, and General Stratemeyer reduced sorties and on October 27 suspended all aerial operations. Two bombardment groups, the 22nd and 92nd, were shipped back to the United States on October 27.

But up north, the ROK II Corps was beginning to fall apart. The Sixth Division had taken that beating from the Chinese on October 25. On October 26 the Seventh Regiment had fallen afoul of the Chinese, and lost 75 percent of its 3,500 men.

By October 27, 1950, The ROK II Corps was in retreat, and the pace was quickening. This corps, which had been decimated in earlier fighting, had not really been given time to rebuild. The officers were uncertain of themselves and the men even more so. The Chinese Red Army, with its weird practices, unnerved the troops, who had been trained to fight a mechanized army, not a horde.

On October 28, 1950, General Li Tianyu, commander of the Chinese 13th Army Group, held a briefing at his headquarters north of the Chungchon River. The Americans and the South Koreans had been slowed but not yet stopped, said General Li. The U.S. First Cavalry Division had been brought up to plug the hole left by the retreat of the ROK II Corps.

On the far west of the UN force, the Australians of the 27th Commonwealth Brigade began to encounter stiffer opposition on its drive to take Sinuiju. The Australians who were out in front were later relieved by the American 24th Division, which continued the drive but again noticed heavy opposition. On October 30 elements of the 24th Division came within 20 miles of Sinuiju and the Yalu.

On November 1 the Americans saw their first Soviet MIG fighters (there would soon be Chinese planes as well). On the night of November 1, part of the First Cavalry Division was attacked very heavily by Chinese forces, including elements of cavalry on Mongolian ponies.

The Americans did not quite know what to make of all this. They simply did not know that the Chinese were in a waiting period, not quite sure of what to do.

The fighting continued. On November 1, the Chinese units followed their instructions and rolled the UN forces back. This was not a new offensive, just the reflex actions of the first. The forests of North Korea were covered with smoke—the Chinese were moving under cover of smoke screens from forest fires they set, getting into position for a major offensive if it became necessary. The determination of Marshal Peng and his men was complete, while even now it was not recognized at MacArthur's headquarters that the Chinese were in Korea in enormous force.

In Washington the Truman Administration was quicker to believe that the Chinese had entered the war. Zhou Enlai's pronouncements and signaling had finally been accepted. Secretary of State Acheson, who in his famous "Press Club speech" denied that the United States had any special interest in South Korea, had first opposed the crossing of the parallel, then approved it, and now had come to oppose it once again. It had never been in the minds of Truman and his advisors to drive to the Yalu and confront the Chinese there; that had been MacArthur's contribution.

Washington was extremely fretful. Secretary Acheson later said that the Chinese would have accepted it if MacArthur had drawn back even to the Pyongyang-Wonsan line and set up a purely defensive position. Almost certainly Acheson was wrong in this, for the Chinese had made their intentions clear previously.

By November 2, General MacArthur's staff had almost all shifted around to accept the concept of a Chinese army in Korea, a definite threat to the UN victory, but MacArthur vacillated. One moment he was denying the existence of the Chinese, and the next saying that they were really volunteers, and an unimportant aspect of the fighting.

But that day General Willoughby announced that he had just discovered 600,000 Chinese troops inside North Korea. With that news MacArthur called for help; his whole command was threatened, he said.

The Joint Chiefs of Staff asked MacArthur for an assessment of the situation. Not now, he said. Wait until something really happens.

Even as General MacArthur said the words, that something was just about to occur.

12

Tactics

From the first Chinese attack on the UN Eighth Army on October 25, it was a week before the American command began to realize what it was up against. By the time General Walton Walker realized and went on the defensive in the face of contrary orders from General MacArthur, the UN force had lost the impetus of its drive to the Yalu River, and was sitting in stunned silence. As is noted in the following pages, even then the American command in Tokyo did not pay serious attention. In a way MacArthur seemed to be very much like the old Prussian generals of World War I who had the utmost contempt for intelligence and plowed ahead according to doctrine no matter what the consequences. This pigheadedness was the direct cause of the destruction of the Third Battalion of the Eighth Cavalry Regiment, the first American unit to feel the full brunt of the Chinese attack. . . .

Had the late Evans Carlson been in Korea on October 25, 1950, he would have recognized the tactics of the enemy who suddenly attacked to split the United Nations forces, even as they seemed very near to total victory. The attackers came in the hours before the dawn, making enormous noise with drums, whistles, and off-key bugles. Their attacks were ushered in by machine gun fire and mortar fire, but no artillery. The use of grenades was extensive. The attackers would come out of the night, rush a position, kill and wound men, and then withdraw. The attacks seemed sporadic and uncoordinated, and in the narrowest sense they were. The purpose of the first Chinese attack was to straighten Chinese lines and prepare to engage the enemy on the western and eastern sides of Korea. General MacArthur had split his forces, and if that split could be maintained, and if the Americans still did not heed the warnings, then the second assault would be quite different.

After the first Chinese move was made on October 25, the straightening of the lines occupied more time than had been expected. Meanwhile up north the troops had used the old technique of forest burning to lay down a smoke screen and confuse the enemy as to the movements of the Communist troops. This was working very well indeed. Occasionally a peasant or a village would report the movement of a column of troops to some South Korean authority, but no one really understood the situation, and so the secrecy about the Communist operations in Korea remained.

Shielded by the fires and their smoke, and shielded by the fighting in the Eighth Army area, Marshal Peng was steadily moving troops. He was preparing for the eventuality, which he quite expected, of a major attack, even as the first attack continued on the western side of the peninsula, and on the east around the Chongjin reservoir.

By November 1, since the Chinese attack had slowed so perceptibly, the UN high command concluded that the number of Chinese in Korea was fewer than had been thought, and that they were not offensively inclined. But one officer who wasn't so sure was Major General Hobart R. Gay, commander of the First Cavalry Division, who had reports of Chinese divisions moving around his area on all sides. These reports reflected part of the positioning of Marshal Peng's forces for the real offensive that was to come, if the Americans did not withdraw to the south.

General Gay asked for reinforcements, but he did not get them. There were too many different stories and too many points of view afloat in Korea just then, and the I Corps, which commanded General Gay's movements, did not believe in the Chinese threat.

At one o'clock in the afternoon on November 1, General Walker began trying to get through to General Milburn, the commander of the I Corps, to give him some bad news. The collapse of the

ROK II Corps was now complete. The South Korean soldiers were fleeing along the roads, beside the roads, and across the countryside, and as a fighting unit the II Corps was finished for the moment. Even though the II Corps was still only rudimentarily trained, no one had expected the total collapse that occurred.

This disaster meant that General Milburn's right flank was wide open. When Milburn put down the telephone he began barking orders, and soon every sort of soldier who could be corralled on short notice was being sent to that right flank. The key spot was Kunu-ri. This whole area was vital to the Chinese defense line, and so they were busily cleaning it up, although their care was such that the Americans did not really know what was happening. To the Americans the important matter was the three bridges across the Chongchon River, which controlled their lines of supply and escape routes in case of trouble.

In the matter of road communications the most important point at the north of the reduced American line was Yongsan-dong, the confluence of five roads, through which all the retreating American troops—ordered to take new defensive positions by General Walker—would have to move. A combat patrol from the First Battalion of the Fifth Cavalry Regiment scouted north from Yongsan-dong, but found its way blocked six miles north and turned around. This was all clearly enemy land. The Chinese had moved down almost to the American positions below the Kuryong River. The Chinese were moving steadily, but carefully, south, to position themselves. They were not particularly looking for a fight just now; that was not in their orders. But the Americans were blocking their way.

So important was this area control that the Chinese brought in some of their very limited supply of artillery, the Katushka truck-mounted multiple rocket launchers provided them by the Soviets. The rockets were not long on accuracy, but one struck an American truck in the Eighth Cavalry area, and everyone discovered that the truck was carrying ammunition when it blew up. The American artillery, which was noted for its pinpoint accuracy, then opened up on the rocket launchers, and the Chinese moved them out of the area—they were too valuable to the Chinese to be risked at this point.

In their move south and east, the Chinese kept up the pressure all day long, forcing the Americans to move south, and the South Korean forces to move southeast. That night they hit the ROK 15th Regiment very hard, and that unit began to disintegrate, which put more pressure on the American units alongside.

Once again, the American lack of information about the enemy created a false sense of security. The fact is that the Chinese had two armies in this area, while the Westerners believed it was only two divisions. By the night of November 1, the Chinese had surged along the banks of the Samtan River, to the northeast of the basic American positions, and were threatening to outflank General Milburn's corps. They probably would not actually have done so—they were more interested in position than in battle—but the Americans had no way of knowing that. And so, the Americans prepared for battle.

Not knowing what they were up against, the First and Second battalions of the Eighth Cavalry got in the way of the Chinese, blocking their move in the Unsan area. The two battalions were positioned on the sides of the ridge, and the Chinese, using the technique of total envelopment, found the gap between the units and surged through. That was the great advantage of the mass army. Troops with tanks were holding the bridge at a village on the Samtan River, and suddenly they saw a mass of infantry moving swiftly down on them. They reported and moved out. Already the artillerymen had learned one aspect of Chinese mass tactics; spotters had watched as their guns plastered infantry columns. Such treatment in modern warfare usually results in the destruction of the column, the way balked by broken and burning vehicles. But the Chinese had no vehicles, and when men fell as they did with the zeroed-in artillery fire, their comrades simply stepped over them and went on. That was what they had been trained to do.

General Walker's Eighth Army had passed over from the offensive to the defensive, except on the extreme west flank of the Eighth Army, where American troops, fighting North Korean forces, did get very near to the Yalu before they were ordered to move back and assume defensive stance. General Walker's plan was to hold on the north bank of the Chongchon River with the

British 27th Commonwealth Brigade and the 19th Infantry Regiment of the U.S. 24th Division. The Chinese were to be given Unsan just as soon as the American troops to the north could be rushed back through this communications center.

But the Americans did not make it. There were too many Chinese and they came too fast. By nightfall the Chinese had surrounded Unsan. They attacked the ROK 15th Regiment on the east, drove that unit off the ridge it was holding, and the encirclement was complete. By that time most of the American units up north had filtered through to the east, with the exception of the Third Battalion of the Eighth Cavalry. The battalion officers assembled the troops in their trucks and jeeps, bumper to bumper, and sweated out the night, ready to charge down the road the next morning. And now was fought a battle of the old-fashioned cavalry and the new. In the middle of the night, the Chinese bugles began to blast, and the men of the Eighth Cavalry heard horses' hooves pounding down from the hills. Then they saw them, Chinese soldiers in their padded uniforms, looking like stuffed dolls on their shaggy Mongol ponies, charging down with rifle, bayonet, and sword. They surrounded the Eighth Cavalry caravan like Indians surrounding a wagon train, and they charged in to burn the vehicles and attack the troops at close hand.

At the outset of that first campaign, Marshal Peng had cautioned his troops: They were to move slowly, pick up their dead, and make every effort to lose no men as prisoners of war. Each unit commander was made personally responsible for seeing that the enemy got no information by taking prisoners. Of course, the UN forces did capture some prisoners, but there, too, all were primed by their commanders with the names of fake organizations to which they claimed to belong. Thus the 129th Division some men claimed to belong to was in reality the 29th Field Army, about ten times as strong.

On this night of November 1 the men of the Third Battalion of the Eighth Cavalry had a taste of hand-to-hand fighting, at which the Communists excelled. But these were green Chinese troops, scarcely out of the basic training stage, and they had no clear idea of their mission. The commanders had been told to take ground, to move from point A to point B, but they had not been issued

instructions about what to do with enemy soldiers. Captain Fill-
more McAbee's life was saved because of the Chinese confusion.
In the fighting around the battalion train, he was shot in the shoulder and fell into a ditch. Chinese troops came up to him and
prodded him with bayonets but did not thrust or shoot. He sat up
and pointed down the road, and the Chinese went that way. No
one offered to take him prisoner, and they left him. McAbee finally
reached the battalion command post, a dugout in the side of a hill,
still carrying his carbine.

There was no chance now that the Third Battalion could fight
its way out and to the UN lines. The only solution was a rescue
from the south, and this was discussed for the next two days, while
the Third Battalion resisted Chinese attacks. Many men were
wounded in the fighting. About 170 of them were rounded up
and brought to the command post, where they were placed under
the supervision of Father Emil J. Kapoaun, the chaplain, and Captain Clarence R. Anderson, the battalion surgeon.

The hand-to-hand fighting was furious but sporadic. The battalion held out for three days, in the daytime covered by air strikes,
which kept the Chinese pinned down, or so the Americans thought.
The fact was that the Chinese were warned by their officers to stay
under cover in daylight because the field marshal did not want the
Americans to get any idea of the real Chinese strength.

The Third Battalion remained in its trap. Meanwhile General
Gay, the division commander, was following orders from General
Milburn and moving the rest of the First Cavalry Division south
of the river.

On November 2, an L-5 single-engined liaison plane flew over
the "lost" Third Battalion and dropped medical supplies for the
two hundred wounded men. An evacuation helicopter came to the
area, circled, and then tried to land near the command post. But
the Chinese began firing on the helicopter with rifles, and apparently hit it hard, because the pilot took off and flew away.

In the afternoon a second liaison plane flew over and dropped
a message. One of the men went out under the cover of rifles to
get it. The Chinese did not fire on him, and the message was taken
to the battalion command post. It was good news: A relief column
was on the way, the pilot had written.

But that message was written before General Milburn had ordered the final withdrawal of the First Cavalry to a point below the Chongchon River. In fact, no column had been dispatched, and that evening General Milburn, in the face of requests from various officers of the First Cavalry Division, made the fateful decision. No attempt would be made to rescue the "lost" battalion. If they were to be saved, they must save themselves.

13

Hiatus

In the first week of November, General MacArthur still did not realize what had happened to his war. He just could not believe that the Chinese had come in force to Korea to nullify his dream of victory. He did not know his enemy. Marshal Peng Dehuai did know his enemy, and he correctly predicted what that enemy would do. The American Marines, who had a healthy disrespect for MacArthur and his methods, also had a healthy respect for the Chinese, whom MacArthur and his staff characterized as a mob. Mob they were, but they charged ahead into the guns nevertheless, without apparent regard for casualties. Major General Beierlinden of MacArthur's staff had more than an inkling of the truth, but MacArthur paid no attention. Even after the surprise and defeat of October, the Tokyo headquarters of the UN forces remained foolishly optimistic, not yet understanding the new nature of the Korean struggle. . . .

The "lost" battalion of the Eighth Cavalry never made it back. The wounded were left in the dugout with the chaplain and the surgeon to be taken prisoner. Those 250 men were the principal survivors of the battalion. Meanwhile, the 200 able-bodied men headed east and then southwest. They saw many Chinese all around them, and had some skirmishes, but mostly they tried to keep out of sight. They reached a point near Ipsok, where they broke into small groups and tried to filter through the Chinese lines. Some of them made it. Most of them did not. Including a number who had escaped earlier and some stragglers who came in later, only ten officers and 200 men of the Third Battalion, Eighth Cavalry Regiment, made good their escape from the Chinese; the final figure was a loss of more than 60 percent.

Up on the mountain in the mining camp office, Field Marshal Peng knew none of the details about the fighting around Unsan. His generals said the attack of October 25 had been successful in stopping the UN drive toward the Yalu River. Peng did not even know of the Yongsan-dong battles, and he had heard of the Third Battalion only in that it was a part of the First Cavalry Division.

As far as Peng was concerned, the first campaign was over and successful and to be put out of mind. But the marshal was worried about something and his aides knew it. He was silent most of the time and he was not eating much.

The aides did not understand it. All the news was really very good. The Americans were extremely careless in the dissemination of information that would have been secret in the Chinese forces: unit names, commanders, and assessments of situations. The Chinese were very grateful, for their principal source of news about the United Nations forces was the dispatches of the war correspondents, radioed back home and picked up by the Chinese radio as well. Peng received these intercepts every day, and he and his staff read them carefully and sometimes based their actions on them. They were very much impressed by the accuracy of Reuter, the Associated Press, and the United Press.

At the end of the first actions, Peng was very pleased to read in the dispatches that the Chinese force in Korea must be a token force. If the Americans believed that, which obviously they did, then they would not delay long before launching their renewed attack toward the Yalu, and then they would fall in the trap of Marshal Peng. The trap was set now with the movement across the neck of Korea. The Chinese had forces in the west that could close off the access to the south for General Walker's Eighth Army, and forces in the northeast that could swoop down on the X Corps, which was planning to move north to the reservoirs. Thus Peng had a chance to entrap a hundred thousand UN troops and cripple the American war effort.

But American General Walton Walker had seen what Peng was

aiming to do, which was the main reason that he had pulled back his forces and established the defense line on the Chongchon. Would the Americans avoid the trap? That was what worried Marshal Peng.

Over on the east side of Korea Major General Edward M. Almond, the commander of X Corps, was supremely confident. He shared almost all of General MacArthur's attitudes, as well he might, for he had come to X Corps straight from the job of chief of staff to MacArthur. Since the first of the month, the marines, who were the spearhead of the UN Corps, had been doing some fighting, but it seemed quite localized. There were Chinese about, but it did not seem that there were very many. One Tokyo estimate put the number at 16,500. General Almond was confident that the number was something small. And General Almond had nothing but contempt for the Chinese Red Army. "A bunch of Chinese laundrymen," he was later to call them—but not much later, and not for long.

Major General Oliver P. Smith, commander of the First Marine Division, said he believed there were at least two or three Chinese armies out there in the mountains. General Almond was so confident that he sent Colonel Edward Forney, the chief marine liaison officer on the Almond staff, on a reconnaissance flight over the whole territory just to show him there was nothing out there, no enemy out there. Sure enough, the recon flight produced no sight of Chinese troops.

The marines moved nervously around the northeast, with that feeling that someone was watching them. Occasionally they ran into resistance, but they were never quite sure who it was, because the troop commanders of the Red Army were following Marshal Peng's direction punctiliously, leaving no wounded or dead behind and making sure no men were taken prisoner. The Chinese stayed under cover in the daylight hours. At night they fired a field piece and some 120 mm mortars at the marines. The Chinese were there, all right. The Second Battalion of the Seventh Marines, which was located on two hills on the sides of the Chinghung-ni-dong road in the Sudong valley, could not see or hear many Chinese around, but in fact they faced the entire 124th Chinese Division of about 10,000 troops.

On the night of November 2 the battalion was hit by those

troops trying a double envelopment formation. The Seventh Marines would have been very pleased to learn that night in the midst of the fighting that Marshal Peng considered this nothing but nuisance work, and that he was delaying any offensive to await events. Yes, the Chinese were there, with the North Koreans and a handful of North Korean tanks. And on that night of November 2 they hit the marines hard.

The fighting continued for five days. From the marine point of view, it was certainly no "hiatus" such as Marshal Peng indicated. This again was because of the nature of the Chinese Red Army and the considerable power of decision of local commanders. The Chinese division commander may have wanted to harden his troops by battle. He may have had some other reason. It was not until November 7 that the word reached the far-flung echelons of the Chinese army in Korea that the fighting was to stop and the Chinese troops were to lie low. The marines, who had caused many casualties, thought it was because of the high casualty rate. Once again that showed how little they knew their enemy. Peng had come to Korea with only one basic strength, and that was enormous manpower. Before Peng had left Beijing he and Mao had understood that the manpower must be used—wasted, one might say— to stop the Americans and turn the Korean war around to save the North Korean People's Republic from destruction.

Up on his mountain, Marshal Peng read the intercepts of the UN correspondents' new dispatches. As noted, during the first week of November he was not very happy. General Walker was talking about holding a line. To be sure, from Tokyo came cries of attack, attack, but Walker had pulled back nonetheless.

The whole Korea situation was extremely confused. The chief operations officer of the U.S. army was "concerned." The marines were quoted as saying the situation was "fluid." Those were not the words Marshal Peng wanted to hear. He wanted to hear that the Americans had decided to move—either below the 38th parallel or toward the Yalu. Then he would know what to do. He was certain, however, knowing General MacArthur's character, that the direction would not be a retreat southward.

U.S. Army Chief of Operations Major General Charles Bolte flew to Tokyo to find out what was happening, could not, and then flew to Korea to see General Walker. Back in Tokyo they were still talking about cutting down the UN force because the war was so nearly over. In spite of the capture of Chinese prisoners by the marines in the east as well as by the Eighth Army in the west, MacArthur was blithe. Nothing serious had happened, said the general one day. Although the next day he changed his mind and said there was a threat, two days later there was "no serious threat." But at Pyongyang, Bolte got a sense of "real crisis" and concern over the possibility of victory with a Chinese opponent in the field.

To add to the confusion, the Chinese behaved with great compassion just now. They brought American wounded back to their own lines. They released many prisoners and told them to tell their friends that the Chinese did not want a war; they wanted the foreigners to move south of the 38th parallel.

On the UN side, no one replied.

As of the end of the first week of November, then, all the information necessary for a proper UN decision was available. Major General Beierlinden, MacArthur's personnel officer, told the Joint Chiefs of Staff that if the Chinese entered the war, the American casualties would continue to go up. The danger that the war would be lost now was as great as it had been at the Pusan perimeter. This Chinese intervention was real, he assured the chiefs.

But the Joint Chiefs preferred to believe General MacArthur, who was hell-bent on continuing the war, and whose contempt for the Chinese was so great that he did not believe they were willing to stake their national future on such a gamble.

On his mountaintop in the fastness of North Korea, Marshal Peng had the probable course of the Americans assessed. He was sure that MacArthur would continue to go for victory, not stalemate. He knew what the tactic would be: an attempt to drive swiftly to the Yalu and push the enemy over the border. The Americans wanted a short, clean war. Marshal Peng was planning to give them a long, dirty one.

At the end of the second week of November Marshal Peng was very pleased. He had just read in the American news dispatches that the Chinese had only a token force in Korea. That was just what he wanted. More than two weeks had passed since the Chinese had made their first move, and still the Americans had no real conception of what they faced.

Peng went to the war room one night in mid-November and looked over the situation map by candlelight. He pointed to the west side of the map where the little clusters of blue pins showed that General Walker's Eighth Army had retreated below the Chongchon River. From Tokyo was coming the word that the UN forces would soon begin advancing once again.

"Good," said Marshal Peng, "we'll let them advance."

"Let them advance?" asked an aide.

"Yes," said Marshal Peng. He pointed to a spot north of the Chongchon. "Piho-san. If they want Piho-san let them have it."

"Give them Piho-san?"

"Yes." The marshal made a sweeping movement with his hand across the situation map, making a line from Napchongjong through Ansimdong, Xinhung-dong, Unyung-dong, and Pung-kok-san.

"We can let them advance to here," he said.

His staff members then smiled. They understood. The marshal was planning to draw the Americans into a trap.

In this trapping, the Chinese had to be very careful. They wanted to secure maximum results. They were to let the enemy come, and not make a stand, and they must not use heavy weapons (since the Chinese were extremely short on heavy weapons, this was a more or less rhetorical qualification). And, he told his aides, once again the commanders must be warned: No prisoners should be lost to the UN forces, and no wounded.

"When would they move?" asked the chief of staff.

Peng looked out at the top of the mountain to the west, where sat the new moon, fine as an eyebrow.

"When the moon is full we shall make our move."

That meant November 24. Marshal Peng knew it would give the United Nations time to make its move first. Would MacArthur listen to the growing chorus of non-American UN members, and move back to the 38th parallel? It did not seem likely to Marshal Peng, but Zhou Enlai, in particular, had voiced the hope that the war could thus be averted.

The plan was first approved by the staff of the Volunteer Head-quarters and then sent back to Beijing for Chairman Mao's approval, which was received without delay. The staff began implementing the plan.

Two armies, the First Army and the Fifth Army, were moved to the left flank and kept in total concealment. A few regiments were kept in the line, to do just enough fighting to continue the impression of a "token presence." This was the desultory fighting that continued above the Chongchon and on the east coast of Korea.

On the west, the Piho-san positions of the Chinese were abandoned, and so were positions farther north, but General Walker did not take the bait. His troops patrolled but did not advance. The air forces flew many missions up to the Yalu River, but the ground forces stayed put.

Marshal Peng was worried. Why did the Americans not take the bait? As one of his staff members said, "Chief Peng never smoked many cigarettes, but now he was smoking a lot. He smoked fiercely, smoking half of the cigarette in a few puffs. Light from the cigarette stubs continually flickered in the moonlight. The golden sickle stood in the sky, still a sickle, not a moon."

Each night Peng and his chief of staff discussed the situation and the day's developments. Each day they wondered why the Americans did not take their bait. The chief of staff appraised the situation:

> Our withdrawal has confused the enemy. The various wire services all said the Communist forces withdrawal is unfathomable to the United Nations supreme command. They have a lot of guesses on why we withdrew. One wire service summed it up in four parts:
>
> One: it is estimated that we might be waiting for a political solution;
>
> Two: that we are building up supplies;
>
> Three: that we may be waiting for reinforcements;
>
> Four: that we might be shifting to another front. And that last estimate said that is something perhaps they don't know about.

But Marshal Peng was more interested in what the American military command was thinking.

His chief of staff had an estimate. He handed it to Peng, who put on his glasses and read: "The Chinese Communist forces' surprising withdrawal is almost as surprising as their appearance. They have voluntarily withdrawn without any pressure while the United Nations forces were on the defense. Looking at it from the general scope of their withdrawal, it appears to be deliberate."

He soon had the wire service reports to augment the official one. Reuter said the British 27th Brigade was of the opinion that the situation represented a phony war. This was based on three ideas:

First, the Chinese Communists were satisfied because their intervention let them save face.

Second, they thought they might build a buffer zone to protect their Manchurian border.

Third, winter was approaching and they intended to let the severe cold help them make the United Nations forces suffer a Napoleonic defeat.

Marshal Peng laughed. The Reuter man, he said, had it just about right.

But then Peng began to worry more. If the newsmen could properly assess his secret thoughts, then could not the United Nations command also get the idea?

General MacArthur just then was struggling with decision. "There were but three possible courses," he wrote later. "I could go forward, remain immobile, or withdraw."

The Chinese Communists would be happy enough with either the first or last course. It was the second course that troubled Peng. But fortunately for the marshal, to follow that course would have been completely out of character for General Douglas MacArthur.

── 14 ──

Guessing Game

The following anecdote about the visit of Mao Zedong's son to Marshal Peng is included here to show the informality that exists in the Chinese Red Army, "where even a cat may look at a king." The next anecdote, about the news dispatches from Tokyo, indicates just how little the American high command had learned about the Chinese intentions three weeks after the Chinese appeared on the Korea scene. What Peng was reluctantly doing, of course, was following orders from Beijing to allow the Americans to do what Zhou Enlai hoped they would do and end the conflict. There were in fact two views in Beijing: one the moderate view of Zhou, and the other the view of Mao, shared by Marshal Peng, that the Americans should be driven out of Asia. This week and the next would be Zhou's last chance to achieve settlement without war. But the Americans had so effectively expunged all they ever knew about Red China from their minds that they did not understand what was happening in Beijing. . . .

As Marshal Peng waited in his mountain shack for the full moon, a young staff officer came up from the valley to bring some papers. Peng recognized the young man as Mao Anyang, the eldest son of Mao Zedong. Anyang had worked his way up through the ranks, having spent the years after 1941 in the Soviet Union as a lieutenant in the Soviet Red Army tank corps. He had fought valiantly against the Germans, and had won medals and been presented with a pistol by Stalin.

Young Mao had the temerity to ask the marshal what they were waiting for. First he looked at the map and the little blue pennants inserted north of the Chongchon River on the west. Then he spoke.

"Uncle Peng, why do we still want to withdraw?"

The chief of staff was aghast, but Marshal Peng was amused. He seemed to relish the chance to expound his views, knowing Mao would repeat them through the staff.

He probed a little. "Do you think withdrawing is bad?"

"It's bad," said Mao Anyang. "I felt when we left China that I wasn't prepared for what was coming and that caution was correct. . . . However, we won the First Campaign, and the enemy is in a panic. Why are we withdrawing instead?"

"Well, what is your view?" Peng asked young Mao.

"My opinion is that we should take advantage of the victory to attack, to fight across the Chongchon River."

Marshal Peng referred to the war against the Germans. "Do you feel that that war and this one are alike?"

Mao Anyang thought for a moment. "They're different. Then it was aircraft against aircraft, artillery against artillery, and tank against tank. There is presently a great disparity between our equipment and the enemy's."

"That's right," said Marshal Peng. "Conditions aren't the same, and the tactics aren't the same either. At the present time the enemy is highly mechanized. Our weapons are not uniform— Japanese, German, Russian, American, and even some from the Warlord Era. If we were to take this kind of equipment and try to carry out positional warfare, we would be playing into the hands of the enemy. Do you think we could win?"

Youg Mao was silent.

Chief of Staff Xie Fang took pity on him. Xie Fang knew precisely what Marshal Peng was doing and why. Xie had served as chief of staff at every level of the army, from regiment to army group. Now he spoke up:

"This withdrawal has a profound meaning. Marshal Peng is using the enemy's impatience, deliberately giving the impression of weakness to get him to extend himself. It is a brilliant move!"

Marshal Peng snorted, "What brilliance? This is all from the tactics we created during the revolutionary war and the war against Japan. You might say these are China's tactics. Now we are going to use them to make the Americans suffer a little."

He looked at Mao Anyang. "Did you read your father's 'Problems of Strategy in China's Revolutionary War'?"

Mao Anyang nodded.

"We still have to have a profound grasp of it now. Our problems are the same," said Marshal Peng.

Mao Anyang left the old shack then, and Chief of Staff Xie looked through the papers he had brought. Among them was a radio intercept of a report by a spokesman at General MacArthur's headquarters. Again it was a news dispatch:

"General MacArthur's headquarters still doesn't know from the positions on the routes to the Yalu River whether the enemy is actually going to move into defensive operations (with a sanitary zone below the Yalu) or whether they are preparing for a new attack.

"The spokesman said that he just could not answer that question or questions on the actual strength of the Chinese army forces.

"The spokesman also pointed out that the Chinese in the past had withdrawn before launching a new attack. This sort of withdrawal seems to be like that of the Chinese on the western front for the past ten days. The problem is that we are not able to conclude whether the enemy is withdrawing to previously selected positions, or is setting a trap. This statement partially explains the reason for the United Nations forces having a cautious attitude on the northwestern front."

Marshal Peng listened to the report. Then he picked it up himself and read it over and over. He lit a cigarette and began pacing.

"Perhaps the enemy suspects our intentions," said the chief of staff. "Perhaps we won't be able to hook this fish."

"I don't believe that," said Marshal Peng. "The enemy is puzzled by a mystery. Even if they were to guess our intent, a few basic aspects are unchanged. First, since the First Campaign did not really hurt them, the enemy still estimates that our strength is about 60,000 men. A few days ago we read the report that one American general said nothing can stop them. If the Chinese Communists

want a fifteen-mile buffer zone, he said, then let them build it on
their side of the Yalu River.

"As for Commander-in-Chief MacArthur, he's been very cocky
since the Inchon landings. He basically disregards the Chinese.
The wild arrogance has not changed.

"And another matter: Their strategic plan calls for a war of
quick decision. With a severe winter coming, their desire for a
showdown will become more and more pressing. They are presently very cautious, but this is only a temporary phenomenon, one
that can change very rapidly.

"Their minds are made up and won't be easy to change. You
just have to be patient to catch a fish."

So saying, Marshal Peng indicated the interview was over, and
escorted the chief of staff to the door of the shack. As they stepped
outside, they looked at the moon. It was nearly full.

"Just a few more days," said Marshal Peng. "Just a few more
days." And he turned back to his cot inside the shack. The chief
of staff wrapped his overcoat around him tightly, shivering in the
growing cold, and headed down the mountain to his bed.

By the second week of November 1950, the UN high command
was thoroughly confused. On November 6, a powerful force of
Chinese Communists had been attacking the Australian soldiers
at the end of the UN line on the bank of the Chongchon River.
Suddenly all the Chinese were gone! There seemed to be no reason
for it; they had not suffered undue casualties, there were no
wounded or dead to count, but that was the Chinese way, as the
UN troops had already learned.

On the west was General Walker's Eighth Army, chastened and
cautious under a commander who believed there were plenty of
Chinese around, even if his supreme commander did not. On the
east was General Almond's X Corps, the First Marine Division, the
Seventh Infantry Division, and the Third Infantry Division. Unlike
the marines, the two army divisions were only partly American.
Some of the troops were Korean, brought in under a system de-
vised by MacArthur to hasten the South Korea training program
and fill up holes in the American divisions.

A lugubrious meeting held in Chungking in 1945. *From left:* General Chu Shih Ming of the Chinese Nationalist general staff; Generalissimo Chiang Kaishek; British Lieutenant General Carton D. W. Wiart; Major General Albert C. Wedemeyer, chief of American forces in China; and Brigadier General Benjamin D. Ferris, deputy chief of staff of U.S. forces in China-Burma-India. (*National Archives*)

Zhou Enlai, Mao Zedong, and U.S. Ambassador Patrick J. Hurley with an unidentified Nationalist Army officer on the airfield at Yenan during Hurley's visit to the Communist stronghold in 1945. (*National Archives*)

Colonel David D. Barrett, chief of
the American advisor group at
executive headquarters, with
Mao Zedong in Yenan in 1945.
(*National Archives*)

Zhou Enlai and members of his staff
meet with the Americans of the executive
headquarters in Beijing in the summer
of 1946. (*National Archives*)

John S. Service, one of the ablest of
the State Department experts on
China, in 1950. Along with most
of the other Americans who really
understood what was happening in
China in the 1940s, he was driven
from office by the China Lobby.
Service was in Yokohama, on his way
to India to serve as American consul
in Calcutta, when he was ordered
back to Washington to face charges
by the late Senator Joseph McCarthy
that Service was pro-Communist. It
was the beginning of the end of his
career. (*National Archives*)

John Davies, one of the most knowledgable American diplomats about things Chinese. He was pushed into early retirement from foreign affairs by McCarthyism and the kind of false charges made against many State Department officials in the late 1940s. His crime: knowledge that the Chinese Nationalists had lost the support of the Chinese people and would lose the revolution to the Communists. (*National Archives*)

October 1950. After the first Chinese attack, elements of the First Cavalry Division pause for a brief rest during their withdrawal—a withdrawal that became a virtual rout. Here they are atop a hill five miles north of Pyongyang. (*National Archives*)

General J. Lawton Collins, U.S. Army chief of staff, being greeted by Major General Edward M. Almond, commander of X Corps, on Collins's arrival to inspect forces in North Korea. He had just landed at Yonpo air base on December 5, 1950, as the Chinese were pressing the UN forces south. (*National Archives*)

Men of the Ninth U.S. Infantry of the Second Infantry Division slacken their pace as they march south on the road to Seoul. This regiment suffered very heavy losses during the rush of the Chinese attack in December 1950. (*National Archives*)

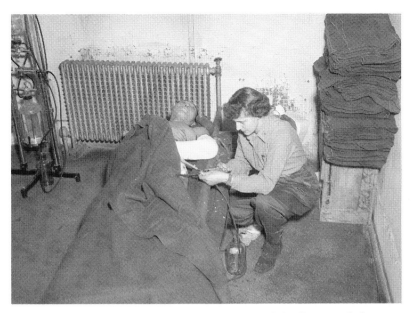

Army nurse Lieutenant Mary C. Jones cares for a badly wounded Chinese POW at a mobile hospital in Korea on the day after Christmas, 1950. (*National Archives*)

There was no time to do it right. This 155mm ammunition was stacked in a temporary dump on the beach during the evacuation of UN forces at Hungnam during the critical period of retreat from the Chinese second offensive. (*National Archives*)

MacArthur visits the front. *From left:* Lieutenant General Walton Walker, commander of the U.S. Eighth Army; General Douglas MacArthur, commander of the UN Forces; and Major General Frank W. Milburn, commander of I Corps. They are just leaving IX Corps headquarters after discussing plans for the "jump-off" to MacArthur's celebrated but disastrous "End-the-War Offensive." (*National Archives*)

Peng Dehuai was closely associated with Mao Zedong from the days before the Long March of the 1930s. By the fall of 1950 he was the army's most highly respected field commander, a member of the Communist Party's Central Committee, and the prime candidate to undertake the defeat of the Americans in Korea. (*Eastfoto*)

General Matthew Ridgway in Korea with a British staff officer. (*National Archives*)

Chinese prisoners of war captured in Korea. Ultimately, the POW problem became acute, because some Chinese, encouraged by the Americans and the South Koreans, did not want to return to Mainland China. This fed Chinese paranoia about America and its supposed aim of destroying the Beijing government. (*National Archives*)

Allied and Chinese POWS became pawns in the peace negotiations at Panmunjom. Here, Corporal E. Dickenson, an American prisoner, is being released to U.S. Army custody. He waves to newsmen at the POW exchange point, while Indian Lieutenant Colonel Uttal Singh looks on. (*National Archives*)

Hill 355, one of the battle sites during the static war that developed at Panmunjom. Here, under fire from the occupying Chinese forces, an M-46 tank of the Heavy Tank Company of the Seventh Infantry Regiment of the Third U.S. Infantry Division takes the hill. (*National Archives*)

Colonel Pu Shan of the Chinese People's Volunteer Army in Korea hurries to a meeting with his UN counterparts at Panmunjom during the peace negotiations. Colonel Pu was once a student at Harvard University. (*National Archives*)

At Panmunjom on October 22, 1951, Chinese representatives (in uniforms without shoulder boards) and representatives from North Korea sign an agreement establishing a neutral zone in Korea. But it would be many weary months before peace really came. (*National Archives*)

Allies at the Korean conference table sign the neutral zone agreement. *From left:* Horace G. Underwood, South Korean Lieutenant Colonel Lee Soo Young, U.S. Army Colonel Andrew J. Kinney, and U.S. Marine Corps Colonel James C. Murray. (*National Archives*)

General Dwight D. Eisenhower, U.S. President-Elect, and General Reuben Jenkins in Korea in the fall of 1952. It was one of Eisenhower's 1952 campaign promises that he would go to Korea, and he did, but what effect that had on the Korean war is debatable. (*National Archives*)

A high-level meeting at a forward airstrip in Korea. *From left:* General J. Lawton Collins of the U.S. Joint Chiefs of Staff; General James A. Van Fleet, commander of the U.S. Eighth Army; Lieutenant General Paul W. Kendall, commander of the U.S. I Corps, and General Mark W. Clark, commander of UN Forces in Korea. The day is January 28, 1953. (*National Archives*)

CHINA IN 1930

(From China in Disintegration by James E. Sheridan. Courtesy of The Free Press)

THE JAPANESE INVASION OF CHINA

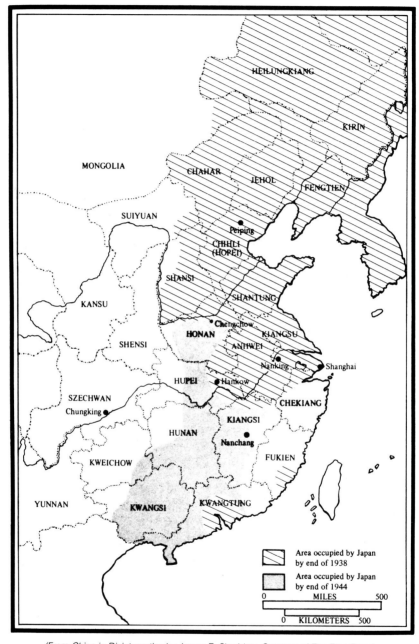

Area occupied by Japan
by end of 1938

Area occupied by Japan
by end of 1944

0 MILES 500

0 KILOMETERS 500

(From *China in Disintegration* by James E. Sheridan. *Courtesy of The Free Press*)

GENERAL MACARTHUR'S PLANS FOR THE INVASION
OF NORTH KOREA

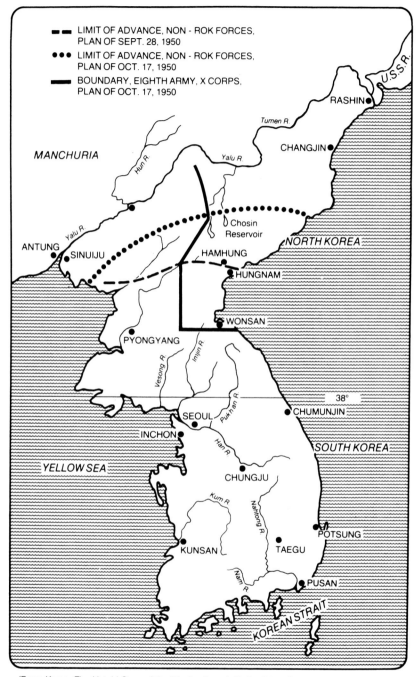

(From *Korea: The Untold Story of the War* by Joseph C. Goulden. *Courtesy of Times Books*)

THE BATTLE OF UNSAN (Night of November 1–2, 1950)

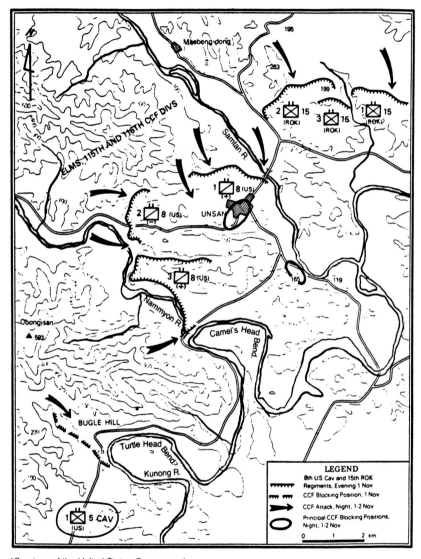

(Courtesy of the United States Government)

THE IRON TRIANGLE AREA

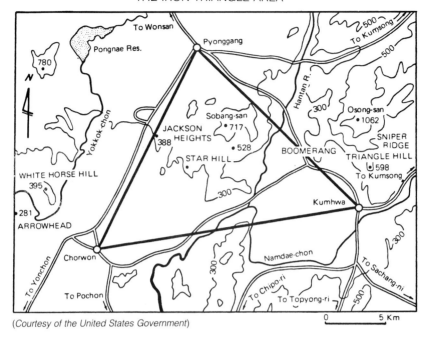

(Courtesy of the United States Government)

ATTACK ON SOBANG-SAN AND PYONGGANG (July 1–4, 1951)

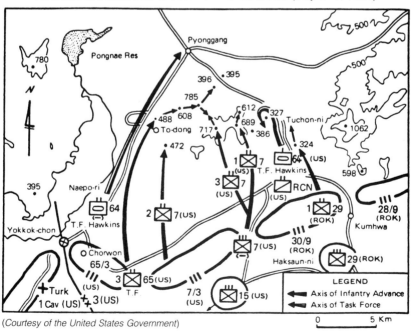

(Courtesy of the United States Government)

THE ARMISTICE LINE (July 27, 1953)

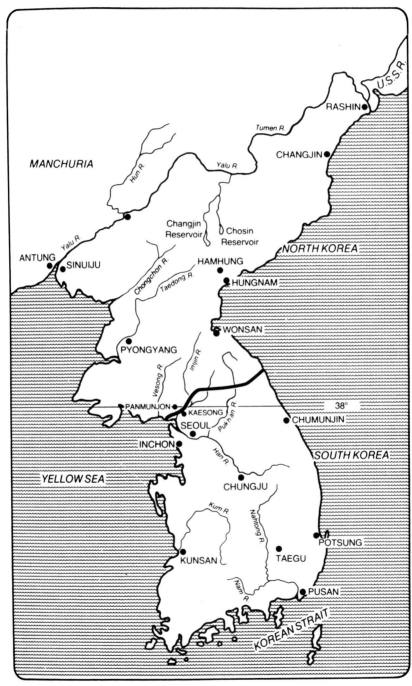

(From *Korea: The Untold Story of the War* by Joseph C. Goulden. *Courtesy of Times Books*)

The marines were sent up a narrow one-lane road to the Chongjin reservoir, high on a windswept plain halfway to the Yalu River. This reservoir provided an enormous amount of hydro-electric power to North Korea and Manchuria. Farther to the east were the army divisions. The army moved up to the Yalu River, and the 17th Infantry Regiment was positioned on the bank. General MacArthur brought a covy of lesser generals up to have their pictures taken, thus illustrating that he had done his job and marched to the Yalu. He congratulated General Almond.

Why, MacArthur wanted to know, wasn't everybody lined up on the banks of the Yalu? The answer was that some of the others were smelling a large rat. General Walker knew there were Chinese all around him. MacArthur ordered the general advance, but General Walker found cause for delay. The marines sensed the presence of the enemy too, and they refused to be pushed. General Smith of the First Marine Division insisted on guarding his main line of retreat, that narrow little road through the gorges, all along the way.

The date for the resumed offensive, to drive to the Yalu and link up forces, driving the North Koreans and Chinese out of Korea, was set by the MacArthur command for November 24, the day after Thanksgiving. Thanksgiving was celebrated in style in most places; even on the line the men had their "turkey and trimmings."

The concern of General Walker and the marines was certainly more than justified. Up in the northwestern corner of Korea the new Chinese Ninth Army Group was assembling to attack the single marine division strung out along its narrow highway.

The 13th Army Group, north of the Chongchon River, had been reinforced and was now 185,000 men.

At the beginning of the third week of November Marshal Peng flew down to Shenyang to meet his generals and put the final touches on the plan. General Song Ohilun's Ninth Army Group would move swiftly east and surprise and overwhelm the marines in the northeast. General Li Tianyu would smash the Eighth Army on the west.

Field Marshal Peng had a bad cold, and his voice was inclined to break as he briefed his generals. But they got the message. It was nearly time. The moon was nearly full. Marshal Peng was very nervous, and so were the generals. Taking on the powerful American war machine was not an easy assignment. Since the October battle the propaganda department had been trying to help out, pointing to the weaknesses of the Americans—they relied heavily on motorized transport and were not toughened to the march the way the Chinese were. The American morale was not very high; most of the troops did not know what they were fighting for. The Communists put great store in the fact that every private had some idea of what was happening on the broad front.

Peng's briefing was part of the Communist method of managing an army, to at least let the troops think they were having a part in the decision-making process, although that was not always true, particularly these days of 1950, with Mao taking ever more power in Beijing.

Indeed, the talk of the military men in Korea was quite different from that of the politicians in Beijing. Zhou Enlai in particular had stressed the possibility of a political solution if the foreigners would respect the territorial integrity of North Korea and the 38th parallel division. This point, however, had been all but forgotten in the past two weeks, and MacArthur did not even listen. So Peng's emphasis now was on "teaching the Americans a lesson." No longer was displayed that great apparent good will that Zhou had exhibited in asking that the foreigners not cross the 38th parallel. The foreigners were to the Yalu now, all the warnings had been unheeded, and it was time to act. Peng issued orders.

Meanwhile in New York and Washington, some awarenesses were making the possibility of political solution seem real. First, official Washington was showing a new appreciation of the problems in Korea. Second, America had always found it hard to see itself as others saw it, but it was beginning to learn, it seemed. Finally, official Washington was waking up to the fact that the Chinese feared the United States, and that that was the reason for their actions. President Truman, who did not want an attenuated war in Asia and already had misgivings about MacArthur's behavior, was inclined to seek a political settlement.

That week the Americans at the United Nations accepted a French resolution that called on the Americans to stop the advance northward fifty miles south of the Yalu River. And then came the major political failure of the war as far as the Americans were concerned. Before, one could say that the politicians were numb to the thought of responsibility. But in accepting the French resolution they showed that they now knew what the problem was. And yet the American politicians allowed the military to bulldoze them into thoughts of "victory." Oddly enough, it was a military man, General Omar Bradley, who suddenly realized—although too late to stop it—what the United States was doing: engaging in the "wrong war with the wrong enemy at the wrong place at the wrong time."

The hysteria of the military was such that several proposals were made for the use of the atomic bomb in Korea, and they were taken seriously in high places. MacArthur, now driven to recklessness, would have welcomed the use of the bomb. He took the Chinese intervention very personally, and accused them, in his own words, of ruining his victory just when he had about sewed it up. This showed his complete disregard for the fundamental international political consideration involved: The Chinese insisted on securing their own borders, which precluded the existence there of forces that had shown themselves to be inimical to Red China —those of the United States.

President Truman, forgetting Abraham Lincoln's adage that war was too important a matter to be left to the generals, allowed himself to be persuaded that MacArthur must be allowed to have his own way. And thus Marshal Peng also got his own way: The Americans prepared to walk into the Chinese trap.

In the third week of November, MacArthur's staff prepared to move. He was ready for anything, including war with the Soviet Union, and he so told one of his staff members. He did not really expect war with Russia, nor did he really expect the Chinese to respond with a major attack. Now that it was very late, he recognized the danger of the split up the middle of the UN line, with east side separate from west, and he proposed that the X Corps on the east launch an attack westward from the Chongjin reservoir to link up with the Eighth Army on the Yalu River.

MacArthur was still confident that a lightning thrust would finish the war and bring his boys at least back to Tokyo by Christmas.

But on November 15, when the Seventh Marine Regiment occupied the village of Hagaru, General Smith of the First Marine Division wrote to his superiors in Washington that he was fearful of facing a tough winter campaign in Korea. The temperature that day had already dropped to four degrees below zero, Fahrenheit.

On the western side of Korea, General Walker's intelligence was improving. He reported on a massive buildup of Chinese all along the frontier of North Korea and Manchuria, on both sides of the line. All this information was sent to MacArthur, who ignored it. The main reason for this attitude was MacArthur's personal dislike of General Walker, because he was not one of MacArthur's "boys."

After November 15, the talk in Tokyo was all about the "End-the-War Offensive," which was just about to begin. On Thanksgiving Day, the U.S. Army Seventh Division troops reached Hye-sanjin on the Yalu River, thus establishing the eastern prong for MacArthur's east-west pincers movement, which was to contract from one side of Korea to the other. At the same time, in position behind and around all the South Korean and Western troops were three times as many Chinese, ready with their own north-south pincers movement, which was designed to envelop and seal off the United Nations forces.

How clear it was—MacArthur's insistence that the UN drive to total victory no matter the cost—or, let us say, how clear it is now. For in those days, MacArthur's position in the American political and military hierarchy was such that almost no one was willing to stand up to him.

"He always considered us a bunch of kids," said General Omar Bradley, then chairman of the Joint Chiefs of Staff, and theoretically outranking MacArthur. Others tried to hold MacArthur back. The British suggested establishment of a buffer zone along the Yalu.

"Just like the British appeasing Hitler at Munich," said MacArthur. "The British have already appeased the Communists by recognizing their government."

The records of the meetings of the Joint Chiefs of Staff and the other Presidential advisory groups between November 9 and November 25 indicate a complete lack of foresight on the part of these advisors. They could see plenty of trees, but not the forest.

They misread the Chinese warnings; furthermore, they ignored them and the reasoning behind them. In the narrow view they adopted, they gave three possible reasons for Chinese intervention:

1. To protect the hydroelectric system shared by North Korea and China.
2. To tie U.S. forces down in Korea.
3. To drive the UN out of Korea on behalf of the USSR.

But as of the eve of the decision about movement forward or backward, the Joint Chiefs did not see that the Chinese were bound to protect the integrity of the North Korean government. It was as simple as that. Because of that American blindness, there was no hope of averting the disaster.

15

The American Attack

In telling the following anecdote about the beginning moves of the real war in Korea between the Chinese and the Americans, which began on November 25, 1950, I may be accused of sentimentalism. But there is reason for my telling this tale, which first appeared in Chinese, in a Chinese military magazine. It, like the story of Mao Anyang's call on Marshal Peng described in the preceding chapter, indicates the closeness of the relationships within the high command of Red China. Mao and Peng were old comrades of the Long March and before who had fought shoulder to shoulder in the revolution. Moreover, they were very human, not the stick figures Western accounts of the Korean war have generally painted the Chinese to be. The image of the horde of men in padded uniforms, wearing tennis shoes, blowing off-key bugles and tooting whistles as they plunged into the automatic fire, to be shot down and stacked up like cordwood, is not entirely inaccurate, but it does not tell the whole story. The Chinese soldier was every bit as human as the American or the South Korean, and often showed more compassion than the soldiers of the West. Again it was a question of "Know your enemy, his hopes and his motivations," and this is something the American leadership in Korea failed to do. . . .

By November 24, all the advice had been considered by General MacArthur, who had been permitted to understand that he was to make the decision about the future of the United Nations in

Korea (although this was not strictly true). All the intelligence had been collected and sifted. For example, General Willoughby, MacArthur's intelligence officer, estimated there were 70,000 Chinese troops inside Korea and that many of these had come to Korea with only three days' rations.

Did Willoughby know that three days' rations was normal for a Chinese soldier? Or that General David Barr, commander of the U.S. Seventh Division, was worried because his men up front on the Yalu had only one day's rations?

MacArthur's confidence was so great and the security so lax that the newspapermen—and the Chinese Communists, the most devoted students of the U.S. news dispatches—knew almost exactly what was coming.

On this day, General MacArthur issued a stirring communiqué of the sort made famous by generals and admirals of the Napoleonic wars:

> The United Nations massive compression envelopment in North Korea against the new Red armies operating there is now approaching its decisive effort. The isolating component of the pincer, our air forces of all types, have for the past three weeks in a sustained attack of model coordination and effectiveness successfully interdicted enemy lines of support from the north so that further reinforcement from there has been sharply curtailed and essential supplies markedly limited. The eastern sector of the pincer, with noteworthy and effective naval support, has now reached commanding enveloping position, cutting in two the northern reaches of the enemy's geographical potential. This morning the western sector of the pincer moves forward in general assault in an effort to complete the compression and close the vise. If successful this should for all practical purposes end the war, restore peace and unity to Korea, enable the prompt withdrawal of the United Nations forces, and permit the complete assumption by the Korean people and nation of full sovereignty and international equality. . . .

On that morning of November 24, to show his confidence and to reinforce it too, General MacArthur boarded his command plane and flew to General Walker's headquarters on the Chongchon River for an appearance and a tour of the front. After a five-hour motor tour he boarded the plane again. This time he ordered the pilot to fly up the east coast of Korea to the Yalu River, so the general could see what was going on. They flew at 5000 feet, over the bridges that cross into Manchuria. Below they looked out on mountains, mountains, mountains, thickly forested, thickly blanketed in heavy snow. There was no sign of recent passage of vehicles. The general's confidence that the Chinese had not gotten through into Korea was fully confirmed.

That morning the Eighth Army attacked on a three-corps front: The I Corps on the left, the ROK II Corps on the right, and the IX Corps in the center. It might be wondered why General Walker chose his weakest link for his most dangerous and unknown position, that of the right flank, which butted up against the gap in the UN line that ran straight up the center of Korea and then to the Yellow Sea.

Marshal Peng had told his generals to let the Eighth Army come north to a point about a day's march from the Chongchon River, so up the UN troops came, starting at 10 A.M. and meeting almost no opposition. General Walker did not much like this lack of opposition, for he knew that there were thousands of Chinese out there. By the end of that first day, moving steadily but cautiously, the Eighth Army had ranged forward from six to ten miles across that broad front. That night, the Chinese launched some probes and discovered they faced Koreans on the east flank and the west flank, and that the east flank, the area of ROK II Corps, butted up against nothing at all. It was an ideal situation for an envelopment. The gap between the right side of the Eighth Army and the left side of the X Corps to the east was twenty-five miles wide.

On the second day, November 25, the ROK II Corps moved out from Tokchon, but soon began to encounter heavy resistance from the Chinese. As they had done before, the South Koreans bunched up behind the U.S. troops next to them, for protection. This left the U.S. troops, the Second Division, very vulnerable to attack.

The Second Division also reached its objective, Kujang-dong, on that first day, and set up its artillery there for the next morning's opening firing. Then it was expected that the artillery would move forward rapidly. But there Major General Laurence Keiser, commander of the Second Division, learned from a liaison plane pilot that the Chinese were widening the road that led off their right flank, back to Tokchon, where the ROK II Corps was stalled. And Keiser knew he was in for trouble.

While the Eighth Army was moving north toward the Yalu River, over on the eastern side of Korea the marines were supposed to cut across and link up with the Eighth Army. All the movement would be through the Yudam area five miles west of the middle part of the Chosin reservoir. And on that first day, the marines learned from prisoners that the Chinese had more than three divisions in the Yudam area, against the two marine regiments committed. The prisoners said the Chinese plan called for the army to wait until the marines had passed into the Yudam area, and then cut the main supply route south of them. The trap would be sprung. The question was, when?

Communications was one of the great differences between the American-led United Nations forces and the Chinese. With the Americans everything worked like clockwork. If the attack was to begin at 10 A.M., it was all set up in advance through messages. But Chinese communications were, by Western standards, primitive beyond consideration. Marshal Peng's radio, a single communications truck, was scarcely better than a battalion communications center. Yet with this equipment, and hundreds of thousands of men, and officers who knew what their initiatives must be, the marshal had an army of formidable dimensions.

Thus the Chinese were ready for the American offensive when it began. But one could never get ready for one aspect of the American military machine, air power, and it was air power that caused the Chinese the most trouble in these opening hours of the new war.

On the morning of November 24 the UN airmen began plastering anything in the north country that looked even remotely like a military installation.

That morning Marshal Peng and his staff were up early, planning the counteroffensive that would be triggered by the American advance, and waiting for a message from Mao Zedong. This, Peng knew, would also contain some new military order, since that was Mao's way of exerting his authority.

The senior Chinese staff all ate together, a simple breakfast of rice gruel. Marshal Peng was deep in thought and said virtually nothing. After eating two bowls of gruel he left for the situation room. The others stayed long at the table, joked for a while, and then drifted off to their duties.

Then the air raid began. Chief of Staff Xia Wen, standing on the mountainside under shelter of the forest, said he had never before seen so many aircraft massed in one place. (Of course, aircraft had not played a major role in the Chinese civil war, which was the Communist yardstick of comparison.) Down below, in the village that housed all army headquarters except for Marshal Peng's situation room in the old shack on the mountain, the staff came out to watch the air show.

Xia Wen came down and stood under a big walnut tree with the others. They saw a squadron of American Shooting Star jets in formation heading north. Then came more planes, more and more.

"The enemy offensive is starting," said Deputy Commander Qin Peng.

"I'm afraid it has already started," said Teng Yunhan, the second deputy commander.

As he was talking, a large aircraft came flying up from the south. It came slowly, leisurely, calm and unhurried. Fighters escorted the plane on all sides. Everyone gazed at this large aircraft in amazement. It flew north and shortly after circled and began to broadcast. Xia Wen, who understood English, listened carefully. It was a broadcast from General MacArthur, to the American troops below. Someone in the crowd said it was *by* MacArthur!

Xia Wen then interpreted for the others:

"MacArthur said this war originally could have ended by Thanksgiving. The situation became complicated later on because of the appearance of unidentified foreign forces. He believes, however, that there are no obstacles in front of the United Nations forces that can't be overcome. The offensive was launched today, a general offensive to end the Korean war by Christmas. If the war ends by Christmas the enlisted men can return home and spend Christmas with their families."

Qin Peng laughed. "Well, we'll invite them to spend Christmas in heaven."

While the members of the staff were talking and watching the planes, they heard explosions on a distant mountain. Then they saw four enemy aircraft, in line, flying very low along the ridge line.

"I'm afraid they've got plans for us," said Qin Peng. He turned to Feng Hui, a staff officer who was a favorite chess companion of Marshal Peng's. He knew that the sometimes recalcitrant marshal would listen to Feng.

"Go ask Chief Peng to come out. . . ."

Feng went up the mountain to the old shack. There Peng was standing silently before the big situation map, an ivory-handled magnifying glass in hand. Telegraph forms were spread out on the table, the ink box was open, and the still-wet brush, cap off, lay on the edge of the table. Two staff men were standing in the doorway, silent. Feng spoke up. "Chief Peng, the enemy offensive has started. There are many, many aircraft today. Do you know that?"

"I know it. At last they are coming as we expected they would."

Peng did not move. Feng saw him staring at the situation map. What could he do to get the commander out of there? He gave the two young staff men a worried look and pretended to criticize them.

"The aircraft will be dropping bombs soon. You aren't worried? You are so irresponsible about the safety of a senior officer? Hurry! Help the marshal to the cave."

The acid of his words was wiped out by the big wink he gave the two young men. Hesitantly, because Marshal Peng was a fearsome character of uncertain temper, they approached the writing desk. Peng had already sat down there and was picking up the writing brush.

"Go! Go!" he said. "You go along to the shelter. I want to write this message first."

Feng Hui listened to the sound of bombing reverberating through the mountains. There was no time to be lost. He stepped forward and, smiling, grabbed the ink box and writing brush and handed them to one of the young men.

"Commander, you must go to the cave to write this message." The marshal glared.

"Pockmark Feng, what are you doing?" he demanded.

The use of Feng's nickname softened the harsh words.

"I'm coordinating your air defense," said Feng. "Come on!"

"You are too frivolous," Marshal Peng grumbled.

"Right, right! I'm too frivolous."

"You are afraid to die?"

"Right. I'm not only afraid of dying. Also afraid you will die."

Without another word, Feng pulled the hefty frame of the field marshal from his chair. The two young staff officers then each took an arm and hustled him out of the situation room.

As Marshal Peng and the others emerged from the wooden shack, they saw an American airplane diving on it. And as they reached the pine trees a little bit up the side of the mountain, another plane joined in the attack. Feng quickly pushed the marshal down to the ground, and held him down. Bombs began dropping, too close for comfort. And then came a burst of shells from automatic cannon on one of the planes, and tree limbs began dropping around them.

"Run for it!" shouted Feng, helping the marshal to his feet and holding his arm as they ran for the cave.

The others came in, all excited, but soon began to calm down. The marshal's runner, Young Zhang, came in with telegraph forms, the copper ink box, and a thermos jug of hot water for tea. His face was ashen. Peng looked at him and laughed.

"Little devil," he said, "How did you get so scared?"

"Just after you left the building your cot got four big holes in it from an automatic cannon. I looked at those holes and the more I looked at them the more scared I got. It was not long before my legs were like jelly. If it continues to be like this I want to transfer to another post. . . ."

Now Feng laughed.

"You see," he said to the marshal, "even your bodyguard objects. You say I'm afraid to die. If I hadn't taken decisive action I'm afraid we would have played our last game of chess already."

The marshal patted his chest and smiled.

"Thanks for the spirit of Marx in heaven." [For a time the Chinese tried to adopt Marxism-Leninism in all its ways, but it didn't really work.]

Peng and Feng were just considering a game of chess to while away the air raid, when a staff officer came up, white-faced.

"Commander Peng, the chief of staff asked me to report to you. Staff officer Mao Anyang and Staff Officer Gao did not escape from the situation room."

"Why not? Where are they?"

"They were on duty in the war room and said they would not leave."

Peng was silent. He knew his men and he knew what the staff officer was saying.

"Go and rescue them," he said.

"Someone has already gone," said the staff officer, and all the room could tell from his expression that there was more to be said, but he was reluctant to speak.

Qing Lin squeezed in between the others and the marshal. "I'll go right now and take a look," he said.

The marshal waved his gratitude. "Good. Hurry."

Qing went to the edge of the cave and waited. An enemy airplane flashed past the mouth of the cave. Qing rushed out of the cave, and looked down to the center of the village. Enemy aircraft were blanketing the area, bombing and strafing. One dived and made a drop, but there was no explosion. Rather, a sheet of flame shot up, followed immediately by billowing smoke.

"Napalm!" somebody screamed, "They're dropping napalm!"

More enemy aircraft came over the village; they had obviously seen soldiers scurrying about to escape burning buildings. They dropped more silent bombs, and more gouts of flame and billows of greasy smoke filled the air above the village.

Young Zhang went partway down and then came back to the cave. The whole area was enveloped in smoke and flame, and the smell of petroleum had already permeated the cave.

Marshal Peng came to the entrance of the cave and looked out.

He began to cough. Young Zhang urged him back inside, but the marshal stood staring down at the village, watching the smoke and flames blankly. He would not move.

He stood there thus for half an hour, not smoking, not moving. Then Qing Lin came struggling up from the village, his body covered with dirt and his face black. He stopped at the mouth of the cave, panting, and stood there for a moment, looking at the marshal.

"Well?"

"They're both done for."

The marshal made a tortured sound in his chest.

"Were there bodies?"

"Don't ask. They were both burned beyond recognition."

Qing Lin pulled a wristwatch out of his pocket and gave it to Peng with trembling hand. "This is Mao Anyang's. I picked it up from the ground."

With a heavy hand, Marshal Peng took the watch. Roma brand. And very worn. The son of the chairman of the party, and he did not even own a decent watch.

Marshal Peng's thoughts went back. He had known Mao's son since his babyhood, long before the Long March. He had seen him grow, and then lost track of young Mao after his mother was killed by the Kuomintang and the children had dispersed.

Young Mao had spent the anti-Japanese years in the USSR and served with distinction in Stalin's army. He was by far the most international of the group around them—only Li Li San would surpass him in that. But whether or not this internationalism would last would now never be known.

Peng remembered the cold night in Beijing when young Mao had come privately to him after the Central Committee meeting, to ask if he could serve with Peng in Korea.

And he had not even known then, although he had since learned, that when young Mao came and asked so movingly to be allowed to come, the boy had been married for only a few weeks.

Peng suddenly felt very close to the young man and his memory. He recalled how, just a few days before, young Mao had asked an impertinent question, but so movingly that Peng had not cared.

Imagine it! The real offensive had not yet started, and already the son of Chairman Mao was a victim of the imperialists. Peng hardly dared give a thought to what this would mean in the greater consequences of the war. Certainly any indication of compromise would now face hard going in the mind of the chairman.

Chief Peng looked as though he might break into tears. He stepped out of the cave into the darkness and stood there for a while, out of sight of the others.

And then he turned to Qing Lin.

"Give this watch to his wife when we return to China," he said.

The American strike ended with that suddenness that always marked the end of an air raid; one moment the planes were surging everywhere, and the next moment you could hear a tree branch break a mile away in the forest. Marshal Peng and his staff emerged from the cave and walked slowly down the hill into the center of the ruined village. Not much was left, but the staff was already improvising a new camp for the headquarters. That afternoon, on a hillside nearby, the staff held a funeral service for the two dead staff officers. They buried them in a clearing on this quiet hill, so their souls could look down on what had been, and once again would be, a peaceful village.

Marshal Peng took off his cap and stood, listening to the simple service. They all stood silent for a long time. Then they put on their caps and walked back down the hillside. The atmosphere changed swiftly. It was now time to go back to the matter of the war and the destruction of the enemy. Chief of Staff Xia Wen spoke up:

"Do you want to report this to Chairman Mao?"

Marshal Peng muttered and did not answer. It was just the question he had been asking himself all afternoon.

One by one the deputies and other senior staff members offered their opinions to the marshal, as they knew he wanted them to do.

Should they bother the chairman?

Mao Zedong's responsibility was enormous just now, with the war, and the problems of the new government scarcely dealt with. Was it fair to thrust this tragedy upon him at this time?

Everyone knew that the problems of the war rested heavily on Mao's shoulders, and that he was sleeping very badly. Someone said he had grown thin. Marshal Peng did not believe that, but he did believe that the chairman had grown worried, for when he had last seen him, he had appeared pale and nervous. Did Marshal Peng have the right just now to inflict on him a personal tragedy of this nature?

But on the other hand, did they have the right to withhold from a father the word that his son had been killed? And did they have the right to withhold from the chairman the news that the war was going to be even more desperate than anyone might have expected? Already the signs were showing.

By midafternoon everyone had had his say, and everyone was waiting for Marshal Peng to make his decision.

"No," he said, "we'll tell Chairman Mao. He is a great politician and he can take it. He sent his child here, and naturally he had to be mentally prepared."

"Do you want to notify Staff Officer Gao's family?"

The marshal thought that over.

"Don't say anything about it right now. His wife is going to have a baby in three months. If they heard this news, the young lady might not be able to take it."

Everyone nodded, glad to be able to show some compassion in the midst of this dreadful war.

"Listen," said Marshal Peng. "Whoever returns to China soon can buy some children's clothing and take them to her. . . ."

────16────

Chinese Counterattack

A month after the Chinese had first entered the Korean war, they began their first serious counterstrike. To be sure, the battle that began on October 25 was called by Marshal Peng the "First Campaign," but its objectives were limited and were really political in nature. When it failed and General MacArthur showed he had learned nothing from it, but rather stubbornly pressed for "real victory" in Korea, then the war became serious, and from the Chinese point of view, it became a determined drive to throw the Americans off the Asian mainland. Zhou Enlai's temporization had not worked, so now the extremists were to have their innings. . . .

Until November 25, there was always a chance that some miracle might occur, opening the eyes of the Americans to the realities of Chinese thinking. The Chinese, to this point, were conducting the war on two levels. Inside Korea, Marshal Peng's troops were committed to victory as far as they knew; no one told them of another possibility. But in Beijing, until November 25, Zhou Enlai's peace feelers remained out; the Americans had responded to them at the United Nations level, and there was talk going on. In the end, however, President Truman gave MacArthur his way, and it all came to a head on November 25, the day that Mao Anyang was killed.

Now it was a new kind of war, with the Chinese determined to teach the arrogant Americans some lessons.

"We employed the tactic of purposely showing ourselves to be weak, increasing the arrogance of the enemy, letting him run amok, and luring him deep into our areas."

Thus spoke Marshal Peng.

But, as noted, all this had been done with a handful of small units, which gave General MacArthur's intelligence officers the impression that the Chinese were confused, and only there in token force.

Meanwhile, as Marshal Peng said, "Our main force assembled in areas east and west of Bukjin and made use of the favorable terrain to build camouflaged positions thirty kilometers from the point where the enemy set out to attack us."

The Americans were to be lured to the Unxon-Kusong line, where the Chinese were lying in wait.

On the afternoon of November 25, the Americans and the South Koreans approached the area.

Peng's new war room had been constructed hastily in the village to replace the shack on the mountain. Here the senior staff of the People's Liberation Army Volunteer Group in Korea looked over the plan for the Second Campaign, which had been approved by Chairman Mao and the military commission back in Beijing.

A few adjustments had to made in light of the enemy's recent maneuvers.

The plan was to drive a wedge down between the Eighth Army on the western side of Korea and the X Corps over on the eastern side, and then to turn the wedge to the Red Army right, thus sealing off General Walker's Eighth Army from escape to the south. If the Americans wanted to get away, they would have to go to the western shore and swim.

For this task, Chairman Mao had suggested an increase of from two to three armies—God knows, the Chinese had enough of them—and on this afternoon of November 25 the official telegram arrived, delegating the new army to the field.

The problem Marshal Peng and his staff faced was to move that new army across the Manchurian border and into position without destroying the system already set up. This was going to be difficult. To be safe, the staff agreed that they should ask Beijing for further instructions while they integrated the new force. That would stall off any recriminations. It was a matter of dealing with higher military authority in a Communist Party system of government, and all these men around Peng were old hands at that sort of maneuver.

The best approach, the staff decided, was to establish a new western front command post.

"I want that job," said Deputy Commander Teng Yunhan.

Marshal Peng thought it over. Teng was a very good man, and he had plenty of combat experience. He also had a reputation for stabilizing any situation almost immediately. The most apparent danger of bringing in a new army was that it could fall into confusion. Yes, Teng was the man. Marshal Peng agreed.

After supper, Teng excitedly got ready to set out. He would travel in a camouflaged jeep that had once belonged to the Americans but had come over with one of the Kuomintang armies that had deserted to the Communists the year before.

It was a nice evening in the valley, with no wind, and Marshal Peng and other members of the staff accompanied Teng down to the place where the jeep was waiting, carrying small items of his equipment and chatting.

Teng got into the jeep and turned to Marshal Peng.

"What instructions?"

The marshal laughed.

"Instructions?" he jeered. "None." He smiled and waved, and Teng's driver took off. The jeep went running down the snowy road in the pale moonlight.

The staff looked at the marshal. He was staring upward at a copper-colored full moon that rose above the shoulder of the mountain like a great wheel.

"What a nice full moon," exclaimed Qing Lin.

"Yes," said Marshal Peng. "It wasn't easy waiting for this day."

While Marshal Peng and his armies had been waiting, they had prepared strong defensive positions along the line they proposed to hold. There the defense was nothing like that farther south, where several small units had been assigned to entice the Americans.

Everyone knew the plan, even down to the privates in the ranks. It would take a while for the Americans to learn that private soldiers in the Chinese army knew more than most junior officers in the American ranks, but it was true. Because of the basic lack of swift communication between units, it was essential that the Chinese soldier know the plans and be able to implement them in time of trouble.

The United Nations forces had been given the latitude to move up, which they had now done. But, as noted, they had made the mistake of putting their weakest link, the ROK II Corps, into position on the right flank of the Eighth Army line, with twenty odd miles separating that flank from the X Corps troops on the north and east. And it was here, on the UN right, that the Chinese struck hardest. Of course, with so many men—three whole armies—the Chinese struck everywhere, but their concentration was to break through the gap left by General MacArthur and then roll around his army and trap it. All along the line, the Chinese searched for, and then concentrated on, ROK units, knowing them to be the most vulnerable. The ROK II Corps was the primary victim. It collapsed that night of November 25, which put the pressure on the American Second Division, right next door. The Ninth Infantry Regiment of the Second Division felt the shock next.

No real soldier would call the Ninth Infantry a superb fighting machine. The reason was the same that affected the American troops all along the line: the overconfidence of the command. The Americans had entered the Korean war unready. In June, the 24th Division had been hustled up to middle Korea to stop the North Korean drive, and had been unable to do so because the soldiers were so badly trained and equipped. In those early days some ignorant Americans had thrown away their steel helmets, entrenching tools, and other battle equipment, as well as their canned rations, as too heavy to carry. That carelessness and ignorance had cost the division dearly, and many men found themselves in battle with no equipment, and sometimes no weapons and no food.

During the grim days of the Pusan perimeter these men had learned war the hard way, and the survivors had shaped up into soldiers. But then came the Inchon landing, the lightning thrusts forward, and the feeling, engendered at the top in Tokyo, that the war was over. And so here was the Ninth Infantry, in November 1950, not much more ready for battle than the 24th Division had been in June, yet thinking they knew how to fight, and planning on going home in a matter of days. The worst thing that had happened to them was that they had succumbed to the lure of the easy life. Korean porters brought up bedrolls and food, and provided the services of supply. The soldiers did not know how to fend for themselves. Also, because of MacArthur's planning, the Ninth Infantry was nothing like a homogeneous unit. It was made of rank recruits from all over America, battle-scarred troops, and South Koreans, assigned as body power, snatched to fill the gaps. The table of organization looked stronger than the regiment really was.

The Ninth Infantry was moving along on the afternoon of November 25, and no one had any complaints. They were assigned to take a series of ridges on the east bank of the Chongchon River, and they found, although at first they did not know it, that they had reached that limit of advance set by the Chinese. While the going had been so easy at first, suddenly the resistance hardened, and by that afternoon the regiment was in trouble.

It lost its company commander that night. When Colonel Charles C. Sloane came up to the line, he observed to the division that things were getting rough and the real war seemed to be about ready to start. How right the colonel was! For that night the Chinese unleashed their attack, following principles laid down for them by Mao Zedong in the anti-Japanese war.

The Mao technique was to select a position and to lure the enemy to that position with hopes of a huge victory. It was also very useful to make sure that the enemy arrived at the trap area at about nightfall, when his men, who had been moving all day, were at a low point. That's how it was with the Ninth Infantry this night. The men were tired. They had been facing strong resistance all day. They were hungry, and they were not ready for a major attack, yet that is what they received. A horde of Chinese descended on their half-prepared positions, and began hurling grenades. The fighting lasted for more than twenty-four hours, and the Americans comported themselves very well, but they were simply overwhelmed. At the end of the fighting one company of the Ninth Infantry was down from 129 men to 36.

Night attack, close quarters, no chance to use heavy weapons, the grenade and the rifle and the machine gun—this was the kind of warfare at which the Chinese Communists excelled, the warfare in which bodies counted, bodies capable of hurling grenades or just rushing forward.

"The enemy troops had been worn out after a day's fighting and were not ready to dig themselves in when small detachments of our troops began to strike at their rear. Then our main force swept into the enemy ranks with the strength of an avalanche and engaged the enemy at close quarters, with grenades and bayonets."

Thus wrote Marshal Peng after the war had ended.

"The superior fire power of the enemy became useless. Overturned and damaged enemy vehicles were strewn over the road, blocking retreating enemy troops."

There was plenty of heroism among the United Nations troops. The ROK First Division, the republic's top fighting unit, comported itself admirably as always. But what good did heroism do when they were absolutely overwhelmed by enemy manpower at close quarters, hurling grenades in the night? And this was what was happening all up and down the line. At one company position on the side of a hill, the men spent the night kicking grenades out.

When morning came there was no recognition by Tokyo that the war had changed. It was normal, said the suave advisors at MacArthur's headquarters in the Dai Ichi building, "to expect the North Koreans to put up one last dying gasp of effort before it was all over." At the battalion level and the regimental level the men knew they were facing a new enemy. Even the Eighth Army knew. But back in Tokyo General MacArthur stuck with his intelligence estimates; there were only a few thousand Chinese in North Korea, and so what the Eighth Army said was happening could not happen.

General Walker knew that to face up to MacArthur at this stage, a General MacArthur waiting for word of the victory he fully expected, was to put his head into the lion's mouth. Walker delayed a full day, but on November 26 he had to report to his commander that the ROK II Corps had been completely wrecked. Walker had rushed the First Cavalry, the British, and the Turks up to plug the hole, but the Chinese were streaming through. On the west the South Korean First Division and the U.S. 24th Division drew back toward the Chongchon River, but were hampered by thousands of refugees streaming south on those same roads.

Next along the line was the U.S. Second Division, which wanted to go back to the safety of the Chongchon lest they be cut off, but the top commanders were not replying to such requests. No one really knew what to do, it seemed. Actually, General Walker knew what to do—retreat as fast as possible—but he was more frightened of General MacArthur than of the enemy.

On November 26 the Ninth Infantry was still fighting to hold its line. But they could not hold, and at daybreak on November 27 they were ordered to pull back. Then they found the roads jammed.

On November 26 the Turks moved up the Kunu-ri road to the important junction of Tokchon. Here they were to try to hold the Chinese. For a few hours they fought retreating South Koreans who were streaming into their ranks, not knowing who they were, but then on the morning of November 27 they set out from Wawon. They fought their way through, but at 2:30 in the afternoon the situation had so worsened that the plans had to be changed, and the Turks were ordered to link up with the U.S. 38th Regiment and secure a retreat route to the west. If General MacArthur did not yet know that the Chinese were there in hordes, General Walker now knew, and he was trying to save his army.

The Turks scurried back to Wawon, but the Chinese got there first. The Turks launched a bayonet attack and threw the Chinese out.

By the morning of November 27 along the Eighth Army line, the regimental commanders were feeling completely frustrated. General Walker did not command one army fighting another army; he commanded scores of companies fighting company actions, surrounded by Chinese, unable to use their tanks and artillery which had brought victory so often before, and reduced to infantry weapons and company tactics. The Second Division was taking a terrible beating. Colonel George Peploe watched as an entire South Korean regiment came streaming through the lines of the 38th Infantry Regiment. When Peploe asked the Second Division commander what to do, the commander said to use the South Korean troops, but this was impossible. The Koreans were shattered, their morale destroyed. All they wanted to do and all they would do was run.

For a long time the British had been saying that the Americans were soft and did not know how to fight. Perhaps. But it was not a question of hard or soft in the face of this Chinese horde. Nobody claimed the Turks did not know how to fight, and yet on November 27 their force was virtually annihilated by the Chinese. By the end of that day even General Walker no longer cared what General MacArthur thought. He now had to try to save his Eighth Army from annihilation.

By November 27 over in Tokyo the magnitude of the disaster was beginning to quiet the optimists. In the Eighth Army's area those soldiers who had been dreaming of a "stateside Christmas" were now fighting for their lives, and they knew it.

The Second Division was retreating as fast as it could. The Turkish brigade was still instrumental in keeping that retreat orderly. On November 28, the Turks held at the village of Sillim-ni, and let the Second Division come through. The Chinese came at them from three sides, but still they held. The Chinese moved to Kaechon. At Kunu-ri the confusion increased, the Second Division jamming the roads, different commanders giving countering orders. On November 29 the extent of the disaster was apparent to all. The Second Division artillery was no longer firing to the north, but to the east, because the Chinese were outflanking the division and threatened to come around to the south. By evening the firing range was down to ten miles. By the morning of November 30 the range was a mile.

At seven o'clock that morning of November 30 the Turkish brigade was split, and half of it was sent to destroy the Chinese roadblock that was preventing the Second Division from escaping. The Ninth Infantry had been trying for two days to break that block, without success. At noon the Turks reached the roadblock and fought the Chinese off the road and up the hillsides, while the line of vehicles tried to get through. The Turks attacked and attacked again, and each time they broke the roadblock and forced the Chinese back, but each time the Chinese sent hundreds more men to attack. By afternoon the Turks were growing very tired. Yet little by little the vehicle parade moved through the valley and the pass, until a 155-mm howitzer and its tractor stalled in the center of the road and nothing could be done. After that the remaining vehicles had to be abandoned. Altogether, in three days, 7000 men tried to run that roadblock with their vehicles, and 4000 of them got through. What was left of the Turks also got through, fighting their way. All around them was the shambles of the Eighth Army, retreating to a point 40 miles south of the positions they had occupied on the day that General MacArthur announced his "End-the-War Offensive."

The Chinese had lost perhaps four or five times as many men as had the UN forces (and the Second Division alone suffered 5000 casualties), but the Chinese were prepared to lose a million men if they had to, and they had the men to lose. This was the secret strategy of the Mao Zedong force. Mao's enemy had to fight a seventeenth-century war in which his twentieth-century weapons were to no avail.

—— 17 ——

The Overconfidence of Marshal Peng

The most significant thing about the battle of the First Marine Division against the Chinese on the east side of Korea was what was not said by the Chinese. In Peng Dehuai's memoirs he discusses the war but he never mentions the marines or what happened around the reservoir country when General Smith's marines made one of the greatest retreats in history, successfully disengaging from a vastly numerically superior force with minimal casualties. The reason that Marshal Peng does not mention the encounter is twofold: First, the Chinese suffered enormous casualties, with two armies decimated; and second, at the time he was writing that relationships between the Chinese and the Americans were still nonexistent, and then Marshal Peng fell victim to the jealousy and megalomania of Mao Zedong during the Cultural Revolution, once was rehabilitated, but then slipped again into disgrace and was really murdered by Mao's Red Guards who virtually starved him to death. Someday, perhaps, the Chinese will produce a factual account of the Korean war, but the time is not now, with the old hard-line Communists in control. Until they are ousted, history will continue to be an aspect of political propaganda in China as it is today (1990). Indeed, in the halcyon period that ended on June 3, 1989, the contemporary accounts of the Korean war, written while the war was hot, had all disappeared from the bookstores and could be found only in such archives as the Beijing Library and the Library of London University's School of African and East Asian Studies. That was because the propagandistic nature of these anti-American books would be embarrassing to the Chinese. . . .

144

In Marshal Peng Dehaui's account of the Korean war, the marshal says nothing at all about the battle waged on the eastern side of Korea, where the marines had been substituted for the American Army Seventh Division in the pincers in General MacArthur's plan to envelop the enemy.

Perhaps the reason Peng did not mention the Chinese attack against the marines is that it did not succeed; the Chinese lost very heavily in their attempt to entrap the marines.

In defense of General Almond, the commander of the X Corps, it must be said that by November 24 he had a few qualms of his own about the coming "End-the-War Offensive" spoken of so glibly by MacArthur. Out of Almond's doubts came the decision to give the tougher job to the marines and the easier one to the army. The marines, and not the Seventh Army Division, would make the march from Yudam-ni, 55 miles to Yonbu-ni on the Yalu River. There the marines were to link up with the Eighth Army and thus surround the North Koreans and anyone else who was inside the Korean borders. Their southern boundary would be Hagaru; below that the Third U.S. Army Division would have responsibility. The First and Fifth Marines would make the march, while the Seventh Marines would remain in reserve.

What made Marine General Smith nervous was the long twisting road, narrow and heading through mountain passes, which was the one supply route for their march across the country. The road had to be kept open, or they could be cut off.

Under the new plan the Seventh Army Division was not to march to the Yalu River east of the Chosin reservoir.

The First Marines were at Chinghung-ni, Koto-ri, and Hagaru. The Fifth Marines were east of the Chosin reservoir. The Seventh Marines were at Udam-ni. On November 24, the marines began to move as ordered, as the Eighth Army did on the other side of Korea.

On November 26 General Smith flew over the length of the marines' supply road. He saw his marines nicely bunched up. He saw the airstrip at Hagaru, almost finished, which would make the supply problem much easier to solve. Otherwise everything had to be carried over a narrow-gauge railroad and the twisting narrow road, threading through those mountains that were in themselves a trap.

On the 26th the marines learned (from prisoners) of the Chinese plan. More than a hundred thousand troops were in northeast Korea; they had reached the Yudam-ni area, and were setting a trap. The Chinese were to wait until two regiments had passed along the road north, and then cut the road and seal it off. That meant they intended to trap the First and Fifth Marines.

That afternoon of November 26, when General Smith returned from his inspection flight, all his fears were realized. General MacArthur had said his marines were to be the northern arm of the pincers that was to seal off North Korea, trap the enemy troops, and end the war. But that day the ROK II Corps had collapsed, and General Walker's army was in retreat. The northern arm could not pinch anything! They had not even started the offensive, and suddenly their disposition was defensive. Now they had to escape the trap that had been laid for them.

Fortunately for his marines, General Smith had planned well. He had been nervous about that narrow twisting road all along, and had insisted on keeping three major garrisons along the road, so that every section of the road would have a haven at the end.

The Fifth Marines set up a defense perimeter at the town of Yudam-ni. At the end of November 27 the marines found themselves facing a semicircle of Chinese positions in the mountains around the northern side of Yudam-ni.

That night the Chinese Ninth Army Group opened its offensive against Yudam-ni, expecting to take the town. Their major move was over the mountains and along the ridges, accompanied by the cacaphony of Chinese bugles and whistles that always heralded an attack. Hundreds of Chinese fell to the mortars and fifty-caliber machine guns and fast-firing semiautomatic rifles of the marines in their prepared positions. But hundreds more came on, climbing over bodies and trying to dislodge the marines. On a hill called 1403, the marines were surrounded on three sides by Chinese. The fighting lasted for several hours, and the Company H marine commander and all but one officer were killed. Finally the surviving officer, Lieutenant H. H. Harris, had to order his men to move to better protection.

Thus the Chinese gained control of Hill 1403, which commanded the valley floor, and split off the Second Battalion of the Fifth Marines. This was the sort of maneuver at which the Chinese excelled, and which Mao Zedong had perfected in the old days of fighting the Japanese: Split off a segment of the enemy force and, using all the manpower available, chew it up; then split off another segment.

But in this case, the superior firepower, superior communications, and tough spirit of the marines prevented the Chinese from achieving their goal. They had split off the battalion, but chewing it up was going to be another matter, they discovered.

The Chinese were moving, and moving fast. The whole Chinese 78th Division moved across North Ridge—three regiments, or more than 10,000 men, to assault these hills and close the trap.

That night the Chinese attacked Yudam-ni and all the hills around it. The marines on the hills held their places under enormous Chinese rushes and tons of grenades. The Chinese also hit the marines in the valley and the command post of the Third Battalion of the Fifth Marines. But the troops rallied and drove the Chinese out. Marines from the village went up to reinforce the marines on the hills. By morning three Chinese divisions were attacking Yudam-ni. If they could cut the road to Hagaru, they could isolate the marines and then seal their trap.

To the Chinese it seemed almost impossible that the Marines could hold out. They had three sides of the trap, and could see one another's signals. But on a promontory called Hill 1240 the marines held out all night. A company was reduced to only 16 men, but they held the position.

At 2:30 on the morning of November 28 the Chinese attacked again, this time using all three of their divisions, but the marines held, waiting for dawn and the aircraft that would come to drive the enemy away.

All day long the Chinese harried the road that was the lifeline of the marines, and peppered away at the marines. But although the marines took casualties, they maintained the tight defenses, which saved them from the superior manpower of the Chinese.

In Toktong Pass, Company F had driven off several attacks and estimated that 450 Chinese had been shot down, while they had 20 dead and 54 wounded. The Chinese could continue to stage such attacks, but the marines could not continue to take casualties of that sort for long.

Here is the Chinese account of the fighting on Hill 1240 that night:

> The enemy counterattacked very violently. Accordingly, the assistant company commander ordered the First Platoon to strike immediately and determinedly. Before the First Platoon's troops had been deployed, Lee Feng Hsi, the platoon leader, shouted "Charge," and the first and second squads pressed forward in swarms side by side. When they were a little more than ten meters from the top of the hill, they suffered casualties from enemy hand grenades and short-range fire. Consequently they were absolutely unable to advance any farther. At that time the assistant company commander and the majority of the platoon and squad leaders were either killed or wounded.
>
> While the First and Second Squads were encountering the enemy counterattack, the Third Squad also deployed and joined them in an effort to drive the enemy to the back of the hill. As a result, more than half of the Third Squad were either killed or wounded. When the second assistant platoon leader attempted to reorganize his troops, they suffered again from enemy flanking fire and hand grenades. That, after no more than ten minutes of fighting. The entire platoon had lost its power to attack and was forced to draw back.

Thus, November 28 went by with no decision in Toktong Pass. Darkness fell and the marines prepared for another night of siege. The Chinese had controlled the road that day, but the marines got help, food, blood, and ammunition by air drop.

That night, at 2:15 A.M., the Chinese attacked again around Yudam-ni. The marines held, but by some pretty desperate measures. At one point the mass attack broke through the line of the Third Platoon of Company F, but a machine gunner turned his gun on the massed bodies and wiped them all out, so the line was held except for five foxholes. Next, Staff Sergeant John D. Audas led a counterattack that restored the night's position. On the morning of November 29 the marines had air drops, which came inside their lines, and helicopter relief. A ground column began to move out of Yudam-ni, with the mission of rescuing Company F, stuck out on the edge of the perimeter and cut off, and then returning to Yudam-ni that night. The Chinese began moving down to outflank the column, and airmen spotted them and reported, so the column was called back. Company F was still alone on its hill. The day's airdrops had brought them food and ammunition and helped morale no end. Captain Barber told his platoon leaders that they would have to hold. Again the Chinese attack came at about two o'clock in the morning, accompanied by a voice over a loudspeaker that kept calling in English for them to surrender.

The Americans had plenty of 81-mm mortar ammunition, including star shell, and they used it. The star shell showed several columns of Chinese advancing across the valley from the south. The mortars and the machine guns zeroed in and, when they came in range, mowed them down like grain. Three companies of Chinese were put out of action. But the marines still faced almost an entire Chinese army.

This was also the second night force attack on Hagaru. In order to hold that slender road line, General Smith had allocated most of his troops to the front area, and so the base at Hagaru was guarded only by a reinforced infantry battalion and two battalions of artillery.

The Chinese confidently prepared to attack on the night of November 28, expecting to occupy Hagaru. On the afternoon of November 28, General Almond made a quick trip to Hagaru, where General Smith was inspecting, and got the news about the number of Chinese and their intentions of cutting off the marines in the next two days. Almond then hurried back to Tokyo, where he had an appointment to tell General MacArthur that his "End-the-War Offensive" had just become a total fiasco.

When Almond got to MacArthur's headquarters that evening, the place was already a beehive of activity, the public relations officers churning out statements for the press that acknowledged the disaster and blamed everyone on the Allied side except General Douglas MacArthur.

The Joint Chiefs of Staff had erred, said the MacArthur publicists. Only he, MacArthur, had saved the day by staging a quick offensive, which in turn had forced the Chinese to act before they were ready, thus preventing the destruction of the Allied command. If MacArthur had not been ready, "in one invincible movement" the Chinese hordes would have surged from one end of Korea to the other.

MacArthur denied that his decision to drive to the Yalu had forced the Chinese hand. Everything he had done, he said, had been in strict obedience to orders (he ignored the directives that he not send troops other than Koreans north across the 38th parallel). MacArthur denied that his troops were retreating on the west, and in danger of being entrapped on the east. He said the correspondents could not tell the difference between a skilled withdrawal and a rout. The fact was, of course, that most of those correspondents knew a rout when they saw one, and they had just seen one of the worst in American history.

Finally, General MacArthur blamed his superiors in Washington for tying his hands, which meant he could not bomb the Chinese in Manchuria, or use the atomic bomb at all. Altogether, he said, no commander in history ever had so much trouble with his superiors.

Washington listened but said nothing.

At Hagaru the marines prepared for a hard night. They knew they were totally surrounded by the enemy in enormous numbers and that here, if not elsewhere, the enemy had artillery. But they settled down for a tight defense. They did everything they could do, from blasting their foxholes with explosives in C ration cans (not in the manuals of procedure), to installing trip flares, booby traps, and thermite bombs rigged to gas cans to make long-burning flares, to hedging the area with barbed wire. As darkness fell, they had sighted in the artillery and established fields of fire.

The Chinese were eager this night, and the probes set out at 10:30 with red flares and a whistle. These patrols were ordered to bring back word of the weak spots they found. But the probing fingers ran into booby traps and tripped flares that lighted up the area. The Chinese then began firing white phosphorous mortar shells at the marine line, and started coming head on by the hundreds. The marines responded with devastating small arms and machine-gun fire on an 800-yard front. The Chinese platoons were mowed down, but they were followed by more platoons, until around midnight they broke through and headed for the airstrip, where the bulldozers were still working. Lieutenant Colonel Ridge called for every marine who could stand up, and the cooks and the engineers and the clerks got rifles and ran to the scene. It was a very tough battle and the marines took heavy casualties, particularly among the engineer troops who were not used to this razzle-dazzle.

Then the artillery got into action. The fields of fire had been established; now the artillery commanders used them. Battery D distinguished itself that night by firing 1200 rounds of 105-mm howitzer ammunition, most of it in precisely the right place at the right time, breaking up the Chinese troop concentrations before they could mass their attack.

The Chinese artillery threatened from the hills above, and Captain Andrew Strohmenger, the commander of Battery D, was afraid they might hit an ammunition dump, which would play hell with the defense this night, because ammunition was everyplace the marines could store it, and one lucky hit could start a chain reaction. Strohmenger decided on a ruse to entrap the enemy guns.

He moved one howitzer out 150 yards ahead of the others. This was his decoy. All the other marine howitzers held their fire, but the decoy fired constantly, attracting the Chinese attention to its flashes. From afar it might have seemed to be a whole battery.

The other five howitzers then began firing on the Chinese flashes, and soon they had put two of the Chinese field pieces out of action and forced the enemy to move the other two out of range. There was no more trouble that night from the Chinese artillery.

Artillery and light, that was the answer. The light was provided by the flares, by the burning gasoline cans, by burning Korean houses in the village. The fighting continued fiercely until six o'clock in the morning. The casualties were heavy again; Company H alone lost 16 killed and 39 wounded. But the Chinese 172nd Infantry had suffered 90 percent casualties, and the regiment that had attacked on the other side had taken almost as bad a beating. The problem was that the Chinese could come back again with a whole new division to throw against Hagaru.

That day the marines sent a column of two hundred men to

their outpost on East Hill, which was nearly surrounded by the enemy. Another column was coming up from Koto-ri, this one led by the Army Third Division, to keep that road open and bring relief to Hagaru.

On November 30 the Chinese tried very hard to spring the trap, cut the road, and stop the column. They did stop the column, and fighting was general all along the road. But they did not cut the road. The part of the battle involving the relief column from Koto-ri was called the Battle of Hellfire Valley. Here the Americans were victims of their own technology, in a way. Their trucks stalled under attack and burned out, and the men then had to try to make their way out on foot. There was surrender that night at Hell Valley, finally, but while the commander surrendered, most of his men infiltrated and escaped. The next day a pale weak sun came out. The marine main line of supply was still there—ragged and almost broken, but still there—and the marines still had a chance of fighting their way out of the Chinese trap.

The marine situation in northeast Korea was bad enough. They were being saved by their training, and by the prescience of the commander of the First Division, who had distrusted this operation from the beginning and done all he could to make it salvageable. But the army troops in the northeast were in a much worse situation in that last week of November 1950.

On November 25 the men of the Seventh Division had moved through Hagaru, and then gone off to the little road that led to the east side of the Chosin reservoir. They were moving like a long finger out of the American perimeter. They did not know that all around them the Chinese were concentrating. So they moved to the north, and into the heart of the enemy. The land was hilly, and without forest cover. They dug in and cut fields of fire through the scrub brush around their highly exposed positions. It was easy for the Chinese to have a good picture of those positions; they stuck out like white chalk on a blackboard.

The Chinese began their assault on the night of November 27. The problem of the cold was as serious as the problem of the enemy. The army soldiers did not know the terrain or the climate.

They had not set up warming tents, so there was no way to give anyone on the line even brief relief from the terrible, terrible cold. Every man was wearing army cold weather gear: long woolen underwear, two pairs of socks, wool shirt, wool trousers, cotton trousers over the wool, shoe pacs, pile jacket, parka with hood, and trigger-finger mittens. It was not enough. No clothing would have been enough. The rifles sometimes failed to work; the carbines failed more often.

On November 28, after he had stopped to see General Smith, Almond came up to the end of the line, where his aides rounded up some men of the Seventh Infantry, to make a speech, while the helicopter kept its engines running. The general made his "Chinese laundryman" speech.

After General Almond had characterized the entire Chinese army as "a bunch of goddamn laundrymen," he began handing medals to anyone who seemed interested. Most people were not. In spite of the general's brave words about the incompetence of the Chinese, these men had seen the Chinese army in action, and it was a fearsome prospect, being stuck out here on the finger of the hand that was supposed to be chopped off.

In the next two days the Seventh Army Division troops at the Chosin reservoir were decimated. Their alternative to standing and holding with nothing to hold onto was to try to make their way down to the marine lines; this they did, but no one could help them, and very few of them made it. They were the sacrificial lambs of General MacArthur's brave swing up to the reservoirs. They were sent air drops, at least a third of which went to the Chinese troops. Their army compatriots tried to save them, and wanted to send a rescue mission. But General Almond's X Corps headquarters was so completely disorganized that there was no transportation for the relief corps.

The breakout was a failure. Men died by the hundreds, and the few who escaped through to the marine lines were very lucky indeed. The fate of the First Battalion of the 32nd U. S. Infantry regiment was typical. The battalion went up to the Chosin reservoir, hearts light, expecting victory, more than 1000 strong. A week later the remnants returned, fewer than 200 men.

The fate of the Seventh Division was the fate that Marshal Peng

Dehuai had ordained for the entire American army in North Korea, and particularly all the troops on the eastern side. General Walker had saved his own Eighth Army, although the losses were high. General Smith was in the process of saving his marines, by force of prescience and discipline. But the army had let the Seventh Division down very badly. General Almond and General Mac-Arthur had sacrificed them, having created a situation in which nothing could be done to save these troops if the tide turned, because they did not even know when the tides moved or that there was a tide.

On November 28, 1950, General MacArthur held an emergency meeting at the American Embassy in Tokyo. General Almond was ordered to come, as was General Walker of the Eighth Army. At 9:30 at night the commanders and the staff assembled in a warm room in quarters to hear what MacArthur reported was happening on the frigid hills of Korea and, after the shock subsided, to ascertain what could be done to stop the disaster.

MacArthur was ready for any desperate maneuver, including sending the Army Third Division into the Taebaek Mountains to link up with the Eighth Army. If he had been paying attention earlier, he would have discovered that the road through the mountains, although showing very clearly on the map, did not exist at all. It was like many another road written on these maps derived from Japanese maps, which were drawn to confuse rather than enlighten, since the Japanese military always had their own maps that were extremely accurate but not passed around to the public.

At this meeting for the first time General MacArthur admitted that he was in a new sort of war, and that there was no possibility of having the boys home for Christmas. Typically, he went from overconfidence to despair. "This command," he said at the end of the meeting, "faces conditions beyond its control and strength." This was true, but only because of the bullheaded manner in which MacArthur had refused to take any advice or listen to any appraisals with which he did not agree. He, with the agreement of the American establishment, had brought the situation to this desperate turn.

MacArthur's message of despair was the one transmitted to Washington, and it got General Bradley, the chairman of the Joint Chiefs of Staff, out of bed just after six o'clock on a cold Washington morning. He put through a call to President Truman and got him up, and the American high command began to assemble to try to figure out what to make of the disaster.

MacArthur was like a madman. He wanted to use atomic weapons. He wanted to bomb China indiscriminately. He wanted to bring Chiang Kaishek into the war, he and some others still spoke of "unleashing" Chiang, although that was not quite how it would have been.

Out of all this came some serious rethinking in Washington, including that of General Bradley, who awoke from the shock to realize that the Korean war had taken an entirely unnecessary turn, and that it was the wrong war at the wrong time in the wrong place with the wrong people. Only because of the restraint shown in Washington at this late hour did it not become a general war; MacArthur would have been very happy to have forced war with the USSR in order to conceal his vital error; and his actions showed this absolutely.

Immediately, MacArthur demanded a series of local attacks by General Walker to take the pressure off the marines and allow them and what was left of the army up north on the eastern side of Korea to escape the trap. MacArthur wanted the X Corps to stay where it was while the United States brought all the rest of the American military over for his use—or so it seemed. The Joint Chiefs were not listening to MacArthur. General Lawton J. Collins was sent to Tokyo and Korea to find out what was really going on. He went to see General Walker, whom Collins had some difficulty in finding, because he was now on the retreat, forced back, first to Pyongyang and then below, by the Chinese drive. Collins caught Walker at the Imjin River, where he had set up a temporary line. But Walker told Collins he couldn't hold that line, and that he could not hold Seoul. He suggested that the UN forces fall back to the Pusan perimeter. There, he said, he was pretty sure he could hold out.

While General Collins was moving about, learning that nothing was as he had expected it would be, the marines in the north were holding out against very powerful Chinese forces, and making their way steadily out of the trap set for them by Marshal Peng Dehuai.

On November 30 the marines moved out of Yudam-ni to open

the road that would lead the whole force to safety. The dead were buried in the field, and the artillery was put at the tail end of the column, to give support to the front. Three marine battalions occupied a defense line three and a half miles long, stretching from the hills north of Yudam-ni to the Chosin reservoir. Thus they established a protective barrier on the east side of the main route of supply.

The marines moved out of Yudam-ni to force their way south along the road. It was December 2. By dawn, after heavy fighting, they had moved down the road and wiped out a Chinese roadblock. They were on their way to Toktong Pass. All the way they picked up little knots of marines who had been fighting and holding positions along the road so that this movement could be carried out. All the way they piled up hundreds of Chinese dead.

Steadily they moved down that narrow, twisting road. During the daylight hours they were covered by marine aircraft, which did their own part of breaking up Chinese troop concentrations with napalm and rocket fire. On the morning of December 3 the marines fought their way to hold the ridge northeast of Toktong Pass, and wrecked another Chinese regiment. Colonel Taplett's battalion had been reduced from 437 men to 194 in three days, but they had done this part of the job, and now tanks and British royal marine commandos came up from Hagaru to meet them.

That night the troops from the end of the line reached Hagaru and marched in, and then the whole column fought its way into Hagaru. The worst part of the retreat was over. They had successfully escaped from the trap set by Marshal Peng.

It had taken the column three days to cover 14 miles. They had left their dead buried behind them, and they had left many vehicles and much equipment along that road, but they had gotten out. The next step was to break out to absolute safety by way of the port of Hamhung.

During the first five days of December, a thousand sick and wounded men were flown out to safety in South Korea. Now General Smith was entrusted with the entire retreat. It was one of the greatest retreats in the course of military history, made against an enemy powerful enough to close a vise, it seemed, but operating in such a fashion that the vise could never be closed.

The marines prepared to fight their way along the rest of the road to Hamhung. Five hundred replacements were brought up to strengthen the First Marine Division, but it was intact—casualty-ridden and tired, but intact. On December 6 the division prepared to attack toward Koto-ri.

The Fifth Marines took over the rear guard, to protect the division from Hagaru, and marched south. This was going to have to be an evacuation on foot, for the most part. The remnants of the Seventh Division of the army were organized into a task force of their own. The supplies and ammunition that could not be carried were to be destroyed. The trucks were filled with the men with frostbite and minor wounds.

During the first five days of December the marines prepared. The Chinese surrounding Hagaru waited and did nothing. In fact, Marshal Peng was now suffering from some of the same overconfidence that had assailed General MacArthur for so long. His plan had succeeded so far. To be sure, the marines on the east side had not been swallowed up as quickly as expected, but they were on the run, and the Chinese armies around them believed they would trap them and destroy the column. The talk at Peng's headquarters was of driving the UN forces out of Korea altogether. The Second Campaign was not over yet, and would not be until the marines were dealt with, but Peng was already planning the Third Campaign, which would be the recapture of Seoul.

As General Smith pondered the problems of his withdrawal, getting the men out of the trap, Washington pondered the plans of general withdrawal. On December 6 General Collins was with General MacArthur in Tokyo, listening to discussion that was largely inchoate, receiving a barrage of comments that still ranged from a demand for the use of the atomic bomb to a general complaint against everyone in authority in Washington for betraying MacArthur.

In Washington it was apparent that America's UN allies were nearly ready to break into open rebellion. The American political leaders were looking for some solution. They got very little information or hope from Tokyo. The Joint Chiefs of Staff wanted to stabilize the line somewhere in Korea, but where? The X Corps had to be evacuated from the north and put solidly in position with no enemy behind it. Until that could be done, nothing could be done, and perhaps Marshal Peng's dream of driving the UN forces into the sea was not so wild after all.

Three Chinese armies—the 20th, 26th, and 27th—had closed around the X Corps. They had taken enormous casualties, but still there were some 60,000 men surrounding the X Corps, not an easy gauntlet for General Smith to run. The marines would have help, of course: all the air power the UN could muster, naval support from offshore, helicopters to come and pick up the wounded and carry them out. But the road from Hagaru to Ham-hung is 56 miles long, and they had to be prepared to fight along every foot of it.

The key was to be the artillery. The 11th Marines split into batteries, some at the head, some in the middle, some at the end of the column. Some would stay with the rear guard at Hagaru and work their way out at the end.

And so it began upon the night of December 5, with a con-centration of fire from the artillery along the road between Hagaru and Koto-ri.

On the night of December 5 the Chinese launched what they had hoped to be a decisive attack against Hagaru, coming in from three sides, in one wave after another. War correspondents who had not really seen the Chinese in action were in Hagaru this night, and they were surprised by this taste of Chinese tactics, so they wrote much about it.

The Chinese attack failed, although it was very spectacular and included all the usual tactics: bugles, whistles, and apparently end-less waves of men surging against the hillside positions. Again the Chinese lost thousands of dead, but also, this time, hundreds of prisoners—some 300 Chinese prisoners of war were taken—which indicated that the morale of some of Peng's troops was not what it should have been and that some of these troops thrown against the line were little more than untrained cannon fodder.

That night's surprise victory enabled the marines to make an easy passage out of Hagaru the next morning. The weather was with them, too—thick fog surrounded the road—and so they moved. Chinese troops contested the road itself and knocked out a tank, but when air support came down as the fog lifted, the

Chinese melted away. By nightfall of December 6 the marine column had moved three miles down the road. Colonel Litzenberg, commander of the Seventh Marines, decided against stopping, because he knew the perimeter would be fiercely attacked, and felt that the best way to meet the attack was on the road. So down they went, another two miles, and the attacks began. The casualties were heavy, but by dawn the column reached Koto-ri, and now the air support came back again. The column moved in segments, and every time a segment moved forward, the Chinese closed in behind and began harrying. Thus the air support was invaluable in driving the enemy away from the rear of the column.

By late afternoon of December 7, the anniversary of another American debacle, all the vehicles of the Seventh Marines were safe inside Koto-ri.

Now came the second element of the column, the division train. This consisted largely of service troops. The general had expected that the riflemen and artillery in front would clear the way, but it did not happen that way. The Chinese, determined, attacked every element, so every man had to fight his way out.

The Chinese attacks never let up. Here is one account showing how the Chinese did not relieve the pressure for a moment:

About two miles south of Hagaru the column was stopped when several vehicles were set afire by Chinese mortar shells and blocked the road. As day broke on December 7 the Chinese attacked the column fiercely, and the guns of G and H batteries were turned on the enemy at point-blank range. There was not even time to dig in the trails of the guns. Fuses were cut for ranges of 500 yards. And the range kept decreasing. Some Chinese got within forty yards of the guns before they were stopped, but after two hours of continuous fire, that advance was eliminated. An estimated 800 Chinese soldiers had died in the attempt to take the American guns.

Everyone fought. The convoy from the division headquarters company was made up of clerks and specialty men. They were marines, and riflemen now. The trucks mounted light machine guns on top and all able-bodied men except the drivers walked in single file alongside the vehicles which carried the wounded. At 1:30 in the morning the column was stopped by Chinese fire.

A strike of night fighters was called in to help keep the Chinese at bay. Lieutenant Albert Clark and Lieutenant Truman Clark's fighter planes flew strafing runs just thirty yards from the main line. That helped. But just before daylight a company of Chinese penetrated to within thirty yards of the convoy. The marines then fought like demons. Lieutenant Charles H. Sullivan fired his carbine until it ran out of ammunition and then hurled it like a javelin at a Chinese infantryman just fifteen feet away. The bayonet impaled the Chinese.

That night the convoy was safe within the perimeter of Koto-ri, like a wagon train that had found the safety of a fort and did not have to worry about the Indians. But at dawn on December 8 they would be moving again, in this desperate attempt to break out of the Chinese trap.

With first light, also, the air drops began, those air drops that meant the difference between an orderly retreat and a rout. The men could never have carried the ammunition needed to get them out. As it was, only about 25 percent of the ammunition dropped actually got to the proper places, but that was enough to keep them going.

That night at Koto-ri General Smith and his staff planned the next step of this difficult evacuation. They fully expected a major attack from the Chinese on the mountain stretch of the roads ten miles between Koto-ri and Chinghung-ni. That being the case, General Smith ordered a marine attack first thing, to clear the road to Chinghung-ni. Of course, clearing it and keeping it cleared were two different matters. There were so many Chinese that it would be difficult to keep the road clear, but they had to try.

But even before the attack there was a job to be done; the repair of the bridge three miles outside of Koto-ri where the waters of the Chongjin reservoir came down to a power plant. The Chinese had blown the bridge, 24 feet across. The marines had to have a bridge, so they had Treadway bridge sections dropped by helicopter. They needed four sections, so eight were dropped, seven of which were recovered by the Americans. On the afternoon of December 7 the bridging had been started.

On the morning of December 8, just after dawn, the Seventh Marines were on the road to attack Chinese points that controlled the narrow winding road. They were followed by a battalion of the Fifth Marines which moved on through to the next set of objectives, and then came the evacuation train. The First Marines would stage an attack later, and the rest of the Fifth Marines would protect the rear.

The marine intelligence estimate now placed ten divisions of Chinese troops in this area of Korea, attempting to block the escape of one marine division reinforced by the remnants of the U.S. Army Seventh Division.

A key position was a hill called 1081, which controlled the passage over the Treadway bridge. The First Marines, who had spent the past few days south in the relative quiet of Chinghung-ni, were rested and ready to make the assault on this hill. They set out at 2 A.M., the morning of December 8, to approach the hill from two sides and take it. Practically speaking, the First Marines here were fighting a Chinese-style war. They wore white parkas that blended with the snow, and when more snow began to fall, they were well concealed. They did not have vehicles, except for two ambulances and a control jeep with a radio, so they made very little noise. They traveled fast, and they surprised the Chinese. By 10 A.M. they had their first objective in hand.

Soon they had made another surprise attack and taken the height.

As morning wore along, the column moved out and down the road, and the column had its difficulties with the Chinese. The marine units were all under strength; the Third Battalion of the Seventh Marines numbered only 120 men when it should have been nearer seven hundred. But slow as the advance was, by 8 A.M. on December 9 they reached their first objective, after forcing a number of small Chinese bunkers. The bridge across the gap was rebuilt by the engineers, and the vehicles began their descent into the pass. There was trouble in rigging the bridge to take the many different sorts of vehicles, from jeeps to construction carryalls, but somehow it was done, continuing in the night by flashlight and headlight. The convoy kept moving, with a steady stream of Korean refugees coming along behind.

The cold was intense, so intense that it affected the Chinese too, and there was very little fighting during the night. At 2:45 on the morning of December 10 the First Marines moved into the Chinghung-ni area. Two vehicles broke down, stopping the column for three hours. During that time the Chinese launched a major attack, but it failed. The rest of the Chinese had been ordered to move south swiftly and prepare to cut off the marines there, so that is what they were doing.

The Chinese now mingled with the Korean refugees. Sometimes they pretended they wanted to surrender, and then they attacked when the marines were supposedly off guard.

The marines took casualties from these attacks, but they did not falter. That night the last tank made it across the Treadway bridge. At one o'clock on the afternoon of December 11 the last of the Americans had left Chinghung-ni, and by nine o'clock that night all but the tanks had reached the Hamhung area. They had made the long trek, sometimes moving for 20 hours at a time. They had fought all the way down, facing six Chinese divisions in the process, and they had decimated those six divisions. But the problem in dealing with Chinese military statistics is that the mauling was expected; it was the price the Chinese army had to pay for its methods and its deficiencies in modern weapons.

The U.S. Army historians also referred to this period, December 1950, as "The Brink of Disaster," and it was. General MacArthur had led the troops brilliantly from the Pusan perimeter to Seoul, but then his vision had failed. So charged was he with the idea of a clean victory to sweep away the North Koreans that he paid no attention to the warning signs, nor did the Americans in Washington pay attention to the political warning flags put up by Zhou Enlai. The end of 1950 had indeed brought crises. What was to be done?

The advice in Washington ranged from "hold," to "retreat," to "withdraw" from Korea. That was the problem that Peng Dehuai posed for the United States at the end of the Second Chinese Campaign, in December 1950.

——18——

Peng's Victory Fever

After Peng Dehuai's offensive of November 25 began, the word came from Beijing that the Americans were to be driven south and chased into the sea. It looked so easy to Mao Zedong, and he was beginning to suffer from the same victory mania that had assailed MacArthur. Peng was sure his forces could do it; the conduct of the American troops they had met on the west side of Korea was conducive to such thinking, for there was a great deal of "bugging out" in the retreat south by American troops, who never had a very clear idea of what they were fighting for in this second phase of the war. That was because the Joint Chiefs of Staff refrained from announcing an intention of which they were half ashamed: to destroy by force the North Korean government and create a cordon sanitaire against Red China. The membership of the United Nations was also losing its taste for the war, since the American war aims had changed so drastically in October and November of 1950. But as the war continued and a new American commander, General Matthew Ridgway, came to Korea, Peng began to have new problems and new doubts. The biggest problem was supply, for which the nineteenth-century Chinese army was not ready. And to add to that, the Americans once more changed their war aims and their strategy. . . .

On December 6, the Chinese occupied Pyongyang and struck south with no indication of slowing down. General MacArthur was telling

Washington that without massive reinforcement he could not possibly hold the line in Korea. But from General Walker, General Collins, the Joint Chiefs' representative, learned that there was better morale among the Americans than MacArthur indicated. Collins left Korea with the thought that the Eighth Army could survive. He had also spoken to General Almond, and believed the X Corps could hold the Hungnam area until all the troops could be moved out. Thus, the panic of the moment was almost entirely confined to MacArthur's headquarters, where it was nursed by the deep sense of hurt MacArthur felt in being deprived of his big victory.

Now the Americans were finally willing to do all the things they had refused to do earlier. They would stop the assault if the Chinese would stop. They would agree to a renewal of the 38th parallel division line and not send troops north again, if the Chinese would agree. But with the United Nations forces on the run, the Chinese ignored the pleas. In Beijing Mao Zedong was now developing his own delusions: The Chinese could smash the UN forces, drive them completely out of Korea, and do for the North Koreans what they had failed to do for themselves: give them the entire Korean peninsula.

Again there was misunderstanding, this time on the Chinese side. Mao and his associates did not realize that the United States was determined not to be pushed out of Korea.

At the United Nations there was much talk about cease-fire, but not by the Chinese. They had sent a special representative, General Wu Hsiu-chan, to New York on invitation. On orders from Beijing, General Wu would not even meet with the UN cease-fire committee. To emphasize the decision, General Wu was ordered home to Beijing.

Egged on by their North Korean friends, the Chinese were as full of themselves as the Americans had been earlier. Following the capture of Pyongyang, the city was cleaned up and sanitized and prepared for a victory celebration. The Chinese began to arrive from headquarters on December 10.

Marshal Peng Dehuai had been ill for a week with pneumonia. It had not really mattered. He had laid the plans and his subordinates had carried them out faithfully. But now new plans were needed. Peng was very pleased with the results of the attack; they were all he could have expected, really. As he noted in his dispatches to Beijing, he had destroyed one American division, the Seventh Army Division. He didn't say much about the First Marine Division; that was a different story, one whose results might have been more to Peng's liking. The less said about that encounter the better.

Peng had just returned from a tour of the battlefields and had expressed himself to Beijing as well pleased.

Up from Beijing for the victory celebration at Pyongyang came a delegation from the Central Committee of the party led by Guo Mo-ro, a theorist and poet. He brought the respects of Zhou Enlai and an indication that the Central Committee wanted to put an end once and for all to the American influence on the continent.

How quickly they all forgot back in Beijing! The campaign had been begun with heavy hearts, half expecting disaster, and with fully expressed understanding of the difficulties that Peng and his volunteer army would face in matters of supply and reinforcement. And here, with only two victories, all this was forgotten and Beijing was ready to demand miracles.

The celebration was attended by Kim il Sung, the Soviet chief general Terentyi Shtykov, Marshal Peng, and the Beijing delegation. It was suitably impressive, with national anthems, speeches, and much good will, all expressed fervently, if a little nervously. They talked about "driving the Americans into the sea," but privately Peng had some serious reservations. He knew, and the others could only surmise, what his logistic problems were already: A handful of trucks and a handful of promises and thousands of strong backs still did not make a supply force tuned to rapid movement.

Liberation Day officially was December 12, and on this occasion the Koreans were in the limelight. Credit for liberating Pyongyang was given not to the Chinese army but to a young Korean officer who had driven into the city in a jeep. The guerillas who had fought the UN troops behind the lines were honored, and so were the North Korean army forces. Kim Il Sung made an appearance and was cheered. He responded with the words "March south."

With those words ringing in his ears, Marshal Peng drove down to the 50th Field Army headquarters on a hill above Pyongyang.

He inspected the troops and noted that they were going to

need heavier boots and clothing for the months to come. But he also noted that they were fresh and ready for action, and he sensed that the mood of Beijing was just the same as the mood of Pyongyang.

Marshal Peng had expected to stop here, along the Pyongyang line, mop up and consolidate, and straighten out the line on the east where the marines, holed up in Hamhung, were preparing to move out under the watchful eyes of the U.S. fleet.

But with the word from Beijing and the celebration, Peng's own officers were singing a different tune, and he was quick to recognize that just now the badly defeated UN forces were in confusion. This was the time to strike and take Seoul, and the 50th Army, fresh, was the striking iron. Marshal Peng issued orders to the 50th Army: March south.

After the enormous success of the Second Campaign of the Chinese, the governing Communist Central Committee and Mao Zedong hoped to have a victory of enormous proportions. The Chinese Communists in Beijing really believed they might drive the Americans out of Korea altogether, and as usually happens, particularly with such dogmatic oligarchic governments, the wish had become the philosophy and the plan.

The intelligence officers of the Eighth Army had sharpened their techniques remarkably in the past two months, and now they had a good idea of the order of battle of the Chinese. There would be no more of this foolery where prisoners told them that a regiment was a company and the Westerners believed. The marines, who were sometimes more adept at estimating than the army, put the figure of Chinese and North Korean soldiers in Korea at 750,000 men.

This new Chinese winter offensive was designed to capture Seoul, leaving the Americans gasping, and then run to Pusan and the end of the Korean peninsula. It began on an empty countryside, for the Americans had already retreated to Kesong, just about on the 38th parallel. The Chinese 13th Army Group moved laterally as it came down to the 38th parallel, stacking up on the north side of the line, and making ready for a major assault on Seoul. Six Chinese armies marched, and so did the newly rebuilt North Korean II Corps, wrecked by the Americans in the early fall.

Peng's plans were endorsed heartily by the Communist leadership in Beijing. Mao Zedong had caught victory fever. From Beijing came early urgings to drive on to Pusan. Marshal Peng's drive would be three-pronged. One element would drive directly for Seoul down the coast highway, to the airfields at Suwon and Osan. The second prong would move down toward Wonju along the Pukhan River valley. On the far left another army would drive down with the North Koreans. The air in Beijing was much like it had been in Washington two months earlier. Zhou Enlai, the prime minister, was talking about cutting down recruiting for the army. Mao Zedong was talking about having the boys home in time to celebrate spring festival (Chinese New Year). General Zhu De, the defense minister, said the plan was so sound it could not possibly fail, and that the Americans were as good as run out of Korea already.

The one man in the Chinese leadership who entertained some real doubts was Marshal Peng. There was something not quite right about the swift victories over the Americans. It was all right for the propagandists to sneer at the American military ability, but Peng had fired too many American weapons to sneer with them. The victories had been won, there was no doubt about it. The Americans had been soundly defeated at the reservoir area, and for the first time a whole division had been decimated. But still there was something that did not quite fit, and Peng did not know what it was.

And then he came to the real problem of the Chinese: supply. When they got to Seoul, their supply line would already run some 200 miles from the Manchurian border. Every mile farther south of that meant an enormous strain on the Chinese supply system, which was still not mechanized.

Just now the troops did not notice the problem, because they were living on the loot of victory. The armies were supplied from the enemy's supply dumps, captured along the Chungchon River line and south.

General Zhou Chunquan, director of services of supply, told Peng that he would mobilize nearly 200,000 men and women to manage the supply train. They were also working on the railroads, with the aim to repair them as fast as the Americans could bomb them. They would not ship by train by day—it would be foolhardy in the face of all those aircraft—but they would ship by night, and the general said he could guarantee the 13th Army Group a thousand tons of supply each day. Since a Chinese army could operate on 50 tons of supply a day (as compared to more than 300 tons for an American mechanized force of similar size), this would be adequate. The general was confident that he could manage the supply services all the way to Pusan, and then they would again have the advantage of raiding the enemy's capacious supply dumps in the south.

But Peng knew the Americans had now begun blowing up those supply dumps and carrying out a scorched earth policy as they retreated. That harsh policy resulted in some UN atrocities against school children and others which left a bad smell in the air along the 38th parallel. But it showed how unpredictable this enemy was.

Even to the Chinese, who shared this frigid northern climate with the Koreans and the Russians, the last few days of 1950 seemed unusually cold. The wind swept down from the Siberian plain, through the valleys long denuded of the timber that eased the pressure of the winds, and the snow began to fall—dry, flaky, hard snow. Marshal Peng was not a great commander of the Napoleonic or MacArthur school: He did not relish perorations to the troops. But some of his commanders had that ability, and one was Li Tianyu, commander of the Ninth Army Group.

His men marched with his order of the day ringing in their ears.

"A final blow against imperialism," the general had said. "Once more our glorious Red Army is about to strike the enemy. An assault on all fronts will liberate the capital at Seoul, and drive the foreign enemy into the sea."

In late December Marshal Peng made an emergency trip to Beijing—the reason, supply. The Chinese armies marching south from the Pyongyang line had not yet met the enemy, and already they were in trouble. The fierce weather bit through their inadequate clothing, and their shoes were falling apart. They were running out of food, and the men were scratching and scrabbling to keep alive.

Peng, who had known Mao Zedong for thirty years, burst into

the chairman's apartment full of fury and suppressed resentment, and unloaded his fears. Mao was ready: He made promises and more than promises. On the Manchurian border were freshly provisioned and armed troops, given Soviet weapons, trucks, and field kitchens. So Marshal Peng went back to the battle, knowing that his losses were going to be enormous, knowing that he was ordered to take those losses, but knowing at least that Chairman Mao understood what he was doing and was prepared to take the responsibility.

Marshal Peng had recovered from his pneumonia well enough now to make extensive inspections of the forces all along the line in Korea to decide what he should do, for he knew that he would be held responsible as well.

It was the same as he moved from area to area to see what should be done with the rest of the armies. Those on the northeast had taken a more serious beating than he had expected, and the major units were up against enemy concentrations. Nothing was moving, and nothing could move until he gave the flat order to go.

At this point there were nearly 350,000 Chinese troops in Korea; the Ninth Army Group on the east, still in action to try to destroy the marines and army troops of the X Corps; and the 13th Army Group, which was poised again to pursue the Eighth Army down deep into South Korea. On the west side in mid-month, the Eighth Army was retreating toward Seoul.

On the east side, the Chinese faced a problem: The UN forces, having reached Hungnam, had set up there inside a perimeter and were going to be a tough nut to crack, even with 180,000 Chinese soldiers at the disposal of General Song Shilun. Offshore stood several warships which offered support by bombarding Chinese positions. The air was busy with UN aircraft making airstrikes all day long in support of the ground forces. On December 10 and 11 the Chinese could see what the marines were up to, loading onto transports by which they proposed to escape.

When word of preparations for escape reached Marshal Peng he was more pleased than distressed. It was one thing to talk about annihilating forces, and another thing to do it. If the marines were to move out of Hungnam, the bridgehead would be eliminated;

and once Seoul was taken and the Americans were driven far south, this would not be quite as resounding a propaganda victory as otherwise, but still a perfectly satisfactory victory, and one that would soon enough be followed by the capture of Seoul. For Marshal Peng knew he had the enemy on the run, although he did not know how near panic the Americans were.

In Washington, President Truman had been persuaded to declare a state of national emergency, the next thing to war, and hurried plans were made to beef up the American army to a million and a half men.

The American plan now was to retreat all the way back to Pusan, where General Walker had said he could hold. The X Corps was now to be joined with the Eighth Army. The important thing was to move all of the X Corps out of Hungnam before something awful happened.

On the night of December 14 all the marines were aboard the transports, and they sailed the next day. That left two divisions of army troops, an ROK Corps, and thousands of Korean refugees inside the perimeter.

On December 6 the Chinese had decided to attack the north side of the perimeter, but they were so swiftly repelled that they thought better of it. Every hour now the Hungnam perimeter was shrinking. The trick was to get the troops and the rear guard out before they could be trapped. This was done under the cover of the battleship *Missouri* with its 16-inch naval guns, two cruisers, and seven destroyers, plus small craft. On Christmas Eve the beaches were cleared and the UN force sailed. The trap no longer existed.

As the Chinese generals prepared the Third Campaign, the Chinese propagandists were making hay with the results of the second. They claimed that the Americans were very bad fighters, and would soon be wiped out in Korea. Already, they said, they had captured 1000 tanks and 6000 motor vehicles. But they had to admit that they did not get much benefit from the equipment, because the Americans destroyed it with shellfire and napalm before they left it.

The Chinese army was going to have to travel in the old way, using pack animals—and human pack animals—to bring their supplies along with the troops. Marshal Peng made a habit of going out to the regiments and carrying a packboard himself for a while. This was a little revolutionary strategy from the early Red Army days which did not do a bit of harm. He encouraged his officers to do the same; it was a reminder of the roots of the Red Army and good for morale.

Had the Chinese been able to capitalize on their first victory, as Beijing seemed to sense, they could have gone all the way to Seoul in the panic that had seized Washington and Tokyo in the early days of December. But by Christmastime the marines were safely out of Hamhung, the Eighth Army retreat to the south was proceeding in an orderly fashion, and the American leaders stopped trembling. Now the United States was opting for a cease-fire. The Chinese had stiffened, telling them that the only sort of cease-fire would be one in which the Americans would withdraw entirely from the Asian continent and the Seventh Fleet would stop prowling around Asian waters. The American presence would be limited to Japan. Furthermore, the Americans would have to end their rearmament program (that was a fillip stuck in to infuriate the Americans and please the Russians).

Did the Chinese really believe they could push the United States that far? They might have. They tended to become the victims of their own propaganda just as the Americans did. Their demands were so insulting that they hardened the American backbone.

America's allies had been equally concerned about the turn of events in Korea, but they too rallied, or the important ones did. By the end of the year the British and the Americans had agreed to stand together and bring about a peace in Korea that the Western world could accept.

The defense line was established along the 38th parallel for the moment, but no one in the UN camp expected it to remain there. Up north Kim Il Sung was making aggressive noises about driving the UN troops into the sea.

The UN force received another setback at Christmastime when General Walker was killed in a jeep accident while on an inspection tour of his ragged line. General Matthew Ridgway, a hero of World War II in Europe, was chosen to replace him.

General MacArthur, having been so roundly fooled before,

pressed everyone for ever more intelligence. And when General Ridgway arrived in Korea, MacArthur assured him that Ridgway would have command, without interfering as he had with Walker. MacArthur lived up to his promise and did not interfere.

No American command since the South Pacific command in the fall of 1942, when Admiral William F. Halsey took over a half-beaten American force in the Guadalcanal area, had been so dispirited as that in Korea at this Christmas, 1950. Ridgway had his own way of building morale—to show himself to the troops—and it was an effective technique. Morale began to improve.

Marshal Peng was nearly ready with his preparations for the Third Campaign. General Ridgway had good intelligence, and just before the end of the year he saw what Marshal Peng was going to try to do. Using five armies striking almost simultaneously, the Chinese proposed to so flood Korea with manpower that they would literally sweep the Americans south and off the peninsula.

Studying the Chinese plan, Ridgway came up with an unusual defense, but one he thought would work. He stopped thinking in the common terms of gaining and holding ground. This would never work with the Chinese. They had too many men too close by and they could refurbish their armies in a very short time. To try to play that game would be desperately expensive in terms of UN lives. He had another idea. . . .

In those last few days of December 1950 both sides prepared for the coming Chinese offensive. In Washington the American high command was very gloomy.

"It appears from all estimates that the Chinese Communists possess the capability of forcing UN forces out of Korea if they choose to exercise it. The execution of this capability might be prevented by making the effort so costly that they would abandon it. . . ."

The quotation is part of a long directive sent by the Joint Chiefs of Staff to General MacArthur. There, in a nutshell, was a superb analysis of the situation that existed in Korea, and a clue to policy that was to be followed with success by General Ridgway.

To General MacArthur, the JCS announcement signified the end of American military predominance in the world—which indeed it did. MacArthur's heart was torn to bits by this reversal of everything he had ever held dear: victory at all costs, and to hell with the political consequences.

While MacArthur argued with Washington, Ridgway, the representative of a new breed of general officer, prepared to fight the actual battle that was to be fought.

General Ridgway arrived in Korea on December 31, and within hours the Chinese attacked.

Ridgway knew that there was no possibility of holding Seoul. Every senior officer who had every visited the place could see that there was a normal defense line at Kaesong on the 38th parallel, and another series of lines below the Han River, culminating in the Pusan perimeter. But Seoul stuck out on the plain like a big cake waiting for the enemy to come and slice it up, and there was no way the army could keep the Chinese out.

Early on the morning of December 31, Ridgway had his baptism of fire, Chinese style. The drums beat, the Chinese bugles shrieked their unearthly signals, and the Chinese troops marched into battle all along the 38th parallel line. It was what was called from the days of World War I a "general attack." The purpose was to accomplish Mao Zedong's dream, and with a rush, to throw the Americans into panic, causing them to lose control and race for Pusan, thus totally demoralizing the army of the Republic of Korea.

The reason that the ploy did not work lies largely at the feet of a single man, General Ridgway. His command was dispirited. The death of Walker was only the last blow in a series. The errors of judgment and the favoritism by General MacArthur for months of his own man, General Almond, had sapped the command of much of its resilience.

The South Koreans were virtually defeated. MacArthur's pronouncements, running the gamut from arrogance to despair, had left them feeling that they were about to be deserted by the Americans. Washington's comments and the rush to the United Nations to seek a political solution that had earlier been rejected convinced Syngman Rhee that he was about to be abandoned. It was a vital moment, then, when General Ridgway came to see Rhee and told him that he had come to stay. Rhee believed, and from that moment South Korean morale began to pick up.

There was a lot more to be done, and General Ridgway began

to do it; that was made clear during the first hours of the fighting. Marshal Peng had directed his major assault at the Koreans in the UN line, with the unerring idea that they were the weak link. This was so because of both training and morale. When the Chinese hit that morning, the Koreans began to give way.

Eighth Army headquarters had been moved 35 miles south of Seoul, but Ridgway did not stay there. He stayed up front, prowling around behind the line, finding out what was happening, and he learned.

The first thing he learned was that the UN forces could not possibly hold against this surge of manpower from the north, and he did not try to make them hold. He issued very sensible orders.

"Retreat if you must, but make the enemy pay for every yard."

This was something the Americans knew how to do, once again with their artillery and heavy weapons as the enforcing agency.

The Chinese came fast. They bypassed Seoul on both sides and drove across the Han River, so Seoul was lost. The problem then was extrication of the UN troops. It was done. The UN moved back—fast, but not too fast. It was not a rout. By January 4 the Ridgway army had moved back 35 miles to the Han River line.

Marshal Peng was lost in thought. General Zhou had let him down. Peng was not resentful—he had never believed that Zhou would be able to sustain the effort to keep the supplies coming, without trucks and with the bare resources of the North Korean railways. But the supply problem was there, and it showed in the report. Peng's army, after only five days of operations, was running out of supply and could not maintain the pace. It was not the Americans who were defeating him; it was winter, and the Chinese inability to fight this sort of war on a straight offensive basis. The logistics of an attacking army are perhaps six times more difficult than those of a defending army, and Marshal Peng's logistics, by his own statements, were so ridiculous as to be laughable.

And so the first phase of the battle ended, giving the new American general, Ridgway, a chance to rebuild some of the morale of the badly shattered forces. As Ridgway moved around, he evolved his philosophy for meeting Marshal Peng: "maximum punishment, maximum delay."

What Ridgway was planning, in effect, was what Mao planned

when he saw his enemy, the Japanese, in the earlier war, and evolved the strategy of letting the enemy have the territory if he wanted to pay the price. Mao's own strategy was to be turned against the Chinese by an intelligent American general who made the utmost use of his own resources.

── 19 ──

The Americans Learn

In January 1951, the Chinese began to realize that they were not going to be able to drive the Americans into the sea, but now Mao Zedong fell victim to his own propaganda. He had promised the Chinese people a victory and he was unable, at the moment, to give it to them. Marshal Peng saw this very clearly and said as much, but Mao was never a good listener. All Peng did, perhaps, was sacrifice some of the confidence that Mao had in him and thus help to create the climate for the breach that would come fifteen years later. As General Omar Bradley said, the war with the Chinese in Korea should never have been allowed to start. That was the Americans' fault, the fruit of policies of five years. The war should have ended in January 1951. That it did not was the fault of the Chinese who would not accept stalemate when Peng Dehuai knew that it was coming and adjusted his position to become defensive, as is shown in this chapter. This was all because Mao still insisted that he must have a Chinese victory in Korea, long after the opportunity, had there ever been one, was gone....

It is not easy for a general trained in the ways of modern warfare to be thrust suddenly back into fighting a war in which much of his sophisticated equipment is irrelevant, and it is a great compliment to General Ridgway that, unlike MacArthur, he grasped this point from the very beginning and adapted the American war effort to it.

In his own way, General Ridgway was flamboyant, and he was sometimes castigated by the more sober thinkers as a showman. But the showman, as generals Patton and MacArthur had shown in World War II, had his place, and Ridgway used showmanship but did not adopt it for its own sake. One day in the very beginning of his Korea tour he stopped six ROK trucks that were heading away from the front, and asked where they were going. When they said they were retreating, he turned them around, a carbine pointing, and sent them back into the line.

Everywhere he went he made little speeches to small numbers of men, telling them that they had to pull up their socks. There was nothing wrong with them, he said, and no reason they could not win.

He had heard many stories, including that of the Third Battalion of the Seventh Cavalry and how they were left out in the field to die by a retreating Eighth Army. He promised that this would not happen again. He went around finding out the gripes and the real problems, and he made efforts to resolve them. Within a matter of days the grapevine had begun to relate these stories about Ridgway, and American morale had begun to stiffen. At the same time, the Koreans saw their allies beginning to shape up, and that affected them. So two weeks after the beginning of Marshal Peng's winter offensive, strange things were beginning to happen in Korea.

Ridgway was a soldier's general just as Marshal Peng was. Ridgway did not carry a pack, because that was not the American style, but he went everywhere, he talked to everyone, and he left his impression on the men. He ordered his staff officers to get out into the field and find out what was going on.

Privately he had his doubts and his nightmares, and he wrote about them to General Collins, the Chief of the Army General Staff in Washington. But the troops never knew that their general had those doubts. He put up a brave front, like a Kabuki actor, and it served him well.

Ridgway did something else that Marshal Peng would have found hard to do because of Mao's control of the army. He began replacing officers on the staff and in Eighth Army commands with his friends, with men he knew were tough enough to shape the battle and try to win it. After two weeks in Korea he realized that the desire to win had evaporated. There was no secret about this; it was the kind of war it was. But if it couldn't be won, then it had to have another value to the American military. It certainly could not be lost! This was an attitude the Chinese, on their part, failed to recognize about their old friends, now their enemies, the Americans.

What Ridgway needed to carry out his unusual mission was men with a new mindset, not the sort of officers who had been taught to win wars. Soon the American army saw the almost wholesale replacement of the divisional commanders of the Korean war, not because the men who were running the divisions were incompetent, but because if Ridgway was to succeed in this strange assignment he had to have his own men, the men he trusted, and they had to be ready to do precisely what he wanted. Thus were sacrificed a number of careers: Major General Robert B. McClure of the Second Infantry Division, Major General John H. Church of the 24th Division, Major General Hobart R. Gay of the First Cavalry Division, Major General William H. Kean of the 25th Division, and Major General David G. Barr of the Seventh Division. All those names are familiar to students of the Korean war, all had fought bravely in the past. But they were not attuned to General Ridgway's new sort of warfare, so they had to go. There is an irony here, in the firing of Major General David Barr. He had been the last American general officer in charge of U.S. military affairs in China in the late 1940s, and he had recommended against continuing assistance to the faltering Nationalist government.

Ridgway was a tough commander. Because of that and his constant pushing of the troops, he has had credit for "stopping" the Chinese Third Offensive early in January, when actually that was not quite the case. Marshal Peng had run out of supply and had to wait until it was delivered.

The result was salutary in America, where defeatism had almost become the norm. The newspaper correspondents had been writing home about the bad morale. Marguerite Higgins of the New York *Herald Tribune* wrote one of those "high army sources say" articles for her newspaper (the device used by correspondents to air their own feelings) stating that the situation in Korea was hopeless. Ridgway invoked censorship of Miss Higgins; she had not interviewed anyone in his command, he said, and the view was not that of Eighth Army headquarters. Gradually, the rough Ridgway attitude began to seep through the Eighth Army, and morale rose.

As of January 4, 1951, the UN line extended from Pyongtaek on the west coast to Samchok on the east coast. The Chinese had not crossed the Han River, and could not until their supply lines were firmly established. The fighting now was in the Wonju area, an important road center in the middle of the peninsula, and in particular, the road from Chowon-ni to Hoengsong. French and American forces fought the Chinese here, and in four days prevented a breakout. But this was localized fighting and did not represent the Third Campaign.

The Chinese had, in the vernacular, run out of gas. Not only was the supply situation nearly desperate, and in some areas was desperate, but the officers and men were very tired. These troops had fought three campaigns successively without rest, enduring constant cold.

Marshal Peng recalled:

> They had neither an air force nor sufficient anti-aircraft guns to protect them from enemy bombers. Bombed by aircraft and shelled by long-range guns day and night, our troops could not move about in the daytime and they had not had a single day's good rest in three months. It is easy to imagine how tired they were.

The Chinese, with very little food and very little ammunition, were told to keep on advancing south. Near Suwon they were able to do so. But the main point of assault was to be Wonju, and there the Americans were much tougher. After a fight, the Chinese took the town. But the Americans did not flee; they simply moved back about four miles and set up another line.

The Chinese took Chongju, and so they held all the towns to the east of Wonju. The war should have been over. They had Osan and Suwon, and Ichon, and if they took Wonju, yes, that should have been the end.

The Chinese generals were eager and confident. The Americans had moved swiftly before them, giving little impression of strength (except those marines in the northeast), little impression of having a real will to fight. If the Chinese armies could only maintain their pressure, the generals were sure that within a few days they would push the Americans south of the Pusan perimeter, and then where would they go? There was nowhere to go—but to sail for Japan.

Drive on, said the Chinese generals. The colonels and majors and captains looked at the empty mess buckets and wondered how the men could get the energy to drive on. But one did not question orders in the Red Army, so they tightened their belts and ordered the men to drive on.

Wonju, said the generals. Take Wonju and the Americans were finished.

So the Chinese troops drove south and took Wonju. Now there was no food, and the billets were few. The Wonju force left a small guard and moved back up the line searching for food.

In the same way, the Chinese captured Osan, Suwon, and Ichon, but the towns were nothing but clusters of buildings, hollow shells with nothing to eat in them. The U.S. scorched earth policy had succeeded.

For two weeks General Ridgway had set out to find out what was happening along the front line of his command in a most unorthodox fashion. General Earl Partridge, the commander of the Fifth Air Force, came up with the idea. General Partridge, in violation of all the common-sense regulations about two general officers exposing themselves to the enemy unnecessarily, brought an old AT-6 two-seater training plane up to the line. He picked up General Ridgway and flew him around "down on the deck" to see what the enemy was doing. Sometimes they landed. But it was a real tribute to Marshal Peng's men that these two generals, really looking, still found nothing to give them clues about the Chinese. Everywhere the snow seemed undisturbed. Nowhere did they see a single soldier or a single vehicle. They saw no campfires. As far as observation was concerned, there were no Chinese south of the Han River.

There was only one way to find out what was going on, and that was to send men on the ground. General Ridgway considered that course. But where?

On January 14 intelligence patrols on the edges of the American line reported some sort of buildup north of Osan and Suwon. General Ridgway decided to act. The 20th Infantry attacked on the right flank, supported by armor, and moved along the highway northward. The thrust met only light opposition, almost like sniper fire, all the way. But on the edge of Osan they stirred up a small band of Chinese and had a brief firefight, the Chinese with small arms and the Americans with arms and armor. Quickly enough, the Chinese vanished under this preponderence of enemy fire.

So encouraging was this experience to General Ridgway that he decided to launch a more serious operation the next day. The Americans certainly needed it. They had been on the run for three months, with the solidity of morale about like that of Swiss cheese.

They called this little patrol work "Operation Wolfhound." Despite its only limited success, it *was* a success, and that made all concerned feel a lot better about this new war.

On January 16 the task force moved to Suwon, with the same experience: success and very little fighting.

Still another probing action was taken by the Eighth Cavalry on January 22. Once again Ridgway called for armor, and got the 70th Tank Battalion. The tanks and the infantry moved up the Suwon-Wonju road, and not until they had gone a good way above Suwon did they encounter resistance. When the resistance became firm, they stopped, exchanged a few more rounds, and then pulled back. The general had wanted information and now he had it. The Chinese were there, up above the towns. Why they chose to stay thus Ridgway did not know, but he did know that for some reason Marshal Peng's drive south had stopped of its own accord. He did not need to know any more. Ridgway decided it was time, and the efforts to improve American morale had worked well enough, to carry out an American offensive and prove to the people in Tokyo and the United States that he had meant what he told Dr. Rhee, that he had come to Korea to stay.

General Collins came to Korea at this point, full of concern and the worries of a Washington that was still in shock. He was delighted to see the change, talk of offense instead of retreat. He held a press conference and sent the word back to America that, indeed, the United States was going to stay in Korea.

Marshal Peng read that story in the press dispatches. His staff continued to be punctilious in their examination of the UN news dispatches, which still were their primary source of intelligence about the enemy's plans and strategies.

But that did not matter much to Marshal Peng at this point. He was chain-smoking again, lost in thought—and not very positive thought at the moment. What was a field general to do when the problem was completely beyond his control? Too many of his supply "horses," the soldiers and civilians with the A-frames on their backs, were turning up frozen in the snow. Too many of the supplies destined for the front were not reaching the front.

So the Americans prepared to go on the offensive. Marshal Peng's real efforts just now were devoted along the 38th parallel. He could already see what was going to happen, and his troops were building fortifications along the line, in anticipation of American counterattacks. These would come, and Peng knew they would involve many tanks and much artillery; that was the American way. So he was preparing now to sacrifice the three armies on the southern banks of the Han River.

20

The Meat Grinder

War is never pretty, but most wars until Korea had been fought for definite goals: capture the enemy's territory and capital city, and he is defeated. Or grind him down to defeat as the Allies ground the Germans in 1918, exhausting his manpower and his resources. Or overwhelm him with destruction of his cities and his territory, as did the Allies to the Germans and the Japanese in World War II.

But there is another sort of war, which involves killing, killing, killing, without regard for any of the old considerations, such as position or possession of territory. And that is the sort of war the Korean war became in 1951. This was the antecedent to the "body count" war of Vietnam fifteen years later. And it was invented in Korea by General Ridgway. . . .

General Ridgway really had very few options to govern his offensive conduct of the new Korean war with the Chinese. Washington was not going to reinforce him; they told him so. The reasons were two: first, the shortage of American manpower and to guard against any number of threats from the Soviet Union and its satellite nations. The second reason was enough to give a military man real pause, concern about the world in which he lived and his profession. The American politicians in Washington wanted the American military to take it easy because they were trying to achieve a political solution to the Korean problem in the United

Nations. Of course, the military had to fight and stay in Korea, but it must be "rash." General MacArthur, naturally, found this almost beyond the fringes of reason. But it was the new world politics, and it affected the military operations of the war in every way.

Generally speaking, General Ridgway's solution to his strategic problem was admirable from the political as well as the military point of view. He would not worry about holding or capturing ground once he had straightened out his main line of resistance. What he did intend to do was punish the enemy and cause so many casualties by the controlled use of firepower and by coordination of air and ground attacks that the Chinese would tire of the war.

On January 25 Ridgway began. The idea was to make an assault, draw the Chinese into attack, and then slaughter them with the artillery and the air strikes. In the first week, Ridgway estimated that he was exacting 2100 casualties a day on the Chinese. General MacArthur was now talking in Tokyo about "the recapture of Seoul" and the drive north. Ridgway was more interested in casualties, and in the discomfiture of an enemy that now had very long supply lines.

It was apparent to the Chinese that in mid-January in the Wonju area they met an entirely new sort of American resistance. The Chinese 40th Field Army, here in the Wonju area, was feeling the brunt of it. On January 13 the 120th Division of that army massed around Hoengsong, but then strange things began to happen. The American artillery seemed to gain new eyes, and the artillery fire became a real problem, day and night. There were many Chinese casualties, although there was virtually no infantry action. The Americans were hard to find. They lurked back behind their lines and did not venture out, and then in came the artillery shells. "Hit the ground" became a sort of swear word in the Chinese ranks.

The Chinese soldiers in the line sensed the difference. All the way south from the Chongchon River, where the 40th Field Army had begun the pursuit, the Americans had been quick to move, almost to flee; sometimes they did, indeed, flee. But now, in January, there was no more fleeing.

Marshal Peng counseled his generals: "They are trying to lure us now into their fortified areas along the Rokdong River. We will not go that way."

At Wonju the Americans had put up surprising resistance. When the 40th Field Army stopped and began to take stock, the Americans attacked them!

The shelling continued.

The new orders to the Chinese to advance came just after they captured Wonju, but this time General Ridgway had other ideas, for a move called "Operation Thunderbolt." The Chinese attack south from Wonju petered out after January 15, because the promised rations did not come, and the 40th Field Army was too hungry to launch a major offensive.

The American testing continued. On January 28 General Almond ordered the 23rd Infantry to make a patrol in the Twin Tunnels area north of the Han River. It seemed that there was a soft spot there that would give the UN forces an opportunity to launch an attack and punish the enemy.

The 23rd Infantry patrol ran into trouble and had to climb a hill, set up a defense perimeter, and hold it half the night, while waiting for rescue. The patrol was rescued, after having taken heavy casualties. What was new was that it had succeeded in punishing the Chinese attackers almost as badly as it had been hit. This sort of American spirit was unfamiliar to the Chinese.

General Ridgway was ready to launch his offensive, but the Chinese supply train suddenly tightened up, and Marshal Peng could move again. This time the Chinese decided to continue the drive from Wonju south on the central front.

This came just as General Ridgway ordered the 23rd Infantry to follow its Twin Tunnels patrol with an attack on the town of Chipyong-ni. The Chinese were moving at Hoengsong. And so a major confrontation was inevitable. The 23rd Infantry moved to Chipyong-ni, a town a half mile long, lying like a snake along the single track railroad, encircled by hills that stood above the rice paddies. The town was not much any more; half of it had been destroyed in the last fighting there. But soon, very soon, it would become a symbol of the new war in Korea.

An American artillery battery was moving up the narrow road three miles northwest of Hoengsong to support the Republic of

Korea Eighth Division to the north. They were backed up by a guard of ROK troops. They stopped for the night, and during the night the Chinese attacked. The ROK troops bolted, and many of the American artillerymen were killed in the hand-to-hand fighting. They managed to rally and pull themselves together by morning, but that night they were attacked again, by Chinese in division strength. In the end only two men of the five hundred American artillerymen survived these ambushes.

The loss put a crimp in General Ridgway's plans for an offensive, but it did not stop him. He augmented the forces sent to Chipyong-ni. Colonel Paul Freeman's 23rd Infantry also got support from the 37th Field Artillery Battalion. The plan was to move up to the Han River line, where they would dig in and prepare to punish the Chinese offensive they expected.

Ridgway conceived of the Chipyong-ni salient as important enough to warrant all he could give it. He sent up a battery of anti-aircraft flak wagons and the 603rd Field Artillery Battalion with six 155-mm howitzers. The artillery that the Chinese hated so much was certainly represented here in strength.

The infantry and the artillery set up area defenses and dug in. The artillery set up its fields of fire, as did the machine-gunners. The artillery registered on all the avenues of approach. The mortars were well distributed among the infantry platoons. South of the 23rd Infantry was a French battalion which had moved into the Twin Tunnels area after that American patrol had been ambushed there a few days earlier.

The Americans did not know it, but they were almost in the middle of the Chinese 40th Field Army zone, and they were virtually surrounded by more than a division of Chinese troops.

On February 1, the Chinese attacked, hoping to start once more their offensive to the south. The attack began at about 2 A.M. as usual, with preparation by mortaring and many grenades, and then the bugling and the shuffling of feet and the popping of rifles. The French held, and as light began to shade through the darkness they drove the Chinese out of their position. But the Chinese came back from three sides. So fierce was this fighting that a 57-mm anti-tank gun was turned on the Chinese at point-blank range, and five shells killed 23 Chinese soldiers. Even so the French were in danger of being overrun, until air strikes came in. An airdrop of ammunition saved a company of French who were completely cut off from the others. The Chinese finally retreated, after they had suffered an estimated four hundred casualties.

Then, on February 5, General Ridgway began his winter offensive with an attack on the town of Hongchon, using two ROK corps, plus the American Seventh and Second divisions.

In the beginning the attack did not go too well. The South Koreans were really no match for the Chinese and North Koreans, and the 40th Army shattered three South Korean divisions on the first night. The ROK Eighth Division collapsed. This left the American Second Division in trouble on the left flank, which soon threatened the new American position at Chipyong-ni.

The Chinese claims of victory were broadcast by Radio Pyongyang, although to hear the broadcasts one would think the Chinese had virtually nothing to do with the war, and that the North Koreans had been winning steadily since the previous June. This was the new offensive, said Radio Pyongyang, which would drive the Americans into the sea and put an end to the war.

The Chinese attacked all along the line established by the Americans, and General Ridgway's artillery pounded them as they came. The soldiers quickly had a name for the new strategy, Ridgway's "meat grinder," the idea being to chop the Chinese into little pieces. The Chinese gained ground, but their casualties rose.

The fighting here went on for a week. Chipyong-ni became a salient in the American line. Colonel Freeman wanted to withdraw, but to Ridgway the town was a symbol, and when Freeman learned that, he said cheerfully that they might as well fight it out at Chipyong-ni as anywhere. And so they prepared to resist a major Chinese effort to surround and take the position.

On the night of February 13, the Chinese attacked in great force. They started about 8 P.M. with the usual noises, and then the troops continued to come, although the American machine guns cut them down. As always with the Chinese attacks, the fighting was fierce and close at hand.

When the Chinese swarmed up the French hill, bugles blowing and whistles shrieking, they were in for a surprise. The French had found an old air raid siren that worked (with a hand crank), which they unlimbered. It unnerved the first Chinese soldiers, and when the French soldiers began hurling grenades even faster than the Chinese, the Red line broke and collapsed.

But they came again and again.

Captain John Elledge took five men up to a hillside machine gun post which had been knocked out by a mortar shell. They held the position all night. A group of American soldiers seemed likely to break under the Chinese assault. Captain Thomas Heath shouted at them:

"Get back up on the hill. You'll die here anyway, you might as well go back up on the hill and die there."

The Chinese kept coming, but this time the American artillery was there in force. The "meat grinder" was working. Tanks, planes, and guns chewed up the enemy all day long as the fighting continued. At the end of the day the UN people were still holding. General Ridgway came up that second day and examined the battlefield. These Chinese had removed most of their casualties, as they always did, but Colonel Freeman, who had seen a great deal of this war, estimated the casualties as the highest he had ever seen and the fighting as the most fierce. He estimated 4200 Chinese casualties!

General Ridgway felt that he had found the answer to fighting the Chinese hordes: Fix strong positions, hold them, and bring in plenty of artillery and napalm to punish the enemy. On the line symbolized by Chipyong-ni, the Eighth Army had fought the Chinese to a standstill.

21

The End of MacArthur

*Anyone who wonders why the Korean war lasted so long after stalemate
had been reached will find the answer in the next chapter of this book: The
presence, and then the ghost, of General Douglas MacArthur prolonged
the war. The general's defenders will rise to claim that the prisoner of war
issue and the issues of freedom and the rights of man, not accepted by the
Chinese, prolonged the war. But the fact was that the aggressive statements
made by General MacArthur about the need to carry the war onto Chinese
territory played into Mao Zedong's hands and made it impossible for less
militant members of the Communist Central Committee to have any decisive
influence on the war. . . .*

General Ridgway had found a satisfactory method of fighting the
Chinese hordes, if anything about the new Korean war could be
called satisfactory. The Ridgway method would not produce victory, but then victory was no longer the UN aim in Korea, and
sharp appraisal would say that it never should have been the aim.
The sort of war that General Ridgway was now going to fight would
take enormous patience and seem to be totally unrewarding.
Whether or not it *was* unrewarding would depend on what America
expected to achieve in Korea. The original war aim of restoring
the 38th parallel equilibrium was perfectly valid, although at this
point it was no longer accepted by the Chinese, who had yet to

learn that they could not win the war any more than the Americans could, if the Americans were willing to fight the Ridgway war.

Apparently eclipsed in all this was General Douglas MacArthur, who, after the dreadful miscalculation that thrust the Chinese into the war, had discreetly retired to running his occupation of Japan and letting Ridgway have the headaches of Korea. When Ridgway seemed to be making progress, MacArthur, with an old performer's sense of timing, decided it was time to get back on center stage.

On February 18 General Ridgway prepared a new operation, based on his "meat grinder" theory. It was called "Operation Killer."

In this new operation the Eighth Army would attack across the Han River, using two divisions against four Chinese field armies. This plan was not as unreasonable as it might seem, for Operation Killer was another probe, designed to concentrate enormous firepower on a given area for a brief time, inflict maximum losses on the enemy, and then retire.

Ridgway outlined the plan to his generals on February 19. That same day he held a briefing for the journalists, and told them what he was doing and why. They were not to write anything yet—he did not wish to tip off the enemy as to what was coming—but he wanted them to be ready. The UN forces were going back on the attack, taking the initiative away from the Chinese.

Operation Killer would begin on February 21, he said. Naturally General Ridgway had kept General MacArthur apprised of his plans, but he was hardly ready for what happened next. MacArthur showed up at Ridgway headquarters in Korea on February 20, called a press conference, and told the reporters, "I have just ordered a resumption of the offensive."

It was not true, of course. MacArthur had been skulking in Tokyo for weeks, while Ridgway rebuilt the morale of the Eighth Army. Privately, until now MacArthur's attitude had been almost totally defeatist since the first Chinese attack. Now, seeing that an offensive was to be launched, MacArthur was trying to take credit for it.

That action can certainly be criticized on the grounds of selfishness. But what was even more intolerable and dangerous was that MacArthur tipped off the Chinese that the attack (which was supposed to surprise) would come in 24 hours. If a junior officer had done this he would certainly have been court-martialed.

Operation Killer was launched, but in reality it petered out because MacArthur had cut the ground from under it.

The operation had another effect, very negative from the military point of view. When word reached Washington that the operation was called "Operation Killer" and that its purpose was to kill Chinese in droves, this new aspect of the Korean war provided the opposing Republican Party with a new opportunity to criticize the Democratic Administration. The Republicans were as cynical as they could be in their charge that this was inhuman behavior —the Republicans had certainly not shown any previous sympathy for the Chinese Communists. The State Department also took up the cause, saying that such concepts as Operation Killer made it difficult for them to negotiate with the Chinese to end the war. This also, of course, was nonsense. What made it difficult to negotiate with the Chinese was that at this point Mao Zedong still thought he would win the war and drive American influence out of Asia, so he was not interested in practically any of the proposals the Americans made.

Because of all this, the Joint Chiefs of Staff gave General Ridgway a dressing-down for carelessness in public relations. This reproach certainly did not improve his morale or that of the Eighth Army, whose biggest problem was that the men often were confused about what they were supposed to be fighting for. Small wonder!

Having seen that the war was not lost as he had thought, MacArthur began to take a new interest in it, and to try once again to stamp his imprimatur on the character of the war. The first sign of this was his statement that unless Washington would permit attacks on the Chinese in China, only stalemate could result from the Korean war. The fact was that the Joint Chiefs of Staff had already formulated a new policy: What the Americans now wanted to achieve in Korea was a return to the 38th parallel division. They had rejected all MacArthur's plans, including the employment of the Chiang Kaishek government in the war.

But without regard to Washington, MacArthur was becoming more belligerent once again.

"The concept advanced by some that we should establish a line across Korea and enter into positional warfare is wholly unrealistic and illusory."

Yet, of course, this was precisely the new policy of the government of the United States.

In the winter of 1951 two separate wars were flaming in Korea: one the war of the Joint Chiefs of Staff and General Ridgway, and the other the war of General MacArthur. The latter was waged largely through the world press. Noting the care with which Marshal Peng and the Communist leadership in Beijing read the United Nations war correspondence, it would not be hard to imagine how the Chinese reacted to such statements as this one of mid-February:

". . . Unless the authority is given to strike enemy bases in Manchuria, our ground forces as presently constituted cannot with safety attempt major operations in North Korea."

But who wanted major operations in North Korea? The national policy now called for a cease-fire and a return to the 38th parallel division. The Joint Chiefs of Staff were committed to that policy. Only General MacArthur wanted new operations in North Korea, but the Chinese believed his statements represented American policy.

MacArthur had taken charge before. Who was to believe he would not do it again?

Marshal Peng read on:

"First," MacArthur said, "I would attack the Chinese supply lines. I would regain the Seoul line as the base for future ground operations. I would then clear the enemy rear all across the top of North Korea by massive air attacks."

Imagine those massive air attacks to cut the supply line from the top—when in the past the Americans had not even been able to find the supply line, and still were not able to interdict supplies very successfully from the air, because the Chinese moved on foot and at night under heavy cover.

MacArthur had an idea even more destructive to humanity. "If I were not permitted to attack the massed enemy reinforcements across the Yalu, in order to destroy its bridges, I would sever Korea from China by laying a field of radioactive wastes, the byproducts of atomic manufacture—across all the major lines of enemy supply. . . ."

It was no less than chemical warfare. The Americans claimed stoutly that they did not use chemical warfare in Korea, except napalm, but how were the Chinese to differentiate between the national policy and the man who had been making the national policy in the Korean war since the beginning?

Further, MacArthur promised to use the forces of Chiang Kaishek to fight the Chinese Communists. They would be landed and would fight their way—where? Why, back into China, of course. MacArthur was going to rekindle the Chinese civil war.

Given these statements from the man who was known to have been making the decisions, what were the Chinese to believe? They believed, of course, that soon again MacArthur would have his way, and that unless the Americans could be resoundingly defeated, the danger to the Chinese state would always remain. Small wonder, then, that the Americans and British and other leaders at the United Nations got nowhere with their peace moves.

Ridgway continued his "meat grinder" tactics. MacArthur stood back in Tokyo and warned: "The war of maneuver, with the object of inflicting heavy punishment on the enemy, has worked well, but we must not fall into the error of evaluating such successes as leading to the enemy's defeat. . . ."

And so, as Ridgway rampaged on the ground, causing real problems for Marshal Peng and his generals, MacArthur raged in Tokyo, causing real problems for the Americans in Washington and New York.

At the end of February, MacArthur outdid himself. He demanded the right to bomb the hydroelectric plants of the Yalu River basin. Marshal Peng read and took note, and his generals renewed their determination to fight this war to a finish in which the Americans would be expelled from all Asia.

By March 1, the Ridgway forays had accomplished two purposes: They had killed, wounded, and captured many Chinese; they had also straightened out the UN line, which now ran from a point above the 38th parallel on the east, which was held by the South Koreans, down to a point below the 38th parallel on the west. Seoul had been recaptured, but it was a meaningless gesture, for the city was virtually uninhabitable, after having changed hands four times, each time after heavy fighting.

In the United Nations, a number of countries were beginning to be more sympathetic to China because of the American attitude toward China's admission to the United Nations and particularly to the Security Council. Britain and other nations favored Chinese admission, and American recalcitrance kept China out. The Chinese reaction, incorporating all these fears in Korea and at home, continued to be deep distrust of any American initiatives. A special UN cease-fire committee came up with a five-part peace plan which called for a cease-fire, an attempt to bring the two Koreas together, and a discussion of Chinese entry into the United Nations. The Americans accepted it, but the Chinese, still believing they could win the war, rejected it.

The matter of the 38th parallel came up again soon—on March 7, in fact, with the launching of "Operation Ripper." This was Ridgway's attempt to do to the Chinese on the west and the North Koreans on the east what the Chinese had done in November: to drive a wedge between enemy forces.

The major target was Chunchon, just eight miles from the 38th parallel.

A reporter raised the inevitable question of the 38th parallel at a press conference held by President Truman. Truman refused to discuss it. But that same day the State Department came up with a statement of policy which indicated that the United States (not MacArthur) had given up the idea of unification of Korea by force. The Americans would continue their "meat grinder" policy and might move ten to twenty miles north of the 38th parallel, but when the line reached that point, the Americans were to stop.

That was American policy, but it was not MacArthur's policy, and from Tokyo the general continued to speak out. To whom were Marshal Peng and Mao Zedong to listen—to General Ridgway and President Truman, or to General MacArthur?

By March 1951 Marshal Peng could see that he and the other leaders of Communist China had made a serious miscalculation. They were not going to be able to drive the Americans into the sea. There was just too much firepower, and the caliber of the Chinese troops coming as "volunteers" into Korea was lower and lower. Colonel Yang Shixian, a regimental commander of the 39th Field Army, complained to his general about the replacements:

"Half of them have never seen an M-1 rifle," he said.

This was very important, because much of the Chinese army was equipped with the M-1, an American weapon, courtesy of the U.S. aid program to Chiang Kaishek and the capture of American weapons in the early days of the Chinese intervention in Korea. Some of the troops had trained with Soviet rifles. But most of them had not trained at all. They averaged less than a month of basic training, and most of them could not even march and keep in step. Their weapons training was minuscule—there was no time for it, so rapidly did General Ridgway's "meat grinder" eat up cannon fodder. Many of these men could not even fire a rifle, let alone hit anything with it. Half of them could not read or write; they were for the most part simple peasants. But they could die, and what they lacked in military training they made up in revolutionary zeal. Their political officers were indefatigable, instilling in the troops the reasons for their dying: They were making the world safe from American imperialism. "Manpower will triumph over machines," was the slogan, which had come straight from Chairman Mao.

But now Peng had the unpleasant task of telling the Chairman that manpower was not triumphing over machines. It was able to meet the machines half way, and that was all.

Mao listened gravely to Marshal Peng's report. There was no question of disbelief; Peng had too great a reputation for honesty and openness for that. But Mao was not ready to give up his belief that manpower would win the war for China.

"Have you annihilated many Americans?"

Peng had to admit that they had not. The only complete regiment they had destroyed had been that of the Seventh Infantry in the opening days of the war in the northeast. Since then they had "dealt crushing blows" against the Turks, and against French and Belgian and Luxembourg units, and of course they had wiped out thousands of Syngman Rhee puppet troops. But as for the Americans, they had never been able to use the time-honored tactics of major envelopment and crush. They had enveloped American units of battalion size a number of times. But each time the Americans had held in their perimeter long enough for rescue. And, of course, the American air strikes in the daylight hours and the American artillery firing at night did not help. American firepower was just too great for the Chinese to manage the old way of war.

Mao mused over this. It was a great shock to him. But he could also see—from reading the world press and from reports filtering into China from the Britons in high diplomatic places in Washington and London who were spying for the Russians—that the Western powers were sick of the war. Yes, even the Americans had now adjusted their war aims to a return to the 38th parallel division.

And what about the 38th parallel? Said Peng: "The Americans must be punished. If they want out of Korea and the 38th parallel line resumed, they will have to evacuate Taiwan and promise to keep their fleet away. That way we can solve the Taiwan problem."

Mao was not very pleased when Marshal Peng told him he was withdrawing north of the Hangang River. Actually he had already withdrawn. On March 14 the Americans crossed the river, and the next day, with the ROK First Division, had marched into Seoul.

But Mao was still resilient, and still ready to wait for victory.

He sighed. "Win a quick victory if you can. If you can't, win a slow one."

And so Marshal Peng knew that he was to go back to Korea and continue to feed cannon fodder into the "meat grinder." Marshal Peng returned to Korea with orders to carry out a new campaign, but before he arrived, a new operation was begun by the Americans. It aimed to straighten out the UN line, following the 38th parallel, except on the west, where it would follow the Imjin River to the sea. This was quite satisfactory to the Joint Chiefs of Staff and to President Truman. The Ridgway operations, now minus their fierce names, were devastating to the enemy, but conducted without showmanship or fanfare. They did not interfere with the continuing efforts in the United Nations for a negotiated settlement.

But if the American government forced the army to stop at the 38th parallel, it was going to prevent General MacArthur from carrying out his mission, the general told reporters.

And what was MacArthur's mission?

Why, that was simple: the reunification of Korea as one country.

And how was that to be accomplished?

By bringing Korea under the government of Syngman Rhee, President of the Republic of South Korea, which now was the only legitimate government in Korea, the North Koreans having forfeited their rights by their attack on South Korea.

Whoever told General MacArthur that he was the arbiter of the world's politics is not known, but the fervency of his belief could not be denied.

As "Operation Rugged" was prepared, the problem of MacArthur became more irritating. The CIA agents in Tokyo reported that the general was conducting conversations with many foreign diplomats, trying to use various pressures to force the Truman Administration to give General MacArthur his head. To Truman, this was the intolerable action. He could disagree with MacArthur, and put up with his insubordination, but to go to foreigners was disloyalty he could not tolerate. For two weeks the matter simmered.

MacArthur lent fuel to the fires of discontent with a running barrage of correspondence. Representative Joseph Martin, a right-wing Republican, received a letter which repeated all the MacArthur arguments about the need for any and all measures to win the war.

Once the UN forces had reached the 38th parallel line, Truman decided it was time for a new diplomatic effort to stabilize that line. He informed General MacArthur that he was going to do this. MacArthur thereupon issued his own personal call to the Chinese.

"It is no longer possible for you to win this war," he said. "You must talk peace."

Mao Zedong had just been told the same by his own Marshal Peng and had rejected that advice. Now, furious, he rejected it out of hand and publicly promised a new offensive to drive the Americans out of Korea and win the war.

The Republicans chose this moment to launch a political campaign. Republican Representative Joseph Martin read MacArthur's letter in the House. The letter warned that if the U.S. government did not take MacArthur's advice, and if the United

States did not win the war in Korea and wipe communism off the face of China—then, said the general, the unthinkable would occur and the Russian Communists would take over the world.

General MacArthur had been playing this tune for two years, and Washington was tired of it. Truman and his advisors agreed that something had to be done to stop MacArthur's breach of military protocol, and even more, his defiance of the President, who had called on him to stop talking.

What to do? What to do? moaned the Joint Chiefs, whose authority MacArthur had always spurned.

What to do? asked a young general of the new school who happened into General Collins's office.

"Why, general, when we have somebody who won't obey orders, we get rid of him."

And, so goes the story, General Collins looked at the young general with wide eyes, seeing for the first time that it was possible to commit *lèse majesté* and survive.

Thus General MacArthur was recalled to America, fired by President Truman.

The results were as foreseen. General MacArthur was a legend, an institution, if you will, in all America. Even people who disagreed with him entirely were shocked when he was fired.*

The manner of MacArthur's firing was unfortunate, a result of the democratic process in which the press had every right to pry. Truman had arranged for Army Secretary Frank Pace, Jr., to go to Tokyo, have a quiet talk with the general, and inform him apologetically that he had to be relieved for the good of the nation.

---

*I was a young journalist in those days, working on the *Denver Post*. I disagreed, as an editorial writer, with virtually everything General MacArthur did. I had also felt his lash as a correspondent in Korea just after the end of World War II, when I had accompanied a shipful of Koreans being repatriated from China. I had written about the conditions of the voyage, which were not salutary, and MacArthur had thereupon decreed that no correspondents would be allowed to accompany repatriation. Still, I participated as much as anyone in the emotional bath that Americans underwent in the next two weeks. When MacArthur made his "old soldiers never die" speech to Congress, tears came to my eyes. It was an occasion of national grief, perhaps as much for the situation in which Americans found themselves as much as for the man who put us there.

But in Washington someone leaked the story to the press, and then the White House panicked and issued a statement before Secretary Pace could leave.

MacArthur then assumed the stance of Caesar wronged, and he took every advantage of it. In Tokyo he exhibited the shock of a righteous man but the resignation of a good citizen who takes his medicine. The nation cried and cheered. He flew home, and his flight was chronicled by the media.

He rode up Broadway in a ticker-tape parade, and was invited to address the two houses of Congress in a joint session. He made a highly charged emotional speech, recalling his long years of service. Then he disappeared into a corporate job and the war could go on.

General Ridgway was appointed to take MacArthur's job as commander of American forces in the Far East and commander of the UN forces in Asia. Lieutenant General James A. Van Fleet was ordered to Korea to take over the job as commander of the UN fighting land forces, the Eighth Army.

In America the whole of U.S. policy from the beginning was brought out by the Republicans for a new airing. The current policy survived this attack and remained official. The China lobby and the anticommunist hawks lost another round.

In Korea, the UN forces had been advancing steadily at the end of March and the beginning of April. The idea was not to drive to the Yalu River, but to do enough damage to the Chinese armies to slow down the offense Ridgway knew they would launch in a few weeks.

The MacArthur flap and the changes in command caused a hiatus in movement, of course, but military operations did not come to a total halt.

The Seventh Marines and the First Cavalry Division prepared to attack Chunchon. Then came word that the Chinese had built up their forces in an area called the Iron Triangle, a plain in the mountains bounded by the towns of Kumwha, Corwon, and Pyong-yang. The First Marine Division prepared to attack here.

After a hiatus of a week caused by the MacArthur affair, on

April 21, 1951 the marines moved up the center of Korea. Everything was very quiet in the forest. There was no sign of the enemy, save the smell of wood smoke and the smoke itself that drifted across the forests, the Chinese smoke screen, to shield its own troop movements. So General Van Fleet knew his enemy was there, but as usual he was an elusive enemy, very hard to pin down, and very hard to assess.

22

Chinese Spring Offensive

The "meat grinder" tactics of the Americans continued under General Van Fleet. The war had settled down to trench warfare of the sort that nobody could win, and everyone on both sides knew it. Both sides suffered casualties, and for what? On the Chinese side, the war bolstered the ego of Mao Zedong. He was forever coming up with new advice. After Peng Dehuai had sacrificed thousands of men to try to carry out Mao's orders to destroy whole units of the enemy, and had failed even to destroy anything larger than a battalion, Mao advised Peng to do what he had been doing all along, knocking off outposts and small company- or platoon-sized units. But as Peng knew, it always cost the Chinese three or four times as many men as it cost the Americans. And the local commanders were growing tired of a slaughter that seemed to have no point. . . .

Because the Joint Chiefs of Staff had now adopted a program calling for compromise and return to the 38th parallel division of Korea, the tendency in America was to wonder when it would all be over. But the Chinese had no such feelings of stalemate; they still intended to win the war and drive the Americans out of Asia. That was announced policy. It was also the deep belief of Mao and his associates on the Central Committee that it must be the future policy of China.

To strengthen that policy the Chinese had new commitments

from the Soviet Union for equipment and supplies, and for an air force. Soviet planes had appeared in the skies above Korea a few times in 1950 and early 1951, but with no sustained effort. The Soviets did not want to get directly involved in the Korean struggle, and when some of their planes were shot down and were identified by the Americans, the Soviets desisted from air activity.

The first serious Chinese air activity in Korea began in January, when the Chinese air force brought in about six hundred planes to support their winter offensive. General Wu Xiu Chuan, the commander of the Chinese air forces, said he hoped to bring at least twice that number of planes to Korea by summer.

After the first Chinese victories and the Chinese drive south, the Americans retreated 275 miles from the Chongchon area to the 37th parallel. The UN air forces moved back to the airfields in Japan for operations. There was no point in staying in Korea after the loss of Seoul. The logistics were all wrong. So in the winter of 1951 the Chinese dominated the air over North Korea and the Yalu. They built new airfields and rebuilt old ones. And they brought in their aircraft, which included some MIG jet fighter planes. When the Americans first saw these, they assumed that they were manned by Soviet fliers, but it was not so. For a year the Chinese had been training under Russian teachers, and now they had their own jet air force. They practiced endlessly, patrolling, but usually avoiding any American planes that came their way. Still, that whole area between the Chongchon River and the Yalu was christened by the Americans "MIG Alley."

As the Chinese saw it, the Fifth Campaign of the Korean war covered the next two years. Marshal Peng realized that the Chinese would not be able to throw the Americans out of Korea in one lightning campaign. When he so reported, Chairman Mao ordered a change in tactics, but not in strategy. Mao said China was willing to devote years to the process, and millions of men if necessary. They would attack, retreat, attack, retreat, and they would establish their own "meat grinder" system.

At the beginning of the Chinese intervention, the Chinese pilots had been tyros, but as time wore on they became more skillful.

The Americans began to introduce F-84 E and F-86 jets, which outmatched the Soviet-built MIGs. Beginning in the spring of 1951, the B-29s suffered some losses in MIG Alley. The mission of the American air forces then was to knock out the enemy air potential.

By the spring of 1951 each side had about half a million men fighting in Korea; 227,000 of them American; 400,000 South Korean; 400,000 Chinese and 100,000 North Korean. The war had changed subtly; the Chinese Communists had come in with manpower alone, but through Soviet help they received more sophisticated weapons.

As usual with the Chinese, the 1951 war plans were known to the rank and file. The Americans learned from prisoners that the Chinese spring offensive was to start on April 22 and the main line of assault would be in the center, where the UN IX and X Corps were operating in the Pakyong-Chongnam-Chunchon area.

The Chinese attacked, and once again the ROK force failed. This time the ROK Sixth Division collapsed and the Koreans fled south, clogging the roads so that the U.S. First Marine Division, which had to stop the Chinese advance, had great difficulty in moving vehicles. The Chinese technique was the usual encirclement of battalion-sized units.

The Chinese moved in great strength, but the marines held, although two marine battalions in one area faced two regiments of the 40th Field Army.

On April 24, because the Korean forces had failed, the marines had to retreat, but they did so slowly and methodically.

It was the same all along the line. The Chinese hordes, now equipped with artillery, better machine guns, and better small arms, launched ferocious attacks, hoping to drive the UN forces back past Seoul once more. There, along the Imjin River where the British were fighting, the UN held, about 25 miles north of Seoul, and in less than a week the Chinese suffered so many casualties that they had to abandon the assault.

If the Chinese had assessed the war as they did in the early days, this would have been the Fifth Campaign all by itself, but there was no Chinese victory. Marshal Peng did not want to face the negative reaction to a failed campaign, so the wording in the propaganda was changed. This defeat for the Chinese was ignored and the whole campaign became only a paragraph in the history of the war.

The failed Chinese advance was followed immediately by a UN advance. By May 10, the marines and the army and the Koreans and British had cleared up the Kimpo peninsula and the area around Seoul, which had been partially overrun by the Chinese.

Next, UN forces prepared to grind up some more Chinese troops, inducing the Chinese to counterattack on the new line called "No Name," which ran west from above Seoul, a little north of the 38th parallel.

In the first week of the new campaign, the UN forces moved up about ten miles, just enough to entice the Chinese into attacking, so that the Americans could use superior firepower to make mince-meat of another Chinese division. But the Chinese were learning. This time they planned to renew their air offensive with a thousand planes.

When the Far East Air Force generals learned of the change in Chinese plans, they rounded up all their resources, and sent B-29s and fighter planes from land bases and carriers to strike the 50 new Chinese airfields. What they did at Sinuiju on May 9 was typical: they hit Sinuiju with 312 planes, destroying 100 buildings and 15 planes on the ground. Sinuiju never recovered from the damage.

In the first move the forces of Marshal Peng had hit the center of the UN line. Their second effort would be against the west side, where they were hoping to do what they had done in the first Chinese offensive in October 1950. But this time the Chinese faced a new breed of U.S. officers, typified by Lieutenant Colonel Wallace Hanes of the U.S. Second Division. He was told that his battalion was to defend Hill 800. "Okay," he said, "if we are to defend, we will defend."

Lieutenant Colonel Hanes put his troops to work building deep bunkers and fields of fire. The men hauled logs and made sand-bags. How many sandbags would they need? About 20,000, said the colonel. His men gasped, but they started filling up sandbags. They secured the services of 700 Korean laborers. Twenty thousand sandbags? They carried 37,000 sandbags up the hill, 1385 rolls of barbed wire, and 6000 pickets for the wire. Thirty-two oxen dragged a whole section of 4.2-inch mortars and enough ammunition, said some of the soldiers, to last a month. Lieutenant Colonel Hanes did not think that was enough. They also brought up cases of hand grenades by the score.

The Americans adopted a new defense technique here in the beginning of the second phase of the Chinese Fifth Campaign, because they had served in the line long enough to know how the Chinese would fight.

By May 10, the Second Division reported that the Chinese were massing for a new offensive up the Soyang River. Colonel Hanes continued to dig and to build up the sandbags on top of the diggings.

On May 16 the Chinese struck. They came at night with the usual fright campaign. The Chinese had improved their English, and the epithets were often understandable. The Chinese struck the Second Division, hitting Hill 1051 and taking it. They did not bother with Hill 800 that first night.

The second night they attacked Hill 800.

The fighting was very fierce. In one area of the hill where the company commander had not been too diligent about burying the wires deep for communications, the Chinese cut the communications wires and isolated the whole company for a day.

Some of the men and two of the company commanders did not believe that preparations were necessary, so they shirked the work, and called Colonel Hanes's defenses "Bunker Hill."

Even General Van Fleet, when he came up the line to visit, said he had never seen such defenses. The implication was clear that they were a little too extensive.

But after the Chinese attack, Lieutenant Colonel Hanes went out to look around. One company had been overrun by the enemy, and its bunkers were full of Chinese. So the troops had to counterattack, and use their 4.2-inch mortars to dislodge Chinese from the bunkers the Americans had not dug deep enough. They recaptured the hill, and that afternoon Company K of the

Second Battalion of the 38th Infantry Regiment of the Second U.S. Division rebuilt the defenses. This time they listened to Lieutenant Colonel Hanes. This time the telephone wires were covered by at least eight inches of dirt. Roving fingers could not find them.

While they were doing all this they discovered dozens of unexploded Chinese grenades. That meant they were up against more untrained troops who did not know how to pull the firing pins on their grenades. The Americans faced another set of "cannon fodder."

On this second night the Chinese approached Hill 800 and its surrounding little hills again. Lieutenant Colonel Hanes was ready. The Chinese massed behind Hill 916, on the far side of Hill 800, and prepared for their night attack.

On the east, the Chinese had overrun another ROK division and the First Battalion of the Second Infantry, so the holding of Hill 800 was vital.

As night fell and the Chinese began mortaring, Hanes called for artillery fire behind Hill 916. The spotters reported that the barrage blew up many Chinese. But within the half hour the enemy had firmed up again and the Chinese bugles were blowing.

Hanes had instructed his men that when the Chinese attacked, they were to go down into their bunkers and stay there. He was going to bring artillery fire onto his own position.

The Chinese came with a rush, breaking through barbed wire on the hill. They reached the top and milled around in the communications trenches, but they did not find any Americans.

Then Colonel Hanes called for the artillery barrage, and it rattled in. The 38th Field Artillery Battalion fired 10,000 rounds of ammunition at those bunkers, and when daylight broke, there was not a Chinese left alive.

Beneath the debris the men of Company K and Company C were perfectly safe.

It was really just an exercise, as it turned out. General Van Fleet's staff found that Hill 800 was a great salient stuck out in front of the line. All the other units had been forced by the Chinese assault to pull back.

And so the men of Lieutenant Colonel Hanes's battalion had

to walk away and leave their deep-dug bunkers to the Chinese. But the Americans had learned something that was going to be vital in the sort of warfare that was now developing in Korea:

For more than a week, the Chinese attacked all up and down the line. They had some successes, and they isolated and wrecked some battalions along the line. They played havoc with the ROK Fifth and Seventh divisions. In the Hangyu and Onju areas, the Chinese actually surrounded the U.S. Second Division, and Marshal Peng hoped to chop it up, but a division was too much for the Chinese to swallow; the artillery, the tanks, and the air strikes prevented that. The 19th Infantry Regiment pushed north, and the 23rd and 38th regiments pushed south, right through the surrounding Chinese. The First Marines doubled back and caught a Chinese division and thrashed them. On May 31, when this struggle was over, the Americans said the casualties of the UN forces were about a thousand men, and the casualties of the Chinese were 70,000. The Allies estimated that the Chinese had suffered at least 105,000 casualties in the whole offensive, including 10,000 men taken as prisoners of war.

The 10,000 prisoners of war were indisputable, but the Chinese denied having the casualties the Allies claimed. Marshal Peng spoke of 3000 casualties in the entire Fifth Campaign. The UN estimated Chinese casualties as at least a hundred times as many.

By the spring of 1951, with the war having changed from one of position to one of attrition, Mao Zedong was having some second thoughts about his brave words to Peng—"Go ahead and fight and the devil take the casualties." Information was seeping back to Beijing that Chinese casualties were disastrous. The growing number of prisoners of war held in the UN prison camps could hardly be denied. Chairman Mao consulted with Zhu De and the other generals and then sent Marshal Peng a telegram changing the Chinese war policy.

Marshal Peng later wrote:

Chairman Mao sent a telegram instructing us not to try to annihilate large bodies of American troops at a time but to decimate them piecemeal. This was an excellent method, but a transitional period was needed for our men to build strong fortifications without which it would be impossible to carry out this approach.

The fact was that Marshal Peng had exhausted his armies. There was nothing left but to take up positional warfare of the World War I type, although this meant continuing to throw hundreds of thousands of men away into the guns of the Americans.

The 1951 Chinese spring offensive had again made a mess of the line, and General Van Fleet decided to correct this during the month of May. The Chinese had quieted down, and now it was a question of selected attacks, at Hangyu, in the Punchbowl (a piece of geography that looked just like its name), and on several other hill lines.

The trouble was that with the promotion of General Ridgway there was no one to keep the troops—and particularly some of the ambitious officers—from trying to move too fast.

Here was General Van Fleet's plan: The First Marine Division would capture Hangyu on the eastern end of the Hwachon reservoir. The 187th Airborne Division, fighting as infantry, would take Wonju, and the Second Division would support them.

The objective of the 187th Airborne was the town of Kansong, on the east coast. The UN thrust would surround all the troops south of the Injin-Kansong road, perhaps as many as 75,000 men.

But General Almond, commander of the X Corps, was still a very impatient officer. He wanted to close the gap in a hurry. He sent the 187th Airborne to move out immediately to Wonju. Two battalions started out, hit trouble, and made only 40 miles on May 23. That was not enough for Almond, so he ordered a task force to move on through, rush to the Soyang River, and seize the bridge site. This meant getting out far ahead of the main body. The body was led by two companies of tanks, and consisted of an infantry battalion and a battalion of artillery with some half trucks and machine-gun-mounted jeeps.

General Almond was too impatient.

The units of the task force could not all be assembled at once, so he sent them off piecemeal. As a result, the whole effort got into trouble. The tanks got out ahead and ended up surrounded by the enemy in the midst of Chinese country.

The tanks and infantry captured a large number of prisoners—too many for comfort, because they had to take care of them. And the fact was that they were themselves prisoners inside this big Chinese area. They managed to forge on to the Soyang River, but the disarray of this task force had prevented the orderly operation of General Van Fleet's trap, and most of the 70,000 or so Chinese in this pocket managed to get out.

The marines and the 187th Airborne Division pushed north along the southern shore of the Hwachon reservoir. They advanced along the road to Hanggu and took the town. They now held an extended ridge that ran northeast from Hanggu and gave access to the southern rim of the Punchbowl, which would be the scene of many violent actions in the next few months.

The Americans now found the defenses of the enemy growing tougher. The Chinese were building log and even concrete bunkers.

At the Punchbowl the Americans were stopped for ten days, until finally a very brave South Korean action on June 10 carried the place called Taeam-san, a central defense position.

Here, along what became known as the Kansas Line, the fighting would go on for months, assuming an almost monotonous character.

23

The Static War

On the U.S. side the war had grown very unpopular, and President Truman heartily wished he were out of it, but there seemed no escape with honor. Everything about the war had turned upside down for both sides. As the reader will see, the remarkable statement made by Assistant Secretary of State Dean Rusk in 1951 was an indication of the trap in which the United States had caught itself. That's why the war lasted still another year, until the election of Dwight D. Eisenhower to the Presidency of the United States. Then came more American sabre rattling, and finally Mao Zedong was persuaded that Eisenhower, another general, was dangerous enough that he could not be ignored. The Americans by this time were talking about using the atomic bomb. The Chinese relaxed their rigid position on the prisoner of war issue, and the way was set for a sort of solution, an unsatisfactory solution, that persists until this writing. Chinese-American relationships finally settled down, courtesy of President Richard Nixon, and China began to give indications of relaxation that lasted until the spring of 1989, when once more the ghost of Mao Zedong seemed to settle over China like a an evil miasma. . . .

If Lieutenant Colonel Hanes's performance in the bunkers of Hill 800 had taught the Eighth Army staff something about defenses, the Chinese taught them more in the spring and summer of 1951. When Marshal Peng realized that the Americans were moving toward a static war, he ordered the construction of deep defenses.

During this period the Chinese constructed a network of fortifications. The surface defensive positions gave way to fortifications built underground along the 38th parallel. The tunnel fortifications were planned to be so strong that no enemy troops could penetrate them.

Marshal Peng boasted:

With concentrated forces we could now crack the enemy defense line at any given point. Our troops had learned to wage defensive warfare as well as offensive warfare of a positional nature by using tunnel fortifications.

General Ridgway had another name for the sort of war that developed. "Accordion War," he called it.

Meanwhile, the United States had painted itself into a corner in the political negotiations about Korea. The basic problem was the American refusal to recognize the legitimacy of the Beijing government. Dean Rusk, Assistant Secretary of State, stated the American position in 1951:

We do not recognize the authorities of Peking for what they pretend to be. It is not the government of China. It does not pass the first test. It is not Chinese.

Given so ridiculous an American attitude about the de facto government of China, which was very much in control of the Chinese Mainland, there was no way that the American and UN desire for a political settlement could be obtained.

Ultimately a dialogue was begun through George Kennan, the expert on the Soviet Union, a former member of the State Department who was now with the Institute for Advanced Study at Princeton. Kennan got in touch with Soviet UN delegate Yakov Malik. Malik got in touch with Moscow, and Moscow, which saw the continual danger of the Chinese-American confrontation, was also interested in talking peace. That, however, did not mean the Chinese were interested; they really were not. Still, they were persuaded by the Russians that the war was getting nowhere and would get nowhere. Kennan also persuaded the U.S. authorities.

On June 29 the State Department prepared a broadcast for General Ridgway, aimed at the Chinese:

> As Commander in Chief to the United Nations Command, I have been instructed to communicate to you the following: I am informed that you may wish a meeting to discuss an armistice providing for the cessation of hostilities and all acts of armed force in Korea with adequate guarantees for the maintenance of such armistice.

He suggested a meeting aboard a Danish hospital ship in the harbor of Wonsan in North Korea.

When word of the Ridgway broadcast reached Beijing, it brought arguments. Chairman Mao was stubborn in his desire to prosecute the war and punish the Americans. But others argued that the American staying power had already proved much greater than anyone expected, and as long as the United States was backed by the British and the other Commonwealth nations, the war would last and the loss of Chinese soldiers would continue.

Finally Chairman Mao capitulated in the Central Committee meetings. The Chinese suggested that meetings with the United Nations be held at Kaesong, an historic spot just south of the 38th parallel, which was in the hands of the Communists.

The war then became political warfare—with such gestures by the North Koreans and Chinese as seating the UN delegates with the sun in their eyes, and in chairs cut down so that the Chinese and Koreans would loom over their opponents in the propaganda pictures. All this angered the Americans and made dealings difficult. The negotiations proceeded slowly, often broken by arguments and walkouts, particularly by the Communists.

By the summer of 1951, each side recognized the staying power of the other, and that there was no way the war could be won. In the background stood the atomic bomb, then still an American monopoly. It was not mentioned at first. President Truman had specifically shied away from discussion of the A-bomb since some misplaced words to the press during the MacArthur period.

The chief American negotiators for the peace were Admiral C. Turner Joy, a naval technician whose career had been spent in the development of military explosives; an army general, Henry Hodes; an air force general, Laurence C. Craigie; and Rear Admiral Arleigh A. Burke, a line officer. The South Koreans were represented by Paik Sunyup, the most talented military man in the Republic.

For face-saving purposes, the Communist side was led by General Nam Il of the Korean People's Army. But the real leader was Hsieh Fang, who represented the Chinese. Marshal Peng was also a negotiator for the Communist side.

The negotiations were attenuated and extremely difficult, as might be expected when neither side has a true advantage over the other. It was nothing like the armistice of 1918 that ended the first European war, where the Germans were defeated and had to accept the Allied conditions, or World War II, where the victorious Allies insisted on "unconditional surrender" by their enemies. At Panmunjon, the 38th parallel site of the peace negotiations, the enmity showed every day, and it was not just for the purposes of propaganda. The hatreds ran deep: hatred and fear by the Americans of "communism," and hatred and fear by the Chinese and North Koreans of "imperialism."

The talks began in the summer of 1951, but the Korean war was far from ended.

At the meetings, the North Koreans and the Chinese insisted that the 38th parallel be the division of the sides to end the war. And why not? Historically there was precedent reaching back to the 38th parallel division of the spheres of interest by the Japanese and the Czarist Russians since the nineteenth century. The division of the occupation zones fixed at Yalta had been based on this historic factor. The Americans did not realize this at the time of Yalta, but the Soviets could not be blamed if the Americans had not learned their history lessons properly. They knew what they were doing, and the Chinese and Koreans now also knew.

There really was no static defense line. The fighting surged back and forth across the 38th parallel as one side or the other gained an advantage for a time, but these were not real advantages and were not sustainable by either side. The UN side could not forget that the North Koreans had started the whole aggression, and the element of punishment for that act was never far from the minds of the delegates of their governments. But the Chinese and the North Koreans took the position that the UN forces had crossed the line and threatened the very existence of North Korea and the safety of China.

Many times the American military were ready to break off the talks and start fighting again. President Truman insisted the talks continue. He suspected that the Chinese were as sick of the war as the Americans were. The problem for both sides was disengagement without losing face. Each side accused the other of many truce violations. There were, of course, violations on both sides, as both sides kept their military machinery well oiled. The talks broke down in the late summer of 1951. The UN force was not unhappy; General Ridgway felt that the UN military position was much stronger than the Chinese, and he wouldn't have minded fighting more to secure some advantages. Unfortunately, the various UN advisors and negotiators kept compromising, interrupting and contradicting each other. Every time there was an interruption in meetings there was another attack by the United Nations or by the Communists, and the zigzag situational war continued, more or less along the 38th parallel, costing lives and gaining nothing for anyone. By December 1952 the talks were stale and the people were stale, but the war continued.

A new issue was interjected: the situation of war prisoners. The American feeling was that any Chinese who wanted to go to Taiwan instead of back to Mainland China ought to be allowed to do so. This attitude was, of course, infuriating to the Chinese, because it showed once again the American position that the government of China was neither real nor governing China. A part of the American attitudes of the past, it was the biggest stumbling block to negotiations, and underlay almost all the arguments.

The prisoner of war issue involved, on the Chinese and North Korean side, the question of prisoners who did not wish to be repatriated to North Korea or to Communist China, either because they had been forcibly enlisted in the service, or because they had changed their allegiance. There was also some of this attitude in South Korea.

It was not the sort of issue that could be dealt with easily by truce negotiators.

The issue grew heated in 1952, and riots and other violence in the Allied prisoner of war camps became commonplace. On occasion the United Nations used troops to control the prisoners of war.

The Communists also charged that the Americans used germ warfare in Korea. The charge was given credence by some confessions of American airmen. But the fact was that the Communists did anything they could to get confessions of wrongdoing, and under certain pressures some Americans collapsed and confessed to anything.

As for the charges, they are still unbelievable and surrounded with mystery. At the time, however, such well-meaning liberals as William S. Powell, who had elected to stay on in Communist China as editor of the family magazine *The China Weekly Review*, were persuaded that the charges were real. (Powell's openness and his sympathy with the legitimate aspirations of the Chinese later resulted in his trial in America on charges of treason. There was no conviction. His tragedy was a personal innocence plus the antipathy for the Nationalist regime that was shared by nearly all Americans who remained for any length of time in the China of the late 1940s.)

1952 was a year of stagnation in the attempts to find peace in Korea. One reason was the forthcoming American presidential election, which was anticipated by both sides as perhaps making a change in American direction.

The presidential election was held. President Truman declined to run, and General Dwight D. Eisenhower defeated Adlai Stevenson of Illinois for the presidency. As it turned out, it did not really make any difference in Korea. The basic problem was still the American refusal to recognize the legitimacy of the Chinese Communist government.

General Ridgway left the Far East command and was replaced by General Mark Clark.

The battlefront settled down to real trench warfare. Both sides dug in deep, making forays against the enemy, causing casualties, but really not changing the situation.

There were hard-fought battles, such as the battle for Bunker Hill, which cost the marines 48 dead and 313 seriously wounded, and cost the Chinese 400 known dead and estimated casualties of 3200. But Bunker Hill, and the Hook, Vegas, and all the other outpost battles changed nothing. The war had gone stagnant. The talks had broken down on October 16, 1952. Marshal Peng wrote the Americans a note saying that the discussions had become futile, and an armistice and total repatriation by both sides of all prisoners of war was the only answer.

The Americans, standing on the principle that they could not forcibly repatriate people who did not want to go home, refused, and the talks broke up.

Once the Eisenhower Administration was being formed, new ideas for ending the war were advanced. The Americans announced that they had perfected an atomic bomb of battlefield size, and the Joint Chiefs of Staff indicated that they were thinking of using such weapons in Korea. They were also thinking of broadening the war if it was to go on, bombing Manchuria and starting a major offensive. The Joint Chiefs recommended naval and air operations against China, including atomic weapons. The Chinese were listening, as were the Soviets. And no one wanted the war either to go on indefinitely or to be extended into China.

The Americans announced that they would not continue to interpose the U.S. Seventh Fleet between Taiwan and the Mainland. (In the first five months of 1953 the Kuomintang sent 200 raids against the coast of the Mainland.)

The Americans did not realize that this announcement was really a hollow threat unless they intended secretly to support an attempt by Chiang Kaishek to invade the Chinese Mainland. That was a possibility in the eyes of the Chinese; they knew that the raids on the Mainland were supported by America's Central Intelligence Agency. But if the U.S. Seventh Fleet was withdrawn from the Taiwan region, the chances that the Communists would invade Taiwan were greater than the chances that Chiang might try an invasion. Even in 1953 the Americans—at least the American military—still did not realize that Chiang had no more credence with the Chinese people.

In considering all these matters, the Chinese leadership finally concluded that the continuation of the war was both dangerous and nonproductive. And so the grounds were laid for a settlement.

Epilogue

The Chinese tragedy of Korea could be counted in the number dead. Even in 1990 the total is not known, but it was high in the hundreds of thousands, that much is certain. The American tragedy of Korea is symbolized by the American casualty figures— 142,091 people, 33,629 of them killed—plus the thousands of dead and wounded from other UN nations.

It was all so unnecessary, the product of the American belief in the mid-1940s that we could create instant change in any part of the world if we wished to do so. By 1947 we had learned that American efforts to bring peaceful change to China had failed, and yet we continued to interfere in Chinese affairs, ultimately on the side of the Chinese Nationalists, even after our most knowing leaders, Ambassador Stuart and Secretary of State Marshall, had said it was a losing cause because of the Kuomintang Party's refusal to carry out reforms and serve the Chinese people rather than the party.

The settlement of the Korean war was no victory for anyone. It did not secure for the Chinese their United Nations seat. That would have to wait until the scars of Korea had faded away. The prisoner of war exchange was puzzling, unless one was aware of the intense propaganda campaigns of both sides in the Allied POW camps. Nearly 15,000 Chinese prisoners opted not to return to Communist China, and not quite 6000 opted to return. Many of the Chinese who said they wanted to go to Taiwan had been members of the Nationalist army who had defected. In 1953 they went back to Taiwan and rejoined the Nationalist forces.

Even after the Korean war ended, the United States government maintained its wrongheaded policy toward the Chinese. The brief unnatural honeymoon between the Chinese and the Russians collapsed and became a long enmity, thawing only in the 1980s, and then not completely, even after new reform-minded elements took over the USSR and China.

Throughout the 1950s and 1960s the Americans continued to wear China blinders. It was not until 1972, when a right-wing American President, Richard Nixon, recognized the truth—that the Communists controlled China and were prospering in spite of American intransigeance—that there was any change in American policy. Nixon saw that the Chinese were ready for good relations with the United States. (In fact, the Communists had wanted them from the beginning.) One major problem remained—the American protection of Taiwan—but by the middle 1980s the Chinese were beginning to approach their own accommodation to that problem. China seemed to be marching ahead on a path leading to freedom and social and economic reform. This was all emphasized in 1987 at the 13th Party Congress, when Communist leader Deng Xiaoping announced that his generation was preparing to turn government and party over to younger men and to step back. A whole new plan of reform was established, under Zhao Ziyang as Party leader and Li Peng as government leader. It was known at the time that these men represented opposite ends of the political spectrum within the Communist Party. Zhao Ziyang came from the liberal element that had also brought forth Hu Yaobang a few years earlier, only to see Hu falter when he deserted the doctrine of strict party control in favor of democratization of the society and the Party. Hu had become a non-person then, and lived in obscurity until he died in the spring of 1989.

In the interim, Chinese-American relationships prospered, each year becoming closer than before. Deng Xiaoping indicated that an open China was what he desired, and that the reform program was leading that way. America and other free countries cheered. But beneath the talk of freedom and reform that was so heady to the Chinese people, the structure of Communist China remained the same. It was not a free country. The Chinese had no freedom to travel. For a Chinese a passport was a privilege, hard to get and easy to lose. Foreigners wanting to go to China were scrutinized, and only those invited were permitted to have contact with the Chinese people other than as tourists. The books and periodicals allowed into the country were scrutinized for inflammatory materials. Although China was connected to the world through the international telephone system, Chinese people were not allowed to make telephone calls outside their country, not even outside their province or city, without official sanction. In the 1980s the media of information were still strictly controlled; television was a state institution. It was known that the authorities opened the mail when they felt like it. In the euphoria of watching the emergence of a "new China," most of the world forgot the structure underneath the pleasant facade. Egged on by Deng Xiaoping's pronouncements, the youth began to believe in the emergence of democracy, and so their enthusiasms and their hopes grew.

Hu Yaobang's death in April 1989 was the symbol that set the unquenched fires of student democratic yearning blazing once again. The youth from the universities swarmed into Beijing's Tiananmen Square, the symbol of the Chinese Communist Party's conquest of China, and they demonstrated vigorously but peacefully for freedom and reform of the notably corrupt Chinese government and Communist Party. Soon they were joined by intellectuals, journalists, and teachers, and ultimately by thousands of workers and peasants.

When the Chinese leadership became aware of the depth of the unrest, the leaders, worried, reacted as in any oligarchy: They split on the fundamental issue. Zhao Ziyang, the symbol of moderation, went to Tiananmen Square, promised reform, and asked the students to go back to their classes. Had they done so, perhaps Zhao Ziyang would have won the day for moderation. But so overwhelming had the surge for freedom and liberty become that more was needed, and Zhao Ziyang could not produce it. For three days a dialogue continued between students and leadership spokesmen on the television, but it produced nothing because the Chinese leadership was split and unwilling to make the concessions the students and other freedom seekers demanded.

And here, at the beginning of May, was where the students

lost the battle. The demonstrations continued and grew, but the government announced that there would be no concessions, and demanded the clearing of Tiananmen. Students and others held on. The demonstrations were still peaceful, but they were losing their point, going nowhere. And within the leadership, Zhao Ziyang's support withered in his inability to bring the demonstrations to an end. When Deng Xiaoping realized that he had become a villain in the piece, that the students were calling for his disgrace, and that he had lost their love and support, he became furious and cast his lot with the hard-liners he had previously tried to control. Reform was forgotten in the recognition that Communist Party power might be lost in the democratization process, which the hard line feared more than anything else.

After Zhao Ziyang's importunations failed, Li Peng came forth and demanded in hard words the disbandment of the demonstrations. He was ignored. He threatened. He was ignored. He declared martial law, and the students and others refused to back down.

And so, entrapped by their own past rhetoric, Deng Xiaoping and Li Peng called out the troops. The 38th Army, located around Beijing, refused to move against the demonstrators. Seven retired generals and field marshals, in a letter to the editor of *Ren Min Ri Bao*, cautioned the government against killing its own people. But Deng and Li had already gone too far to back down, and now they brought in the half-savage 27th Army from the steppes, and instructed this semi-rabble in its responsibilities. On the grisly night of June 3, 1989, the 27th Army marched against the peaceful Chinese people and began massacring them. Then they plunged through the streets firing everywhere, to frighten China into submission.

They succeeded, on the face of it. The popular rebellion went underground. The terror remained in charge. But Deng and his colleagues faced one new factor which the Communist Party could not control. The world had seen the terror on television, and the old technique of denying the truth so loudly that the truth could not be heard no longer worked.

Foreigners began to move out of China. Within two weeks twenty years worth of confidence had been destroyed. The Chinese government blustered. They accused the United States and other protesting nations of interfering with China's internal affairs. Government and Party first threatened to purge anyone who objected. But their strong line was counterproductive; China began to lose its diplomats to defection; perhaps a whole generation of Chinese students abroad would be lost to the nation as well. The United States cut off all sales of any technology relative to arms, which meant such things as airliner communication systems. Suddenly the Chinese leaders realized that they had gone so far as to jeopardize the nation's economy.

Abruptly the line changed. The blustering about more and more executions and harsher punishment gave way to a plea for reconciliation and a promise of amnesty to the demonstrators. The Party began to look inward, all the while denying that the demonstrators had any cause for complaint. Officials were dismissed and trials were promised, and all this within a month of the massacre.

So although most of their leadership was underground and some were dead, the Chinese students and other rebels had already won. Within a month, they were forcing the changes they had demanded from a corrupt leadership.

As of the summer of 1989, foreign business was slowly moving back into China, but not quite so starry-eyed as before. It would be months, even years before the damage done by the guns of Tiananmen Square was undone. The Chinese revolution was still unfinished, but it was also still continuing, and the goal of the Chinese people was now apparent, symbolized in the Statue of Liberty erected in Tiananmen Square and destroyed by the soldiers. That symbol would not be forgotten, the students vowed.

And so the Chinese revolution continued, spurred by demands of the people that the Communist Party would never be able to eradicate, no matter how much terror they might apply.

American President Bush, once ambassador to China, reacted to the Chinese government excess with the most admirable moderation. Unfortunately, the members of the U.S. House of Representatives, seeing an issue on which they could not be hurt politically, reacted with a bombast that reflected the past. Once again the demand was for excess, for breach of all but diplomatic relations, and some of the violent wanted even that.

The question arose again in the summer of 1989 about American policy toward China. Would it again be one excess after another, destroying the progress in Sino-American relations of the past fifteen years?

The demonstrations of the spring of 1989 were the largest in China's history. There was another significance to them: The last great demonstrations of the 1940s were critical of the Chiang Kaishek government as the enemy of the people, and the United States was equally regarded as an enemy. From 1946 until the 1970s, that was the picture the Chinese held of the United States. In those years certainly no Statue of Liberty would ever have been erected in Tiananmen Square!

In the summer of 1989 America had once more become a model of freedom for the Chinese people, and the Statue of Liberty its symbol. Whether this atmosphere could prevail in the face of demands from the advocates of excess remained to be seen, but even in the bombast from Congress there were indications that perhaps America had learned that the life of nations is long and individuals are not enduring. The old men of China are dying off, and with their demise must come change. What America needs is patience, and perhaps this time it will be developed.

ACKNOWLEDGMENTS

I am indebted to a large number of people for information and assistance in the production of this book. They include James R. Schiffman, former Beijing correspondent of the *Wall Street Journal*; John M. Allison, former ambassador to Japan and long-time State Department official who was active in China policy making during the period under discussion; John K. Emmerson, also of the Department of State, whom I knew when an Office of War Information employee in World War II; General Patrick J. Hurley, Special Ambassador to China, whom I knew in China and then later in America; General George C. Marshall, Special Ambassador to China and Secretary of State and Secretary of Defense in this period; Lieutenant General Joseph Stilwell, commander of American and Chinese forces in the China, Burma, India theater; Colonel Joseph Stilwell, Jr., U.S. Intelligence officer; John Stewart Service, State Department official and advisor to Lieutenant General Albert C. Wedemeyer; Richard Service, State Department official; John Paton Davies, department advisor; John Davies, OWI official; William P. Gray, Time-Life China manager in 1946; Theodore H. White, Time-Life correspondent in China 1943–45; Richard W. Johnston, United Press Associations and later, Time-Life correspondent in China 1945–46; Eddie Chen, China News Agency; Robert P. Miller, United Press Associations, later UPI; Walter Rundle and Miles W. Vaughan, United Press Associations;

Randall Gould, editor of the Shanghai *Evening Post* and *Morning Mercury*; A. T. Steele, correspondent in China for the New York *Herald Tribune*; J. W. Powell, editor of the *China Weekly Review*; Serge de Gunzbourg, Agence France Presse; Graham Peck, author; Barbara Stevens, Agence France Presse; Lieutenent General John R. Hodge, commander of U.S. forces in Korea 1945–48; Ambassador Leighton Stuart; Madame Chiang Kaishek; Henry R. Luce of Time, Inc.; Pearl Buck; Robert Payne; Robert W. Shaplen; William L. Holland of USOWI, Rewi Alley; Anna Louise Strong; Dr. George Hatem; Edgar Snow; Peter Townsend; Lieutenant Colonel Don Kight; Reynolds Packard, United Press Associations; George Weller; Chicago *Daily News* correspondent in this period; Tilman Durdin, *New York Times* correspondent; Henry R. Lieberman, *New York Times* correspondent; Dixie Tighe, New York *Daily News* correspondent; Charles J. V. Murphy of *Life*; Christopher Rand, New York *Herald Tribune* correspondent; Zhou Enlai, foreign secretary of the Communist Party, later foreign minister and prime minister of the People's Republic of China; Mao Zedong, Communist Party chairman; Li Lisan, Communist Party chief for northeast China; Chao Guanhuan (Chao Mu), assistant to Zhou Enlai; Geng Peng, Chao's wife and also assistant to Zhou Enlai; a number of spokesmen for the Chinese Nationalist Government, including K. C. Wu and Wellington Koo; Charles W. Thayer and Walter S. Robertson of the U.S. Department of State; James W. Grant of UNRRA; Ellis Melvin, scholar of Chinese and former soldier; Xu Xiang Min, Chinese scholar and translator; Xu Jian; Joshua W. Chance, London merchant and former officer in the Red Army; and many, many others met in Korea, China and Japan. Also I am grateful to Olga G. Hoyt for editing, to Diana Hoyt for editing and typing, to Jackie Rose for typing, and to Marc Allen for fixing his computer so it would run when I used it.

NOTES

1. The Reach for Victory

For this chapter I relied on the official U.S. Army records of the MacArthur command of the U.S. Eighth Army.

General Paik Sunyup, the commander who first recognized the Chinese presence, was the best soldier in the Republic of Korea army.

2. Days of Hope in China

The U.S. Department of State's "White Paper on China" is the definitive document covering American China policy from the end of World War II until 1949. John S. Service's dispatches from China during the period, later collected in the book *Lost Chance in China* (see bibliography), were also valuable to this chapter, as was that portion of Mao Zedong's works dealing with the period.

It was apparent in Chongqing early in 1945 that there was something wrong between Ambassador Hurley and the professional staff of diplomats, most of whom were old China hands and many of whom had grown up in the country. Of course, birth or childhood in China was not necessarily a key to attitude. Henry Luce, the publisher, grew up in China and was tenaciously loyal to his vision of the Chinese Nationalist government. John Stewart Service grew up in China, and he was only too cognizant of the regime's fatal flaws.

3. The Marshall Mission

In August 1945, I was sent down to Hanoi to cover the surrender of the Japanese, and remained there for about a month writing about the

Vietnamese revolutionary movement, the French, and the Chinese occupation. On the aircraft going from Kunming to Hanoi I sat with an
acquaintance who was surgeon general to Luhan's troops. He invited me
to stay with the staff at the governor's palace, which Luhan had taken
over. Next morning, I was the recipient of many black looks from General
Luhan's table, and in a few hours was summarily ejected from the palace,
which was perfectly proper; as a journalist I had no business being there.
But at least I was thus able to get a room at the Hotel Metropole when
there were no rooms. To apologize for the ignominy, my doctor friend
took me on a shopping trip in the Chinese community. I found a Rolleiflex
camera that I admired and wanted to buy. No charge, said the doctor.
Yes, no charge, reluctantly agreed the Chinese store proprietor. Thus,
in my own way I saw firsthand (and participated in) the looting of Hanoi.

As a correspondent in China I never had the feeling that any of the
information given us by the Kuomintang's Ministry of Information had
a ring of truth. Usually it consisted of handouts mimeographed on rice
paper, handouts that dealt with facts and figures that most of us felt were
fabricated. Particularly when the facts and figures dealt with some aspect
of life that we saw around us, we knew there was something amiss. The
poverty of the people in the cities from Chongqing to Shanghai was
appalling, yet there was never a mention of any of this in the government
press. In the fall of 1945 I was in Shanghai, and there the correspondents'
press hostel, the Broadway Mansions apartment hotel, sat on Soochow
Creek, overlooking the boat people and the homeless people who somehow managed to live along the creek and the river, with no housing at
all. The best view of this teeming humanity was from the penthouse
apartment maintained on the top of the Broadway Mansions by Henry
R. Luce. In the summer of 1946 I visited Yanan. Then I spent a month
with the Chinese Communists in and around Harbin. I was subjected, as
were all Western journalists, to the full Chinese Communist propaganda
treatment; visits to schools, villages, and an interview with Li Li San, just
back from years in Moscow. One could sense the weight of the propaganda, but nevertheless one could also see that up here the people were
better off and happier than in the Nationalist-controlled rural areas.

Most of the facts regarding the operations of the Executive Headquarters and the Marshall mission came from interviews with members
of the Executive Headquarters (mostly American members), and the staff,
which was led by Americans. Lieutenant Colonel Don Kight, the public
relations officer, sent us around in military aircraft and kept us informed
of the activities of the headquarters. We were kept informed of the Communist position by Geng Peng and Chao Mu, Zhou Enlai's very skillful
assistants, who spoke excellent English and knew the Westerners' ways.
Zhou held regular press conferences in Chongqing, and in Shanghai,
where he had a house that summer of 1946. Of course he answered only

the questions he wanted to answer and in his own way. But the Nationalists, on the other hand, were extremely standoffish and usually unfriendly to any questioning at all.

4. Unyielding Truce

I happened to be in Beijing at the time of the Anping incident, and was thus virtually on the scene, as you might say. That same day we learned about the affair from the Marine Garrison, where everything was confusion. The usual rumors flew about Beijing, indicating that the Communists, whose forces surrounded the city although the Nationalists held Beijing, were about to launch an attack. It was soon enough obvious that the attack had been truly an "incident" manufactured by a zealous local Communist commander; but that incident was made to order from the Communist high command, which showed within a matter of hours. The Communist elements of Executive Headquarters at this point became distinctly less approachable, and old acquaintances like Geng Peng changed too, becoming somehow accusatory in their dealings with the Western press.

Earlier General Marshall had met with the American journalists several times at Nanking, at the press hostel. Shortly before the incident was one dinner at which he held informal conversation with the press. In a free and easy discussion, he expressed real hope that he might effect a settlement. But after August 1946, it was apparent in Marshall's dealing with the journalists that his attitude had changed. He did not say much, and he did not smile even his infrequent smile. We could sense that the general had not much hope left by this point.

I was in Beijing on the day that General Marshall declared the failure of his mission, and asked that he be withdrawn from China. It was a Saturday afternoon, I recall, and a lot of the foreigners had come to James Grant's compound for a pig roast. A handful of the young colonels from Executive Headquarters showed up to give us the information about the general's action. Several of us then rushed forth to write and file to our outlets the story of the failure of the Marshall mission. There would be months more of verbiage, but as everybody knew, the party was over.

I relied on the biography of General Marshall, Bao Shouyi's *An Outline History of China*, John K. Fairbank's *The Great Chinese Revolution, 1800–1985*, hereafter known as Fairbank, Percy J. Fang's *Zhou Enlai*, and Harry S. Truman's *Memoirs*, vols. 1 and 2.

5. The Prophet

Perhaps the most dispirited of all the people in China in the winter of 1946–7 were the intellectuals, the students, teachers at the universities, and the members of the Democratic League. This most admirable of Chinese political organizations stood for real democracy in China, in the manner that students and intellectuals would again stand in the spring of 1989 at Tiananmen Square: peace-loving, dedicated to nonviolence, and completely hopeful. It was an enormous blow to the League when the Communist Party aligned itself with the Soviet Union. For this chapter I relied on Mao's writings, Fang's biography of Zhou, Fairbank, Fitzgerald's *China's Uninterrupted Revolution*, and Sheridan's *China in Disintegration*.

6. China and American Anticommunism

In the fall and winter of 1946, and more so early in 1947, it was apparent to everyone in China that the Nationalist government had lost control. Taxes could not be collected. Chiang Kaishek put his son in charge of tax collections, but it did no good. The Kuomintang directors of industries were salting away the profits in American dollar investments. In this atmosphere the political reporting of the American Embassy continued to be excellent. Ambassador Stuart's people went out into the Communist countryside and saw what was happening. In those liberated areas where the Communists had confidence, the people were remarkably content, as compared to any district under Nationalist control, where taxes were collected at the point of a gun, and young men were recruited to the army with ropes around their necks. Anyone who visited the embassy knew these things. The terror of communism had not yet seized hold in America, although in the spring of 1947 anticommunism was becoming a major credo in Washington. I was in Washington that spring, and still had the sense that Congress was listening to what was happening. By fall 1947, when I visited Washington again, that sense was gone. Anyone who spoke any kind words about any Communist government or party was immediately suspected of being a Communist or a Communist sympathizer, a "fellow traveler." The fall of 1947, then, was the end of any realistic appraisals of the situation in China from Washington.

President Truman's words are from his letter of appointment of General Wedemeyer in July 1947.

I used Truman's *Memoirs*, Mao Zedong, Deng Xiaoping, Qi Wen, and Bao Shouyi.

7. America Leaps into the Morass

The Wedemeyer mission was dispatched to find a way to help the Nationalists, no matter what President Truman said in his public statements. General Marshall, who knew precisely what was going on in China, was virtually muzzled in from China and from Washington. American journalists reported the facts. The uprisings in Shanghai and the student marches in Beijing were reported, but they were meaningless to an American government that had made up its mind: Communism was the greater danger. Therefore, no matter how corrupt China had become, the American support must be given to Chiang Kaishek. As noted in this chapter, General Marshall had to back away from the truth because of the political climate in Washington in the spring of 1948. I had just come out of Czechoslovakia, having watched the Communists engineer a virtually bloodless (Jan Masaryk was the principal victim) coup d'etat in Prague. And to Americans in those days all Communists were clones.

Secretary Marshall's words are from the State Department White Paper. The Chinese reactions are indicated in Mao's works. In Paris in the fall of 1947 I had a long talk with Anna Strong to get the Chinese Communist position on the future possibilities. For this chapter I also used the Truman *Memoirs*.

8. The Wrong Compounded

One can see how much American attitudes had changed in the October 1948 words of Ambassador John Leighton Stuart on the subject of communism in China. By this time he, too, linked it with Soviet communism. But he never joined the frantic claque, and one of his statements ought to be remembered in the 1990s as a great truth about communism: "Evil in communism is moral or political rather than military."

It was this evil that caused Deng Xiaoping to call out the troops to shoot down the unarmed and peaceful students on June 3, 1989, in Tiananmen Square; the evil that best illustrates Lord Acton's adage about the absolutely corrupting influence of absolute power. But the Americans were afraid for the wrong reason; they feared the military spread of Communist power. In China, Communist power was spreading for a simple reason: It was regarded by the people as the lesser of the evils, and in fact it was the lesser. The Communist Party of China was not in 1948 corrupt and venal as it became forty years later.

The real shocker in this period was Li Tsung Jen's serious proposal that the United States should engage in his charade, turning over cheerfully all American influence in China to the Russians. This comes from the news dispatches of the time. I used the Truman *Memoirs*, the Acheson biography, the Zhou biography, Zhou's writings, Swanberg's biography of Henry R. Luce, and Fairbank.

9. Trouble in Korea

For this chapter I relied on Mao's works, the Zhou biography, the China White Paper, the Acheson biography, the Marshall biography, the

MacArthur biography, MacArthur's memoirs, the Luce biography, and Joseph Goulden's *Korea*. The remarks of Secretary of State Dean Acheson that Korea was not within the American defense perimeter were not accidental or faux pas, but a considered statement of the policy laid down by the National Security Council. I was told this at a Washington party by John Davies. For MacArthur's reactions I leaned on his autobiography and the Manchester biography. I had several discussions with my friend John M. Allison regarding the decision to move above the 38th parallel. He was instrumental in many of these decisions at that time. Truman's memoirs traced his changing position in this period. Also here I used the memoirs of Marshal Peng Dehuai in connection with general comments about the Chinese army. Zhou's works and the Fang biography indicate what Zhou was doing and thinking as he surveyed the American advance in Korea.

10. China Prepares for War

For this chapter's beginnings, I relied on Marshal Peng's memoirs, Mao's writings, and Bao Shouyi's history. The assessment by the CIA comes from Goulden's *Korea* and the MacArthur biography. I had a long conversation with Admiral Arleigh Burke about the intelligence reports and the Chinese. Burke was then one of MacArthur's chief naval advisors.

The second part of this chapter depends heavily on materials translated by Ellis Melvin from various Chinese publications. This material did not begin appearing until the middle 1980s, more than thirty years after the end of the Korean war. In fact, when I visited Beijing and Moscow in 1987 seeking materials on the Chinese aspects of the Korea conflict, I found none at all in either city. They have been suppressed in the used book market, although hundreds of volumes exist in the Lenin Library in Moscow and in the Beijing and Beijing University libraries in Beijing. No new books on this subject have been published since the 1950s. When the conflict ended, and the propaganda value was gone, Korea became a nonsubject. I secured a bibliography from Beijing University library through the good efforts of my friend James R. Schiffman, then Beijing correspondent of the Asian Wall Street Journal, which is a part of the general bibliography.

I also used Peng's memoirs, and translations from the Chinese by Ellis Melvin. As a former correspondent for newspapers and radio, it was most interesting to me to learn how heavily the Communists relied on the American news media reports for intelligence about UN operations, and how accurate those reports were. It is a tribute to a free society that a war could be conducted in the open in this manner. The Communists, of course, would never allow such freedom. Indeed, the Chinese Communists were confounded in the spring of 1989 during the demonstrations at Tiananmen Square when they opened fire on their own unarmed civilians, and all the world saw it on television. The puerile attempt of the Chinese government and Chinese Communist Party to deny to the world that people had seen the truth shows just how hidebound and ridiculous the Chinese Communist Party had become by 1989, not yet anywhere near the twenty-first century that the Chinese people want to enter. In the autumn of 1950 the Red Army was a mass people's army, notable for its enormous size and not its weapons. That was understandable at the time, but nearly forty years later, the Chinese army is much modernized physically, not yet in its thinking.

11. *The Red Army Moves*

For this chapter I relied on Mao's works, Peng's autobiography, and the Ellis Melvin translations; also, Gao Yihan's *The History of the Early Days of the U.S. Invasion (Meiguo qinhua chuqi shi shi)*, Liao Gailong's *Resisting the U.S. Invasion (Fankang meiguo qinluezhje)*, and Wang Chun's *History of the Early Days of the U.S. Invasion (Meiguo chuqi qinhua shihua)*. For the story of American and South Korean activity I relied on Joseph Goulden's *Korea*.

12. *Tactics*

The story of the Korean fighting comes from the U.S. Army records and U.S. Marine records of the Korean war and the five-volume history of the Marine activities. The MacArthur memoirs and biography were also important here. The story of the lost battalion is from the regimental history of the Eighth Cavalry and the Fifth Cavalry.

13. *Hiatus*

Again, the regimental histories of the Eighth and Fifth Cavalry regiments were important sources for this chapter, and so were Peng's memoirs and the Ellis Melvin translations. The official Marine history described the actions of General Smith and his men. The activities of Major General Bolte and others come from Goulden.

14. *Guessing Game*

Marshal Peng's memoirs, Mao's works, and the Ellis Melvin translations were important. So was *The History of the U.S. Invasion of China (Meidi qinlue zongguo shihua)* and Tao Juyin's *The Story of the U.S. Attack (Meiguo qinhua shiliao*). The tale of the actions of Mao Zedong's son comes from the Ellis Melvin translations. The events in Washington are from Goulden's *Korea*, and from the pages of *The New York Times* for the period. MacArthur's quotations come from his own memoirs and the MacArthur biography.

15. The American Attack

The story of the American assault of November 24 is from the MacArthur memoirs and various other sources. Marshal Peng's activities are delineated in his memoirs and in the Ellis Melvin translations. The story of the death of Mao Anysing is from the Ellis Melvin translations.

16. Chinese Counterattack

The sources for this chapter were the Mao works, the Peng memoirs, the Ellis Melvin translations, and half a dozen Chinese works on the war, including *Choushi meidi, Bishi meidi, Mieshi meidi*, and *Meidi qinhua shi tujie*. I also had several long conversations with Joshua Chance of London, a former intelligence officer in the Red Army during this war.

17. The Overconfidence of Marshal Peng

Here I used Peng's memoirs, the Marine history, and the U.S. Army history for the story of the Seventh Division and the Ninth Infantry. The story of the Turks comes from Goulden. Events in Washington are depicted in Truman's *Memoirs* and the Goulden book.

18. Peng's Victory Fever

Army and Marine histories were important for the first part of this chapter. So were Peng's memoirs and the Ellis Melvin translations. Peng's account of the supply problems is from the Ellis Melvin translations.

19. The Americans Learn

I used General Ridgway's autobiography for this chapter as well the Goulden book. Marshal Peng's memoirs told the Chinese side, with help from the Ellis Melvin translations and several of the Chinese-language histories listed in the bibliography.

20. The Meat Grinder

General Ridgway's new "meat grinder" technique proved very effective in countering the Chinese hordes in Korea, although this was never admitted by Marshal Peng either before or during the Korean conflict. What really distressed the Chinese and made their chances for victory impossible was the problem of supply, which they were unable to conquer because of the primitive nature of their transportation system. Marshal Peng made this quite clear. But it was also clear, from Mao's writing and others, that this would never be admitted at the highest level in Beijing.

Ridgway's biography explains his methods.

21. The End of MacArthur

Because the Chinese had made so much of General MacArthur as a military personage in planning their war against the Americans, one would expect that when MacArthur was dismissed by President Truman there would have been some Chinese reaction. But no, there seems to have been none whatsoever, no sense of relief that a major enemy was down, no feeling whatsoever. The story of the MacArthur relief comes from the Truman memoirs and several other sources, including the MacArthur biography and the author's own memories. The indications that the Chinese were getting worn down by the war of attrition comes from the Chinese histories and the six-volume Japanese history. Manpower will triumph over machines is from Chairman Mao's works. The discussion between Mao and Peng about the number of Americans annihilated comes from Peng's memoirs.

22. Chinese Spring Offensive

The notes about the air war in Korea come from the Futrell history of Korean air operations. The story of American operations comes from the Marine and Army histories. Marshal Peng's role is described in his own memoirs.

23. The Static War

The material about the last days in Korea with the Allies comes from General Maxwell D. Taylor's *Swords and Plowshares*. He was the last commander of the Eighth Army. Marshal Peng's activities are from his own work. Dean Rusk's remarkable statement about not recognizing the authority of the Chinese over China was printed in *The New York Times*.

BIBLIOGRAPHY

Acheson, Dean. *Present at the Creation*. New York: Norton, 1969.

———— et al. *United States Relations with China, 1945–49*. Washington: Department of State, 1949.

Appleman, Roy E. *U.S. Army in the Korean War*. Washington: Department of the Army, 1960.

Clark, Mark. *From the Danube to the Yalu*. New York: Harper, 1954.

Beijing shifan daxue. *Meidi qinlue zhongguo shihua*. Beijing: Guangming ribaoshe, 1950.

Bao Shouyi. *An Outline History of China*. Beijing: Foreign Languages Press, 1982.

Chen Yiyuan. *Chedi dabai Meidiguozhuyi de xijunzhan*. Beijing: Renmin chubanshe, 1952.

Chiang Kaishek. *Resistance and Reconstruction*. New York: Harper, 1943.

Clark, Elmer T. *The Chiangs of China*. New York: Abingdon-Cokesbury, 1942.

Cohen, Warren A. *America's Response to China*. New York: Wiley, 1972.

Deng Pu. *Meidi qinlue Shanghai de zuizheng*. Shanghai: Shijie zhishishe, 1950.

Deng Xiaoping. *Selected Works*. Beijing: Foreign Languages Press, 1984.

Ding Zemin. *Meiguo pai hua shi*. Shanghai: Zhonghua, 1952.

Donovan, Robert J. *Years of Decision*. New York: Norton, 1977.

Du Mansu. *Meidiguozhuyi shi zongguo renmin*. Beijing: Beijingshi zhong-su you hao xiehui, 1951.

Fairbank, John K. *The Great Chinese Revolution, 1800–1985*. New York: Harper and Row, 1986.

Fang, Percy J. et al. *Zhou Enlai, a Profile*. Beijing: Foreign Languages Press, 1986.

Field, James A. Jr. *History of U.S. Naval Operations in Korea*. Washington: U.S. Navy, 1962.

Gao Yihan. *Meiguo qinhua chuqi shi shi*. Beijing: Guangming ribaoshe, 1950.

George, Alexander L. *The Chinese Communist Army in Action: The Korea War and Its Aftermath*. New York: Columbia, 1967.

Gittings, John. *The Role of the Chinese Army*. London: Oxford University Press, 1967.

Goulden, Joseph C. *Korea: The Untold Story of the War*. New York: Times Books, 1982.

Guo Dajie. *Jiechuan meidi "yuanhua" zhenxiang*. Beijing: Shiyue chubanshe, 1951.

Huang He. *Meidi qinlue Taiwan zhenxiang*. Beijing: Renmin chubanshe, 1951.

Karnow, Stanley. *Mao and China*. New York: Viking, 1972.

Kojima, Noboru. *Chosen Sensao (Korea War)*. 6 vols. Tokyo: Bungei Shunju, 1970–77.

Leckie, Robert. *Conflict: The History of the Korean War*. New York: Putnam, 1962.

Liao Gailong. *Fankang meiguo qinluezhe*. Shanghai: Haiyan shudian.

Lin Cantian. *Kuoda fan Meifuri yundong*. Beijing: Jiulong Zhongguo xue-sheng congkanshe, 1948.

Liu Danian. *Maiguo qinhua jianshi*. Beijing: Xinhua, 1949.

Lu Eting. *Kang Meiyuan chao shishi xuixi xiaocidian*. Beijing: Beijing beixin, 1951.

MacArthur, Douglas. *Reminiscences*. New York: McGraw-Hill, 1964.

Manchester, William. *MacArthur*. Boston: Little Brown, 1981.

Mao Zedong. *Selected Works.* Beijing: Foreign Languages Press, 1977.

McAleavy, Henry. *The Modern History of China.* New York: Praeger, 1977.

Mei Bihua. *Zhong mei zhijian.* Shanghai: Xinshi shudian, 1948.

—— *Lun Mei su guanshi.* Beijing: Shijie zhishishe, 1951.

Meng Mowen. *Mei jiang goujie shiliao.* Beijing: Xinchao shudian, 1951.

Meng Xianszhang. *Meiguo Fujiang qinhua zui xing shi.* Shanghai: Zhong-hua, 1951.

Montross, et al. *U.S. Marine Operations in Korea.* 5 vols. Washington: U.S. Marine Corps, 1960–1968.

Nee, Victor and James Peck. *China's Uninterrupted Revolution.* New York: Pantheon, 1975.

Payne, Robert. *Forever China.* New York: Dodd, Mead, 1945.

Peng Dehuai. *Memoirs.* Beijing: Foreign Languages Press.

Qin Linshu. *Meidi yuan Jiang nuyi zhongguo.* Beijing: Xinhua, 1949.

Qing Ruji. *Meiguo qinhua.* Beijing: Sanlian, 1952.

Ridgway, Matthew. *The Korean War.* New York: Doubleday, 1967.

Seagrave, Sterling. *The Soong Dynasty.* New York: Harper and Row, 1985.

Service, John S. *Lost Chance in China.* New York: Random House, 1974.

Shao Xi. *19 shiji Meiguo duihua yapian qinlue.* Beijing: Sanlian, 1950.

Snow, Edgar. *Red Star over China.* New York: Random House, 1938.

Spurr, Russell. *Enter the Dragon.* New York: Newmarket Press, 1988.

Su Kaiming. *Modern China.* Beijing: New World Press, 1986.

Swanberg, W.A. *Luce and His Empire.* New York: Scribners, 1972.

Tao Juyin. *Meiguo qinhuq shiliao.* Shanghai: Shanghai zhonghua, 1951.

Taylor, Maxwell D. *Swords and Plowshares.* New York: Norton, 1972.

Truman, Harry S. *Memoirs.* Jersey City, N.J.: Da Capo, 1986.

Wang Chun. *Meiguo qinhua shihua.* Beijing: Gongren chubanshe, 1953.

Wang Minzhi. *Meidi zenyang qinlue zhongguo.* Beijing: San lian, 1950.

Wang Yun. *Meiguo qinluexia de dongnanya.* Beijing: Shijie szhishi chu-banshe, 1951.

White, Theodore H. and Annalee Jacoby. *Thunder out of China*. New York: Sloane, 1946.

Whiting, Allen. *China Crosses the Yalu: The Decision to Enter the Korean War*. Stanford: Stanford U. Press, 1960.

Xuan Dizhi. *Meiguo qinhua 100 nian*. Beijing: Shijie zhishishe, 1950.

Xue Chun. *Meiguo tewu zai zhongguo de zuixing*. Beijing: Shijie zhishi, 1951.

Xue Mouhong. *Meiguo zai xi ou de beizhan*. Beijing: Shijie zhishishe, 1950.

Yao Simu. *Meiguo chongxin wuzhuang riben wenti jianghua*. Beijing: Shijie zhishishe, 1950.

Yu Lan. *Meiguo chuqi qinhua shihua*. Beijing: Kaiming, 1951.

Zhai Yirong. *Meidi zenyang furi?* Beijing: Xinhua, 1951.

Zhong Wenxian. *Mao Zedong*. Beijing: Foreign Languages Press, 1986.

INDEX

239